W9-BWO-816

THE SPY CHRONICLES

Previously by A.S. Dulat and Aditya Sinha

Kashmir: The Vajpayee Years (2015)

Previously by Aditya Sinha

The CEO Who Lost His Head (2017)
Death of Dreams: A Terrorist's Tale (2000)
Farooq Abdullah: Kashmir's Prodigal Son (1996)

Forthcoming from Asad Durrani

Pakistan Adrift: Navigating Troubled Waters (2018)

THE SPY CHRONICLES

RAW, ISI and the Illusion of Peace

A.S. Dulat, Asad Durrani
and Aditya Sinha

HarperCollins *Publishers* India

First published in India in 2018 by
HarperCollins *Publishers*
A-75, Sector 57, Noida, Uttar Pradesh 201301, India
www.harpercollins.co.in

2 4 6 8 10 9 7 5 3 1

P-ISBN: 978-93-5277-925-3
E-ISBN: 978-93-5277-926-0

Typeset in 11/15 Berling LT Std
Manipal Digital Systems, Manipal

Printed and bound at
Thomson Press (India) Ltd.

To my late parents, Shamsher and Raj, who spent many joyous hours playing bridge with two successive High Commissioners of Pakistan in India: Syed Fida Hussain, my father's former ICS colleague, and Abdul Sattar.

—A.S. Dulat

To all the faceless agents who take great risks in the service of their country.

—Asad Durrani

To my parents, Neelam and Chandreshwar Narain Sinha, who, in England during 1965-71, were best friends with Gulshan and Nazir Hussain, immigrants from Lahore.

—Aditya Sinha

Contents

IV: KABUKI

V: THE FLASHPOINTS

VI: NEW GREAT GAME

VII: LOOKING AHEAD

If only somehow you could have been mine,
what would not have been possible in the world?

—Agha Shahid Ali, 'The Country
without a Post Office'

Preface

In the dedication, A.S. Dulat and I have each mentioned India-Pakistan friendships that were deep and, silly as it may sound, beautiful. It is a growing fear that in the age of shouting heads on TV and hyper-nationalistic NRIs, we are reminiscing about a bygone era. All hope is not lost—my elder daughter was best friends with a Karachi-ite during her undergraduate years at New York University. On the whole, however, she seems part of a shrinking minority, and a window of opportunity for goodwill between the people of the two nations may be closing. It is to keep that window open, and show that through the window one may see endless possibilities, that this book was written.

The hostilities that are ceasefire violations across the Line of Control erupt occasionally, but the norm is of long periods of peace. Similarly, armed conflict between India and Pakistan has broken out on four occasions in their 71 years of independence. Even the proxy war of terrorism is characterised by intense bursts of violence that occasionally puncture everyday peace.

The cold war between nations, conducted by their spy agencies, is continuous, however. There is no let-up. There are no uniforms, or counter-measures that force terrorists to opt for soft targets. Spies and their networks live 24x7 lies at great risk to themselves. They are a last line of defence. If a Kargil happens, then it is ultimately attributed to intelligence failure. Terrorism is seen as a slippage through an invisible net put up by the agencies. War is either pursued or averted mainly due to intelligence efforts.

The army's Inter-Services Intelligence (ISI) directorate has been Pakistan's main intelligence agency since immediately after independence. The cabinet secretariat's Research and Analysis Wing (RAW), founded 50 years ago as of September 2018, was created out of India's Intelligence Bureau (IB) due to perceived failures of the 1962 and 1965 wars with China and Pakistan, respectively. Due to Pakistan's unique history, the ISI has gained a larger-than-life aura, often seen in India as Pakistan's Deep State. The RAW has a similarly sinister image, if not among its own citizens then at least among those across the western border.

This book brings together two men who each had a stint at heading their respective agencies. As such, they have been privy to their nation's greatest secrets—whether they relate to secret agents placed in sensitive foreign locations, nuclear weaponry, strategic intelligence, or secret liaison with foreign agencies and governments. They are the keepers of their nation's dark matter.

Indians and Pakistanis keep trying to talk to one another. Politicians and diplomats speak to their counterparts; peaceniks exchange notes; sportsmen share locker-room chat; and businessmen drool over each other's markets. This is open. Spychiefs rarely talk to each other—you can be certain that the spies never do—though there have been occasions when their governments have directed them to do so. In the last two decades, some former spychiefs have come together to exchange views in Track-II dialogues. But they have never spoken openly.

As the two spymasters say, they are aware of the stakes. What they say to each other, around a table, their guards down, counts for something. Their conversation goes to the heart of the India-Pakistan relationship; a deep dive into the Deep State, if you will.

This book was Dulat's suggestion after the encouraging success of the 2015 book we co-wrote, *Kashmir: The Vajpayee Years*. Since he and Durrani had earlier co-authored two papers, his idea was to follow that format. Chiki Sarkar, the publisher at Juggernaut Books, suggested to me that to reach a wider audience as well as to make it an interesting read, it ought to be in a dialogue format. She pulled Hitchcock/Truffaut out of her living room library as an example. It was a winning suggestion, in my opinion.

After Dulat got Durrani on board, they enlisted the help of Peter Jones, of the University of Ottawa's Centre for International Policy Studies. He helms the Track-II 'Intel Dialogue' between India and Pakistan, and he graciously agreed to host me at the meetings in Istanbul (May 24-26, 2016) and Bangkok (February 1-3, 2017 and October 28-30, 2017), so that we could spend a couple of days after the official engagement to produce material for this book. There was a meeting that we did on our own in Kathmandu, Nepal (March 25-29, 2017), though Sudheendra Kulkarni of the Observer Research Foundation, an ardent supporter of the project throughout, offered to facilitate.

These meetings produced a total of over 1.7 lakh words. The manuscript prepared for publication was half that size. The transcripts had a lot of spontaneity and the two former chiefs got into the spirit of each discussion; I have tried to retain that tone in the manuscript, despite the second thoughts of each participant at different points. I have also attempted to provide the flowing literary style that Dr Farooq Abdullah told me he admired most about *Kashmir: The Vajpayee Years*.

Unlike *Kashmir: The Vajpayee Years*, which was essentially Dulat's narrative and thus demanded to be read chronologically, this conversation between Dulat, Durrani and myself can also be read differently: that is, one may read chapters or sections out of order or in isolation, and drift back and forth through the book as one fancies. The choice is the reader's.

In acknowledgement, mention must go to Krishan Chopra, who seized the project with both hands and did not let go; Siddhesh Inamdar, who put in much effort to produce this book; my friends Mayank Tewari, who at difficult moments reminded me that Philip

Roth would have treated this project as 'material', V. Sudarshan, who reminded me that this project was an enviable journalistic exercise, and P. Krishnakumar, who gave me a gig at *Mid-Day* which was invaluable in more ways than one; and of course my spouse, Bonita Baruah, whom I regard as my better 51 per cent.

Aditya Sinha

New Delhi, India
March 2018

Introduction

Pointing to the horizon where the sea and sky are joined, he says, 'It is only an illusion because they can't really meet, but isn't it beautiful, this union which isn't really there.'

—Saadat Hasan Manto

Kaash ke hum dost hote.

General Asad Durrani and I have gelled ever since we met at a Track-II dialogue named after Thailand's Chao Phraya River. It was held in the aftermath of 26/11, in the wake of Western apprehension of what may come to pass. Who knows, if a madman was in control we could all still be blown to kingdom come, in revenge for 1971 or even 1947.

General Saheb has been a friend. His straightforwardness is striking. There is no bullshit; for him a spade is always a spade, which is at times disappointing for me. He has never hesitated to speak up or render help.

When Prime Minister Narendra Modi was preparing to take the oath of office in 2014, two notables from Srinagar called and suggested that Pakistan's prime minister, Mian Nawaz Sharif, be invited. They said he was keen to come. Since it was early days, people in high places were prepared to listen, so I passed the message along. There was excitement in government, but the bigwigs wanted an assurance that Mian Saheb would come if invited.

To confirm, I first called a senior diplomat in Pakistan. His advice was to not risk it, because Nawaz Sharif might not be allowed to come to India. Somewhat disappointed I called the General. His response was unequivocal; there was no reason for Nawaz Sharif not to come. Generals in Pakistan are generally right, and more so Asad Durrani.

Our wives met at one of the Track-II meetings on Kashmir, held in December 2015 at a Dead Sea resort in Jordan. My wife Paran and the Begum are poles apart. Paran enjoys an occasional smoke with the General whereas the Begum approves of neither smoking nor drinking. Yet they got along like a house on fire. Incidentally, at the same meeting, the Pakistanis enquired whether there was any hope of forward movement between India and Pakistan. I stuck my neck out and said something should happen soon. Lo and behold, we were in Abu Dhabi on Christmas Day on our way home when we learnt that Modiji had dropped in at Lahore. Since then, however, the process has gone nowhere.

If it's any consolation, Pakistan is in a bigger mess than we are. The man India put its faith in, Nawaz Sharif, is likely to be kept out of power (along with his family) by the military when the next elections are held, likely in August 2018; the military's preferred choice is the current PM, Shahid Khaqan Abbasi, whom Mian Saheb had handpicked to replace him.

In any India-Pakistan conversation, Kashmir will inevitably come up. In January 2018, during my annual pilgrimage to Goa, I met a Kashmiri in a tailoring shop. He told me that Kashmir wanted independence.

'Whatever for?' I enquired.

'How would you expect me to react if you walked into my shop and slapped me?' he said.

That's what the security forces do in Kashmir. Anyone can be stopped and beaten, he claimed. The slightest protest or stone-pelting leads to tear gas and pellet guns. Kashmir remains on the boil: the

Line of Control (LoC) and border are more volatile than usual and questions are being raised about the government's muscular policy.

A reformed militant who had flirted with the Lashkar-e-Toiba visited me more recently and spoke of the threat of increasing radicalism in the Valley. He said the youth in South Kashmir prepared for martyrdom and had no concern for Pakistan as they believed they were fighting for Allah. As former Pakistan Foreign Secretary Riaz Mohammad Khan acknowledged, the 2008 Mumbai terrorist attack did irreparable damage to the Kashmiri cause and tarnished Islamabad's image as well. Pakistan had been out of it since then, until we brought them back into the picture in 2016.

The militant, who now resembles a professor more than a terrorist, warned that the Jamaat-e-Islami, once with pockets only in Sopore, Shopian, Kulgam and Pulwama, was now omnipresent in radicalising the youth. It had made inroads in the state government and infiltrated the J&K Police as well. The central jail in Srinagar was the hub of radical indoctrination, he said from personal experience. Militancy was a thriving industry, where everyone was someone with a vested interest in the status quo—except that the status quo is never static. The Kashmiris who crave peace live in fear of the next explosion, not knowing where or when it will happen. What a change this is from the time when Srinagar was a city of great style, from the 1960s to the early '80s.

The situation in Kashmir, like our relationship with Pakistan, is going nowhere. It waits for another Vajpayee. Could General Pervez Musharraf and Dr Farooq Abdullah, sharing many similarities, given an opportunity, have found a solution on the LoC? Kashmiris crave peace but there can be no peace or forward movement in Kashmir so long as we keep relating it to elections elsewhere in the country, just as we do in our relationship with Pakistan. We need to talk to Pakistan as much as we need to engage with Kashmir. As Chief Minister Mehbooba Mufti said in the state assembly in February 2018, with the risk of being called anti-national, there is no alternative to engagement with Pakistan. Or, as the old Kashmiri communist Mohammed Yousuf Tarigami said, seeking a 'security solution' to a fundamentally political problem will not succeed.

Finding a way out of any mess requires a willingness to listen. It connects us to Kashmir and to ourselves as well. But we are so caught up in the noise around us that very few have the time to listen. Sentiments at times are more illuminating than facts. Empathy is the key to understanding Kashmir.

I have learnt much from Track-II, including the similarities between Kashmir, Afghanistan and Balochistan. Noted Pakistani author Ahmed Rashid once said that if Kashmir were resolved, Afghanistan would be a cakewalk. At one of our meetings, Rustom Shah Mohmand, a Pakistani bureaucrat, diplomat, and a gem of a human being, remarked that Pakistan needed to put its own house in order in Balochistan before finding fault with India in Kashmir.

Surprising as it may sound, I was as happy leaving the Prime Minister's Office in 2004 as I was joining it in 2001, even though these were by far my best years in government. Yes, there was a tinge of sadness at leaving the RAW just when I was beginning to enjoy it; 17 months is not enough for a chief. But there are so many worlds, so much to do. Retirement is the beginning not the end of life. Who could have imagined I could even become an author in the bargain? As someone said, there is no pleasure in having nothing to do; the fun is in having lots to do and doing nothing.

Having lived more than my life of secrecy, spookiness still clings to me. A Kashmiri friend, not knowing we had shifted residence to Defence Colony in Delhi, dropped in and enquired if this was my 'new safe house'. Pakistani friends still don't believe that my only e-mail ID is my wife's. And my wife tells all her friends that you can never get the whole truth out of this spook. A 'cover story' is still useful at times.

When the idea of a joint project was first mooted by Peter Jones at one of our Track-II meetings in Istanbul, the General laughed and said nobody would believe us even if we wrote fiction. We have tried to stay as close to the truth as we believe it to be even if some of it is regarded as fiction. The reality is that there are normally more than two sides to most stories. Truth is a kaleidoscope.

I know there will be people in the fraternity who will say how did these swines get so chummy: who was working for whom?

After all we have each been a part of licensed skulduggery on either side.

Not everyone will agree with what we have said, possibly nobody. But the effort here has been to make some sense of the India-Pakistan conundrum in the hope that sanity will someday prevail.

I have often been labelled an optimist. If so, it's only a way of life and I have no regrets, or as General Saheb says, he doesn't give a damn. All I can say it's been a great life. As Mark Twain puts it, good friends, good books and a sleepy conscience: this is the ideal life. And this, I believe, is how the General and I have gone about it, even though he is much more of a realist.

Finally, this project could never have taken off without our friend, philosopher and guide, Aditya Sinha.

A.S. Dulat

New Delhi, India
March 2018

I was born an Indian—there was no Pakistan then. Rawalpindi, my birthplace and now the headquarters of the Pakistan Army in which I served for over three decades, is where I live after retirement. When British India was divided, I was a schoolgoing kid in Sheikhupura, a city that fell on the Pakistani side. I was spared the horrors of the Great Divide, except for a brief glimpse when we visited our relatives in Delhi during summer vacation in 1947. The riots forced us to return post-haste, but strangely I have no memories of the journey back home. It must have been one of the lucky trains that got away.

One change I recall from soon after Partition was the absence of a matka. The shop halfway to school where we often stopped to sip water had a new owner. Unlike his Hindu predecessor, he had no use for the pitcher that contained the elixir of life. The next episode to remind me that the worst was not yet over was when we moved from Matka to Mucca. I can't remember what caused tension between the recently dissected twins some time in 1950, but I do remember that our prime minister responded by raising a fist—which became known as 'Liaqat's Mucca'. Throughout those years, though the Kashmir issue was simmering somewhere in the background, the study of history in our schools was mostly about the glory of the Muslim rule in India. Little surprise that it led to some fascination with the seat of power, both political and spiritual: broadly the region bounded by Delhi, Agra and Ajmer. Any link with our eastern neighbour thus continued to be followed with great interest.

I grew up watching Indian movies; even knew all the great names from show business based in 'Bombay', a name that still sounds more familiar than Mumbai. Indeed, it took some time before someone explained to me why Muslim actors like Dilip Kumar and Meena Kumari had to take non-Muslim names. Episodes that dealt with the Mughal period were generally watched with nostalgia. But my memories of those earlier years were more influenced by the sporting scene. Cricket duels were keenly listened to, as radio commentary was the only way to follow them. But unlike present times, these were not a matter of life and death.

In a test match in Montgomery—now Sahiwal—where we had a world-class stadium, an Indian batsman, Sanjay Manjrekar, was the crowd's favourite. In the same city, when it hosted the National Games, the Indian Punjab was also represented. After the event some Sikhs dropped in to see my father, who at that time was in charge of Central Jail. They came to get a few durrees (cotton woven carpets)—the place was famous for this product—and pleaded for immediate delivery so that these could be taken as personal baggage—let's say 'duty free'. Over time the legacies of the past had to be shed because the realpolitik overrode.

I may have joined the army in 1959 because Ayub Khan had putsched only a year earlier, or because the girls in Government College Lahore, where I was studying, clearly fancied those who showed off in uniform. But after I did, it turned out that I had to appear more often in combat than in my former alma mater.

While training for war, we were taught that though we had to fight better than our larger adversary, but must also keep in mind that our enemy too was doing his duty for his country. And when we saw that both in the 1965 and 1971 wars, the Indian and the Pakistani armies deliberately spared non-combatants—fighting gentlemanly wars, in other words—mutual respect amongst the two militaries was reinforced—but so did the belief that our countries were not likely to become friends anytime soon. Post-'71, even within the uniformed clans—despite professional correctness—the assessment of the antagonist became hard-nosed, and the attitude harder.

In due course, I went for training and visits abroad, and met our eastern neighbours on neutral ground. That helped me make the best of a bad relationship. Once on a course in the north German town of Hamburg, I bumped into a south Indian professor. The next day he walked into our apartment with his wife to invite us to his home. When returning the courtesy, I asked him if he had any dietary restrictions. He said that as a Brahmin he was forbidden to eat even eggs. His German spouse, however, assured us that she could make him devour whatever we served.

When I returned to Germany as an attaché a few years later, my Indian counterparts walked up to me at the first opportunity to introduce themselves. Though irritated by our host's special favours since Pakistan was the frontline ally in Afghanistan, they did not let our domestic battles affect our personal relationship. It was during that period that the first Indian officer was to come for the German General Staff Course, and from amongst the alumni I was the first person to be contacted for advice. Operation Blue Star took place soon after I left. Otherwise I would have tickled one of them that the days of one Singh or the other representing the Indian Army in Germany were over, and I am sure he would have taken it sportingly.

Ever since, there has never been 'any quiet on our eastern front'. The Siachen violation; Indira Gandhi's assassination; Brasstacks—if it was an exercise or an operation depended upon its design; the Sikh insurgency and the Kashmir uprising; the nuclear tests; the

Kargil ingress; and indeed all the post-9/11 turmoil ensured that our relationship was alive and (literally) kicking. Indeed, the period was dotted, even if sparsely, by peace efforts like the Composite Dialogue, Vajpayee's bus yatra, 'they met at Agra', and the Kashmir bus service. The toxic, or the intoxicating, mix helped people like me, who had been in and out of hot seats, join post-retirement the ever-expanding club fatuously called 'the strategic community'.

No surprise, therefore, that some of us are bursting with wisdom that can hardly wait to be shared. One of the more useful means to do so would indeed be an exchange amongst key players on the opposite sides—provided of course we were prepared to concede our faults and provide a different narrative, even alternative facts. How far my 'comrade in arms'—as he describes our equation—Amarjit Singh Dulat, and I have succeeded in this mission is obviously for the reader to judge.

Asad Durrani

Rawalpindi, Pakistan
March 2018

I

SETTING THE STAGE

In the opening chapters, Dulat and Durrani explain how this book came about and why they thought it relevant. They speak about their backgrounds as professional intelligence officers, and narrate an episode that not only solidified their friendship but also firmed up their belief that a healthy India and Pakistan relationship has more benefits than downsides.

Setting the scene

May 25, 2016: Our first set of meetings was in Istanbul, at an upmarket hotel in the historic Old Town. The first time the three of us met was for lunch at the rooftop restaurant, the mild sun pleasantly shining through the windows, the waterfront visible in the distance. General Durrani looked at me intensely, as if to size me up. Peter Jones was even more wary, perhaps the effect of a full plate of Turkish kebab.

1

'Even if we were to write fiction, no one would believe us'

———

Aditya Sinha: The trust between you and Mr Dulat would seem unusual to a layperson. How did it come about?

Asad Durrani: In my experience, once people believe they are going to get together and exchange their views as professionals, more often than not they have no problem. Also, when we speak and one says—this is how we read a particular situation at the time; and then the other says—well, we were reading it like this. This is of great mutual benefit.

For example, when I read Dulat's book,[1] I found so many things beneficial, but also clarified. For instance, how the other side reacted to a particular development.

Sinha: An example of an eye-opener?

Durrani: The Kashmir uprising. I was involved in aspects for a couple of years. When it happened, I was heading Military Intelligence. We were looking for more information. It was not my subject, more for the foreign office or the ISI directorate. And it happened during Benazir Bhutto's first government, probably early 1990; she asked all three for their assessments.

Some were saying, it's happened before, it's another type of development taking place, more youth, and not likely to last. Such people had known about commotion in Kashmir.

It, of course, went on longer than expected. The deficiency on our side was that those who got involved were surprised; they weren't experts, maybe ignorant, and their assessment was not up to the mark.

Dulat's book showed that on the other side they had a man dealing with Kashmir for a long time, ten years, I think, before he became RAW chief, in different capacities. He was asked to do something about it, manage it as well as possible, and that focus continued. That continuity of personalities, of knowledge and experience, and probably also of policy.

On our side, the Pakistani side, most of the time we dealt with the development from event to event, as a person saw it fit, not clear till late what actually happened, how far it would go. And even if one figured out the best way forward, the government changed, the personalities changed, and even the policy, so continuity does not happen. Just reading Dulat's book highlighted this for me. It was not a complete surprise, one knew about him and the tenures on the other side.

I remember in MI someone told me that on the Jammu side there was a lieutenant colonel posted there for 15-16 years, I forget his assignment. I was tempted to recruit him. He probably knew more about us than our own people did because they changed so often. That may be peculiar to the system.

Sinha: What do you hope for from this book?

Durrani: Frankly, the idea was Amarjit's. He said, let's do a book. We've done joint projects, the first on intelligence cooperation, after the Pugwash Conference[2] in Berlin in 2011, and that was a good experience. The second was a paper published by the University of Ottawa on Kashmir in 2013, and it was encouraging.

Dulat's book was also interesting for its London launch. Indians and Pakistanis were there, including some Pakistani academics and others with whom I once spent an evening. One of them messaged me: 'We were at the book launch and the relaxed way in which the former RAW chief spoke, with a bit of humour, reminded us of our meeting with you. And we thought someone with a similar background might do a similar project.'

If our being together gets traction and creates interest, one can give perspective on some matters. If one would say one's piece as frankly and honestly as possible, without being defensive or offensive, then this was a project worth pursuing.

Amarjit Singh Dulat: We had done two papers. Some people provoked and prodded us: 'You guys seem to be comfortable with each other, why don't you do some writing?' Let's attempt something a little more serious, and we wrote on intelligence cooperation. As General Saheb says, when professionals meet they exchange views. I agree, there has to be a comfort level.

We have different types of personalities. Our backgrounds are different, apart from being from the (intelligence) agencies. But there are commonalities also. He doesn't bother to watch television, nor do I. I realised he can be laid-back. I thought I was the only one who was laid-back. It gives you comfort.

The interesting thing was he's my senior. When we met I was actually looking in this Track-II business to meet someone from the ISI. It was a huge opportunity and I didn't want to just spend my time with diplomats, drinking whiskey. I wanted to talk our kind of business.

I first went to Pakistan for the Balusa Group[3] meeting in January 2010, thanks to Salman Haidar.[4] When I got to Lahore the first thing I asked the generals there was—isn't there anyone from ISI who lives in Lahore. I actually said this.

'No, you'll have to go to "Pindi",' came the response, 'or at least to Islamabad. If you had told us, we might have arranged it.'

And then I came across General Saheb.

Durrani: It was in a Chao Phraya Dialogue[5] in Bangkok. We co-chaired a session on terrorism.

Dulat: I wanted to say things but it was my first time. I wanted to be more truthful than we normally are, but found myself waffling. And when he spoke, he spoke so directly, about proxies, and how they were legitimate for every intelligence agency.

During the coffee break, I said: 'General Saheb, what are you saying about proxies?'

'Why?' he said. 'Don't you use proxies? What did you do in Bangladesh? What was the Mukti Vahini?'[6]

The man was direct. 'No, Sir, I understand,' I said. 'I've figured it out.'

There were three of us at the first few meetings, including Vicky Sood,[7] and we were laughing about 'happy hours'. General Saheb said these sessions would go on, but that the three of us should talk separately. The three of us sat down with glasses of whiskey and started talking. More openly and honestly.

I was surprised by the things he said. He said amazing things which I frankly couldn't think of, because spooks don't talk easily. And for a former ISI chief to be talking candidly. Even Vicky was pleasantly surprised.

After the second meeting Vicky went off to greener pastures in Europe. We were left by ourselves, a certain relationship built.

In Islamabad in 2011, when we got a bottle of Black Label (whiskey) from General Saheb's car and had a drink in my room, he spoke to me about how it would be if we had an understanding. For instance, if Mumbai[8] happened again, there would be an understanding that India had to retaliate. And that it could be managed. That India could do what (Prime Minister Narendra) Modi did, a surgical strike.

It was interesting. Here was a former ISI chief with a considerable reputation, suggesting how to choreograph surgical strikes. How can a person get more candid?

The ISI is supposed to have the most difficult rogues. I have gotten to know General Saheb over a period of time and he has surprised me more and more.

These sessions went on. One interesting morning the two of us sat together, at a conference in Istanbul, and Malini Parthasarathy of the *Hindu* was so excited she took out her phone and took a photograph, saying, 'I've got the two spooks together.' It sounded so funny.

It was in that session that Peter Jones[9] made a suggestion that we write something.

Durrani: A joint paper.

Dulat: We wrote a joint paper on intelligence cooperation. General Saheb initially remarked that even if we wrote fiction nobody would believe it, but okay, we'll give it a try. It was published simultaneously in the *Hindu* and in *Dawn*.

Then Peter suggested we do a Kashmir paper. That is now on the University of Ottawa website.

Sinha: What was the reaction to your joint paper?

Durrani: (American academic) Stephen P. Cohen sent a message that he was very impressed by our paper on intelligence cooperation. He's a specialist on Indo-Pak affairs. I got emails from elsewhere.

Sinha: What do the governments say about such meetings or papers?

Durrani: Not a word.

Dulat: Same on our side. And because General Saheb is internationally renowned, Stephen Cohen may have called him, but nobody called me!

Durrani: I'm sure there are people on your side, like a couple on ours who are upset and say: 'These chaps? What do they know? Having messed up royally in their own time, they want to have a joint anti-terror mechanism and a joint intelligence? They want another paradigm?' They think we are looking not only for recognition but further employment.

Even in the US think-tanks like Brookings Institute, which are 'Inside the Beltway', they keep churning out papers, earmarking them to Senate committees. Unless what they say supports existing government policy, they will not get due attention. They make recommendations but the government is following a policy in the belief that it's doing the right thing. Rarely is a report seen and is the basis for help.

Dulat: Absolutely right, Sir. That's what gives the IDSA or now the Vivekananda Foundation importance, because they toe a certain line. These are almost government think-tanks.

Sinha: They uphold the status quo.

General Saheb, after interacting with a few chiefs from the other side, do you see Mr Dulat as representative of Indian spooks or is he a maverick?

Durrani: Of course he's different. We are all different in our own ways, but he is different in a number of ways.

First of all, his hands-on experience. More than ten years looking at Kashmir, at the IB, then as the RAW chief, then at the PMO (Prime Minister's Office). That he was a former IB man coming to head RAW and that he was accepted means his approach was different. I know institutions resist outsiders gatecrashing their domain. They would like to show that this intruder fails. Otherwise, inducting outsiders might become the norm. I know from personal experience, and also within the military.

Certainly his book also shows that he's not stuck on a particular idea. He understands the Kashmir issue's genesis, not thinking of what to do now, a response here, a tit-for-tat there, but seeing the bigger picture, the people there.

You may manage Kashmir or muddle through it but finally one will have to find a lasting solution. This is when he says we'll have to do something different. My assessment, though, is that we are not likely to do anything that much different, not because we are stuck in a groove but because we have settled conclusions as State policy that we try and make last as long as possible.

My own experience in intelligence was limited, just three and a half years, so he may have more narrative to add, I have less. But we have come to certain conclusions that masla yeh hai and perhaps that can help shift the focus from the usual rut and provide a way forward. Some may be sceptical about the things we come up with, but even if a few thoughts start making sense to them, then it could percolate to decision-makers.

Dulat: Yes, I've learnt an amazing amount through Kashmir in the last 30 years. To understand Kashmir you have to empathise with Kashmir, you have to have a heart to try and see what is happening. And if you start understanding Kashmir you'll find that you understand a lot more happening in the world.

Kashmir took me to Pakistan. And in trying to figure out Pakistan, that took me to Afghanistan. And looking at Afghanistan, I find so many similarities with Kashmir.

(Pakistani writer) Ahmed Rashid once said that if we can sort out Kashmir, Afghanistan would be a cakewalk. Kashmir leads you to Central Asia as well. When I look at the world I find there is a lot to learn from what is happening in Kashmir.

General Saheb once mentioned the Palestinian problem. In many ways it's stuck in the same way as we are in Kashmir.

The interesting thing is that news about our association has travelled in Kashmir. A few Kashmiris say to me that one way out of this whole thing is to get a couple of Indians who understand Kashmir together with a few former ISI chiefs, and the first name always mentioned is General Saheb. They say if you give us a chance to sit with you guys, we can find a way out.

It's interesting that the separatist Kashmiri looks at it like that. He knows that this cannot happen without Pakistan. Now even the mainstream is coming to the same conclusion. Mufti Saheb[10] used to say this. Mehbooba[11] doesn't say anything, rarely does she mention Pakistan. Strangely, Dr Farooq[12] has been repeatedly saying that unless India and Pakistan sit down, we'll not have a solution in Kashmir.

Sinha: Since General Saheb mentioned the book, you received criticism for it and for saying that money played a part in Kashmir, though that may not be a secret to a professional.

Dulat: You were determined to send me to Tihar (jail)! When it came out, like the General said, nobody said a word to me. Officially, directly. But I could sense that the establishment was not happy. And there were people who were critical. Not directly. Like you heard. I'm not surprised, others also told me that people were not happy. I said yeah, so be it, I've written a book and that's it.

What is the big deal about money? This became a big thing for everyone. (Senior journalist) Harinder Baweja took me to lunch just to get me to talk about money. Money is a given all over the world.

Durrani: (Chuckles.)

Dulat: I said it in a certain context, that after I left government and the PMO in 2004, some blamed me for everything that went wrong in Kashmir. It's this guy's fault, he bribed Kashmiris. A senior, senior officer said I bribed my way through Kashmir.

My reaction was: Why don't you try dealing with Kashmir? Or tell me of a better way of doing it?

2

The Accidental Spymaster

Aditya Sinha: General Saheb, how did you reach the ISI? Before you met Mr Dulat, had either of you met counterparts from the opposite agency? Did you picture them to have horns and tails, for example?

Asad Durrani: My entry to intelligence was accidental. I was not trained for this work. I was a normal line officer with a reasonably good career.

The first time I was nominally administered by an organisation called ISI was when I was a full colonel and was posted as defence attaché at our embassy in West Germany, 1980-84. Otherwise, the post is an open one.

Do you know who cleared me for the posting ultimately? I was a senior instructor at the Command and Staff College, for us a prized position. When my name came up for the Germany posting, it had to be cleared by various agencies. One of them went to my in-laws' house in Model Town, Lahore, to ask about me. No one was at home, so they went and asked the neighbours' chowkidar, 'Yeh kaise log hain?' That chap said, 'Yeh acchhe log hain.' I got the green signal and I always say that my neighbours' chowkidar provided the certificate that the intelligence agency sought.

Sinha: So had your in-laws been home, you might not have become defence attaché?

Durrani: Quite possible. You never know with these in-laws!

As defence attaché the ISI was administratively looking after me, but I had no covert missions assigned to me. I was not spying in Germany. The hosts knew me, I would go and get information from them. I was lucky to go there, just after the Soviet invasion[1] of Afghanistan; because of Pakistan's stance we had extraordinarily good relations with the West. Getting information from the Germans was no big deal, and after the NATO attachés, I obtained the maximum. At times, I even got exclusive briefings.

I returned to Pakistan and resumed my career as a line officer. Zia's[2] plane fell from the skies, and the new army chief, General Mirza Aslam Beg, with whom I had served, put me in charge of Military Intelligence (MI). That was a bolt from the blue.

The move to ISI was also accidental. After Benazir Bhutto's[3] dismissal in August 1990 they were looking for a person to keep the seat warm till they found someone else. Just because I was in MI for two years, as a manager of that branch and from the military, doing military assessments on the military front, they grabbed hold of me. Since I was current on Afghanistan, current on Kashmir, current on the impending Iraq/Kuwait crisis, I got the job.

I spent nearly 18 months at the ISI. Surprisingly, when I landed in MI I saw an Indian confidential report describing me as a hawk. No one from the other side had ever talked to me except for your attachés in Germany. Abroad you aren't hawkish or dovish, you are colleagues working in a third country, sometimes exchanging views and talking on 'soft' matters.

Sinha: What was your image of intelligence work before you went to Germany?

Durrani: Any normal person, in Pakistan or in India or elsewhere, is wary of anyone in the spook business. That chap probably has the boss's ears. God knows what else these intelligence chaps are up to, they move covertly, quietly and surreptitiously. So be careful.

When I was in the business I said good heavens. We were assessing threats to the country, external and external-sponsored threats, trying to warn the relevant quarters that these threats are developing, these are the dangerous ones. It wasn't what I used to think, cloak-and-dagger work, but it was an honourable job.

That's why I had the Corps of Intelligence created in the Pakistan Army. The idea had been floating for some time but I said let's go ahead with it. Certain aspects of intelligence should be handled by specialists. Previously there were reservations, and this apprehension was not misplaced, that professionals in this business would acquire the form or character of a mafia, and become a brotherhood. And then, leave aside the country, everyone else in the environment is threatened. But I went ahead with it.

One thing that happens is collateral damage. I'm looking for the people on the payroll of an enemy country, who may be on the payroll of people whose interests are not the same as mine, and in the process stumble on activity that has nothing to do with the interests of the country. I might think it's a good idea to sort him out. Some would even blackmail: look I caught you with a girl, nothing to do with national security, but since one has come to know about this extra-marital relationship one can nail that chap.

These things happen. This is not our main task and if it happens, it has to be resolved. But it makes people see intelligence as something to be shunned. A covert operator can know things we don't want him to know, and he may be at a particular level but can go to high levels because of the nature of the job. If people think they will get exploited and misused, they get scared.

Sinha: You also served under Nawaz Sharif?

Durrani: It never worked out with Mian Saheb when he first headed government and I was DG ISI. People can talk about chemistry or about his way of looking at things. It just did not work out.

Sinha: You didn't think highly of his intellectual capability.

Durrani: That's one. I also thought he was paranoid about certain things. About what the military might do, what the ISI would do, should he not have his own person to head ISI?

When my boss Aslam Beg left, and since the DG ISI serves at the pleasure of the prime minister regardless of the army—the army never says, 'issi ko lagao'—I got ready to go. Since I served as a two-star general it was supposed to be a stopgap arrangement.

Ultimately I became three-star, continuing because Mian Saheb said that Aslam Beg has gone and Asif Nawaz (Janjua) has come in his place as army chief. This is paranoia: thinking that if Asif Nawaz gets his own DG ISI then there'll be an army-ISI nexus that he'd be faced with. Sharif had had his doubts about me, but his expectations suddenly changed and he now thought he had his man.

It was an example of the flawed perception that civilian politicians had of how affiliations and loyalties in the services work. We are not anyone's man. You can be fond of someone but when it comes to work you are loyal to the institution. That still remains a plus point for us, and on many different levels.

For instance, with Aslam Beg I did not agree on the first Gulf War, in 1991. With Nawaz Sharif I did not agree on Afghanistan; he believed that we were working for not only a broader consensus but we were also asking the United Nations—Benon Savan used to be special emissary (formally, the Secretary-General's Personal Representative)—to work for the Loya Jirga, because Pakistan individually or Pakistan-Iran or Saudi Arabia may not be able to. We weren't making headway on Afghanistan, so the reconciliation should be led by the UN, supported by the OIC (Organisation of Islamic Cooperation). We had worked hard. The foreign office may have led that particular strategy and we supported it.

It's well known how Aslam Beg saw the first Gulf crisis. Jehangir Karamat as DG Military Operations (DGMO) did not agree with him. I as DG ISI did not agree with him. But he did not hold it against us. In fact, once his own assessment went wrong, he actually almost publicly admitted he was wrong. That's the greatness of the man.

In Sharif's particular case, he had the fear that this chap can't be trusted. So six months later, he found an opportunity and appointed his man. I left.

It was good for me, I went back to the mainstream. I headed something that no one with my background had ever been in charge of, the military's training. It's a mostly infantry army and I was an artillery man, a gunner. I had served in an infantry formation but that's another story. I was the first non-infantry officer who headed the army's training branch, which also holds inspections. I was happy during that period, and then went on to National Defence College. If any of us gets an all-arms appointment, it was a feather in the cap.

Sinha: This isn't the first time you've talked about your ISI days, is it?

Durrani: There is one thing that Indians share, whether they are friendly towards Pakistan or hostile: nothing gives them greater pleasure than if a former ISI man can be put on the mat.

Twice this was the case: in 2004 at the Pugwash Conference in Delhi, and at the Tehelka meeting in London. I found them a good bunch, Tarun Tejpal and his sister, their father being a former fauji. But on stage, on both occasions, when they asked me to say something, it was usually that I must have been sending infiltrators into India.

How do you avoid that embarrassment, or how do you defend it? I made light of it saying, you people misunderstood. We were not sending infiltrators, we were sending people because your visa regime is so rigid, we were sending them for people-to-people contacts. Go and meet them! Go and talk to them!

Dulat: The General said something very apt that while in service nobody is anybody's man. I have often been referred to as Dr Farooq Abdullah's man, which incidentally I regard as a compliment, but in 2002 when the NC lost the Assembly elections I was made out to be the main villain. I was then Brajesh Mishra's 'henchman' and often on the wrong side of North Block.

3

Brotherhood to the Rescue

Asad Durrani: When you mentioned a lack of hostility towards Pakistan I thought of an episode that should find place in this book. That was when Mr Dulat and some colleagues rescued my son Osman who was stranded in India, in May 2015.

Amarjit Singh Dulat: I got a call from General Saheb while out for dinner, around 11 p.m. He sounded a bit desperate.

Durrani: Osman was in Kochi, on behalf of the company he works for. It's a company that he had a hand in co-founding, in Germany, and had recently established an Indian office. As head of one of the company's software divisions Osman went there for a week for fresh recruitment and to develop an esprit de corps in the new team. That's a culture there that does not exist in many places; it's why a company is successful not just for the product but also for its collegial atmosphere. The way that the Japanese do it.

The crux is: my son was here on a Pakistani passport. Though he's been living in Germany for 20 years or so, and in this company for 15 years, he had kept his Pakistani nationality. He'd say, I'm a patriotic Pakistani.

And people in Kochi were fascinated by him. 'You are from Pakistan, how nice to see you,' they would say. They were very glad to see a Pakistani because they had never seen one before. And these were not Urdu speakers; there he spoke English. Someone told him, next time bring your wife and family. We'd like to see a Pakistani woman.

On this visit he finished up his work in four-five days. He thought of taking a flight from Mumbai. The office people in Kochi sent him to Mumbai not due to bloody-mindedness but out of ignorance. They did not know that if a person came with a Pakistani passport he had to follow a certain procedure: he had to leave via the city his visa allowed. They were only used to handling German passport holders, do their registration and fly away. They didn't know a Pakistani passport holder had to go to the police station, he had to go to Foreigners Regional Registration Office, and that on the way out of the country he would again have to go to both offices for clearance.

At the Mumbai airport, however, the immigration officials said your visa is only for Kochi, what are you doing in Mumbai? And he was sent away from the airport.

He then rang me up for help and advice, and besides talking to our high commissioner in Delhi, Abdul Basit, I called up ASD.

Dulat: Possibly because it happened in Mumbai it was easier for us to help out than it would have been in Delhi. General Saheb was unusually worried and kept inquiring whether it was safe for Osman to stay in Mumbai or whether he should return to Kochi. I said that means accepting that we can't do anything but we will do something, it's such a minor thing. Let's sleep over it, though I don't think the General would have slept peacefully.

I also spoke to a former colleague in RAW, who I'm sure helped without taking any credit for it. More substantively, in 2003 a tip-off from the RAW to the ISI had saved General Musharraf's life.

Durrani: Osman was stuck in some office for three to four hours where no one wanted to deal with him. It was a normal subcontinental bureaucratic office, where whenever he said I have been referred to this gentleman they would say, saheb toh seat par nahin hain. Twice this happened that a name was given to him and they said the officer is not in his seat. I was on the phone with Osman and I said, they obviously don't want to do anything.

We were in a panic because we did not know what would happen.

But even those people did not say to him, you don't have a visa for Bombay, what are you doing, pakdo, andar karo. That could have happened, but it didn't.

All this while my wife and I had another concern—what if someone reported that Osman, the son of a former ISI chief, was roaming around Mumbai, which hadn't forgotten 26/11, without a visa for that city?

Even his taxi driver had a good idea what was happening because he stayed outside for four hours with his luggage in the cab. A porter advised him to go back to Kochi, we know about this thing about leaving the way you came.

Dulat: The General called me six to seven times the next day, often asking the same thing: should I send him back to Kochi? I told him: 'Our boys are on the job and, Inshallah, he will fly out of Mumbai in the evening. You believe in Allah and I have full faith in Waheguru, all will be well.'

As the day passed, the thing was stuck in the police's Special Branch in Mumbai, and it was a Saturday so things were closed. I got a hold of Jeevan Virkar, an old friend from the IB. I knew the Mumbai police commissioner but that was an old link and I hadn't been in touch with him, whereas Jeevan and I had kept meeting. We were in the same social circle, so he was a friend throughout. I called Jeevan and said, bhai yeh karna hai.

Incidentally, Jeevan had met General Saheb because he had attended a couple of these Track-II meetings. He promised to sort it out.

Durrani: A few things happened during this to and fro that could only be sorted out by this cyber-savvy generation. For example, when Osman had earlier tried to board the flight and was offloaded, the chap at the immigration office asked him: 'How do we know that you were ever in Kochi? You may never have gone there!'

Osman quickly went on the internet on his cell phone and downloaded the document of the Kochi police registration. Later, with Jeevan's intervention, the lady in charge of the office arrived to finally force the reluctant staff to provide Osman with the necessary papers.

The man at the desk asked Osman what flight to Munich he would be taking. He hadn't booked a flight yet, so he quickly went to the Lufthansa website and reserved a seat online for the next flight. Then he showed them the reservation and they were satisfied.

It was a combination of his cyber expertise, good luck and help from Dulat and Co. that got him off the hook.

For 24 hours he had been on the phone, and a thing that was declared impossible was pulled off for him.

Sinha: A former RAW chief's IB background helped a former ISI chief.

Durrani: After this episode his company insisted he take a German passport. They say, we've been asking you to change your nationality, then all these restrictions that are imposed on Pakistanis in India, you won't have to deal with them. You were saved by the skin of your teeth by your father's friend, otherwise you would have been in trouble. Imagine, being in Mumbai, after 2008, being a Pakistani and with a father who was the ISI chief. They might have said, what a catch we've got!

Now, with his wife and two daughters Osman has helped retard the decline in the German population.

Dulat: When Osman finally left Mumbai, the General called and said: 'Your faith in Waheguru helped Osman.'

'Our Guru Nanak said there was no Hindu, no Mussalman,' I told him. 'We were at best born into a faith. The Supreme Being had rescued Osman.'

I rang up Jeevan and thanked him profusely. Then I realised I'd better thank my ex-colleague from RAW, so I rang him up. 'Not at all, Sir,' he said. But the best part of his response, which made me extremely happy, was his reference to General Saheb.

'It's our duty,' he said, 'after all, he's a colleague.'

Durrani: I immensely value that remark, and hope to get the opportunity to thank the gentleman personally.

II

THE SECOND OLDEST PROFESSION

In these four chapters, Dulat and Durrani discuss the business of spying. We tackle, head-on, the perceptions of the ISI and compare it to the RAW. They assess the activities of other intelligence agencies, particularly of the US, England, Russia and Germany. They then speak about the advantages of a dialogue of spychiefs, and the need to formalise a spy-spy communication channel between India and Pakistan, with their unique call for an 'open post' in each other's national capitals.

Setting the scene

Istanbul, May 25, 2016: We congregate in Dulat's room for 'happy hours' in the evening, a day of good work behind us. Since the tape recorder is off, a few other retired spychiefs land in the room, their (lubricated) tongues loosen and the jokes begin to fly. It may now be revealed that spies allow themselves a certain degree of bawdiness in a fraternal atmosphere.

4

Pakistan's Deep State

Aditya Sinha: People say the ISI is Pakistan's 'Deep State'.

Asad Durrani: Many intelligence agencies have been called the Deep State. CIA, KGB. It's a term denoting an establishment which runs the affairs of state behind the scenes. The very nomenclature indicates that it is invisible yet influential. In my vocabulary, it's a psy-war term. It's also hypocrisy. The United States has a 'Deep State' and it comprises big money, the military-industrial complex, and the Jewish lobby.

The 'Deep State' in America can even scuttle presidential policy, as it did to President Barack Obama's efforts to end the wars in Afghanistan and the Middle East. The CIA, State Department, Pentagon, and the military-industrial complex make the political leadership helpless. This is not something Pakistan says, various Americans including some former CIA heads say yes, there's no coordination between various organisations, so we do whatever we deem fit.

Deep State, incidentally, is also making life miserable for President Donald Trump, preventing him from improving relations with Russia or fulfilling his election promises to disengage from foreign military ventures.

Sinha: Didn't Pakistan's Deep State keep Osama bin Laden hidden?

Durrani: I've been on TV with my own assessment, whether unko chhupa ke rakha hua hain, or whether at some stage we knew, we had the upper hand. At some stage the ISI probably learnt about it and he was handed over to the US according to a mutually agreed process. Perhaps we are the ones who told the Americans isko le jao, we are going to feign ignorance.[1] If we denied any role, it may have been to avoid political fallout. Cooperating with the US to eliminate a person regarded by many in Pakistan as a 'hero' could have embarrassed the government.

A.S. Dulat: Our assessment is the same. That he was handed over by Pakistan.

Durrani: It was pretty uncomfortable for us.

Dulat: In India we had never heard the term 'military-industrial complex' till a few years ago, that it was becoming powerful.

As for the ISI, it's a great organisation, otherwise it wouldn't get named every day in India. Whatever goes wrong in India is attributed to the ISI. It's very effective, whether you call it the Deep State or the State within the State. It is by far the most exciting of the intelligence agencies.

Sinha: But ISI publicity has come down after Narendra Modi became prime minister. Now everything is blamed on liberals and intellectuals, not on ISI.

Dulat: I was once asked by a TV channel in Karachi what I thought of the ISI. I said, ISI's great, I would have loved to have been the DG ISI!

Sinha: Have prime ministers in Pakistan been fearful, ambivalent or fascinated by the ISI?

Durrani: Quite distrustful. I don't think anyone wants to task the ISI with a good run-down on any subject, though it's their right.

On critical matters the ISI will often impose itself simply because it needs a decision. We needed to take a certain step, but we don't want to warn the military, the civilian leadership, the bureaucracy.

Some think the ISI is powerful enough to order everyone to fall in line. Even if that were true, the ISI would not get civilian cooperation unless they were willing.

Dulat: You're right, but the point is it's a small state, it's a dictatorship. When the ISI focuses on one thing, they have the manpower and capability to do it in many kinds of ways. They'll get it one way or another.

Durrani: The ISI's clout grew probably because of the (1980s) Afghan jehad. The organisation was developed, and given plenty of resources and support because the Soviets had invaded Afghanistan. Otherwise it would never have had the wherewithal that a country facing so many threats, external and internal, would get. It still remained short and had to focus on quality. It could not afford much manpower and had to make do with less.

It developed a reputation for efficiency. It also developed a reputation because many people did not like what the ISI did, due to clashing interests. One example was after the Soviets left, the United States became uneasy: now that the job is done, how do we cut the ISI down to size before it becomes too big for its boots.

There was a particular reason, conceded by General Brent Scowcroft, who was US President George H.W. Bush's NSA (national security adviser). Two years after the 1991 Gulf War he said in London that the ISI assessment of the Iraqi forces' potential when it occupied Kuwait was better than the CIA's. It was my assessment that the CIA highly exaggerated the threat. We hardly had any assets on the ground and required a hard-nosed, cold-blooded, methodical assessment.

The CIA deliberately overblew the threat either to oblige its political masters who were raring for war, or to play safe with dubious satellite images. I don't know where the satellites were looking when India was preparing for its nuclear tests in Pokhran in 1998.

Dulat: General Saheb dismissed electronic surveillance and I agree, I don't believe anything electronic unless it's endorsed by human intelligence.

Durrani: If I was in the CIA's position I would also worry about the type of assessment the ISI was capable of making. I have said this in a piece published in the *Atlantic* a few years ago: the next time you want to sex up the WMD threat in Iraq, as happened in 2003, and if the ISI says, nonsense, you should be worried.

These things created the ISI profile. Larger than life? Probably a little exaggerated. But it had to be efficient given Pakistan's environment: India is big enough, Afghanistan is hot enough, Iran is experienced enough and sometimes independent enough, and the US also still meddles in the region's affairs. The ISI had to juggle many balls.

You people probably did things more discreetly. You could afford to: you had time, we at times were in a hurry. We felt threatened to the extent that we opted for immediate results. One can lose the basic principle of doing things coolly, deliberately, for the long haul.

Dulat: The ISI chief was the last word, he could say anything and get away with it. Right or wrong. He had to be right if he was saying so. Our guys were more circumspect in an assessment, which was supposed to be more serious.

Durrani: ISI's ability to make political assessment has been quite limited. Yahya Khan[2] went ahead and held the 1970 election because the intelligence agencies told him it would be a hung outcome and his regime would thus continue. However, Mujibur Rahman[3] swept in East Pakistan, Bhutto[4] swept in West Pakistan, and Yahya Khan landed nowhere.

When I headed ISI, people reported assessments and likely turnout for the 1990 election. I said the People's Party would suffer, but only marginally. The results showed the PPP was decimated. So much for that assessment.

When it comes to grassroots intelligence, however, the police are more effective. No one is better than the police's Special Branch.

For example, the Lal Masjid[5] episode in which many children and women were victims of a massacre. I believe it was a disaster. It was badly handled by the authorities: wrong force used, wrong means. On occasions like that when you have hundreds of children and women with possibly tens of militants in a place that is open to movement and enough information available, and if you have to take the militants out, it's best to use the Special Forces. They operate stealthily, and would have nabbed the militants while saving the innocent. But they sent the Rangers instead, who burnt down the place.

That incident gave rise to suicide bombers.

A couple of weeks later I was in Rawalpindi. These garrison towns have photography studios and tailor shops where military people go, have a uniform tailored and get a photograph taken. I went to the well-known Bhatti studios, as on many occasions, and an SHO walks in. He recognised me and said: 'General Saheb, ek SHO da kaam si, tussi saari fauj lekar uthhe pahunch gaye?' (It was an SHO's job, why did you take the entire army there?)

A single SHO could have gone in, seen how many militants were there, and then probably bribed a few or probably got a hold of the family members of a few of them and used them to release hostages. And before we know it, the 10-12 militants would have been taken care of. But the government did not trust the effectiveness of the police.

Then the Peshawar school incident,[6] which was a nasty one. The intelligence agencies had been warned that a big place would be hit, but which one of the hundreds? The Special Branch would have noticed unusual activity at the APS (Army Public School), which was on the watchlist, and increased security. That type of near-time information is more useful. And then would come the ISIs, the RAWs and the IBs to build the big picture of terrorist attacks.

The mighty ISI will say, who will implement it? Who's better known to the locals with whom we ultimately deal? That's what the local police are for. All we can do is ensure the police remain effective.

Dulat: I'm happy this whole argument is coming from the General and not me. Because I'm an old IB guy, but he's a General. And chief of the ISI.

Sinha: The most infamous ISI chief in Indian eyes has been the late General Hamid Gul.[7] He was to India what Ajit Doval is to Pakistan.

Durrani: Hamid Gul was my predecessor, though not my immediate one. I have known Hamid ever since we were both lieutenant colonels. He was a professional intelligence man. Very brainy. Read a lot. And his forte was that he would try and hypothesise things, put them in a particular context. I don't know what he himself fabricated, but he had a particular purpose. His presentation was always impressive. Knowledge of history, etc. If he became famous later it is because he talked about these theories or hypotheses.

Hamid liked to sex things up for the necessary impact. We were different types of people but remained friends till he died. We agreed on certain things and disagreed on others but were friends. I admired him, and his knowledge, commitment and dedication.

Dulat: Yes. We used to say he was the villain, the godfather, the ultimate. And yet after he passed away, quite a few tributes were paid, some not very nice.

The most interesting thing was that A.K. Verma[8] wrote a piece in the *Hindu* saying there was a time when Hamid Gul offered peace to us. It was a positive tribute. Reality and perception don't always match. And on our side, if you're looking for hawks, A.K. Verma is a hawk. Yet he's willing to credit Hamid Gul.

Durrani: When Hamid was DG ISI he was monitoring the 1988 election. I was at MI. He said the People's Party would win and came close to the actual number of seats. But he went wrong in Punjab and Sindh; the results were the opposite of what he predicted, by the same margin. In Sindh, he predicted less for the PPP, they swept. In Punjab, he predicted more seats, they got that many less.

Sinha: Around that time, the Bible for reporters like me was *The Bear Trap*.[9]

Durrani: There are many books like *The Bear Trap* that are in a particular mould, with an agenda. That's all that I want to say. It wants to highlight a particular personality or period or contribution. That becomes the problem. When it was published, I think during my period, someone came and said look at what's written. What should we do? Should we get a hold of the man, court martial him, issue a rebuttal? I said, there must be 20 people who have read it but once we do something, 200 people will read it.

I'm not happy with things that are projected out of context or send a message that might not be helpful either to the country or to the organisation.

I don't recall accurately as to what we found at that time that should be vetted or scrutinised. But one said, let it be. Whatever you say about the book will never be as effective as the book itself. Also, it was well-written, a foreign chap was involved. One had heard good things about the author Mohammad Yousaf's contributions. He headed the ISI's Afghan cell under General Akhtar Abdur Rahman,[10] at a crucial stage of the Afghan jihad.

Sinha: Since the ISI is part of the military, can people enter at higher levels without a military background?

Dulat: Let me take the liberty to say that we may be a little more 'on the job'.

Durrani: We had a handicap in this regard. There is experience and continuity in the IB, Special Branches, police.

ISI made its name for different reasons—Afghanistan, military rule—but it has a certain personnel problem. MI came to me when I was a mainstream officer, and I was moved to ISI because I was current on both of our fronts.

This was not unusual. Many heads of ISI and MI came with no intelligence experience for a variety of factors. By the time you start understanding how you're supposed to do field jobs or specialised jobs, you get promoted. It is a gap, though the military sees it as movement within the force.

There was an air force officer who left ISI and went to the IB. Few do that since the IB is mostly police or civilians from the government cadre; some retired military officers have headed the IB but that's an exception. We didn't miss the chap, but he did a reasonable job in IB. The interesting part happened when he fell afoul of the political leadership. They made him stay at home, but gave him his pay, and he kept silent, pursuing leisure like reading, writing, etc. This would not have happened in the military.

One more thing. Back in 2010, Amanullah Gilgiti[11] was leading his people for the October 27[12] march from Muzaffarabad to Chakothi on the Line of Control. I went along. There's an important barrier with a battalion to prevent people from going too close to the LoC, and I thought I would tell them who I was, once upon a time. There was a junior commissioned officer who stopped me and said: 'Saheb, aap kabhi thhe toh thhe, abhi toh nahin hain na.'

Dulat: That happens all the time. They may not openly say it, but nobody takes notice of you once you're out of the system.

Durrani: The first thing I was involved in when I entered the intelligence business was the Maldives invasion.[13] Also at that time,

Nepal was active because it bought six MPA (MasterPiece Arms) guns from China. Thereafter Rajiv Gandhi[14] enforced a weapons embargo.[15] I said, if this is the situation between Nepal and India, where do we fit in? We may have had wishes for a long time, but this was when one started looking at it. How do we make use of this?

Benazir's government was neither interested nor knew what to do. With some colleagues I said, what would General Zia have done? We agreed that Zia would have been proactive. People would have been seen doing something—statements, visiting, calling the ambassador, the works.

So I went and looked up the Nepalese ambassador. Kathmandu usually posted retired military chiefs as ambassadors. In those days a couple of military men had followed one another. The Sri Lankans also did that. I went and asked him, how could we help?

Sinha: They had a military man because of Zia?

Durrani: Probably. For me, it was a development in Indian backwaters, how can we make use of it?

Dulat: How can we exploit it?

Durrani: The Kathmandu dinner we three had, I asked our host despite your presence, whether India makes the Nepalese unhappy. He said, yes, of course. Because here is a big country, India, with hegemonic ambitions. They like prevailing on us, telling us what type of system we should have, whether or not it is good for us. That we could be a part of India, a big province, benignly, positively. That's one way of annexation. What is it they did to Sikkim?

But why only talk of Nepal and India? Afghanistan and Pakistan: we're much smaller than India, and Afghanistan much bigger, more potent and more problematic than Nepal. Yet Afghan generals come and say, you think we are your fifth or sixth province, kya baat kar rahe ho? Some of our people say, you are our younger brother. They immediately respond: 'Younger brother? We were there 200 years before you came along. We had never even heard of you in Afghanistan.'

This equation of an overbearing country and its neighbour exists on our side too.

Dulat: The Nepalese were always willing to concede that they are the younger brothers.

Sinha: What happened with that Nepalese ambassador who was a military man?

Durrani: He said, 'We're only trying to get closer to China, that was the help we got from them. India is not the only one.' Never put your eggs in one basket.

But nothing happened. Pakistan was not in a position to have done much either in Maldives or in Nepal.

Sinha: That ambassador became your friend.

Durrani: I went and met him once or twice. When I was the head, the ISI head did not attend receptions, foreign National Days, nothing. I only attended two National Day functions. One was when Mani Dixit[16] invited me when Foreign Secretary Muchkund Dubey was visiting Islamabad.

I got to know Mani well. I met him while I was at MI and sitting in the army chief's room. Mani had taken over as Indian high commissioner and was making his first call on Aslam Beg, who handled things well though he sometimes got bad press. After half hour or so Aslam Beg says we're going to hold a big exercise (Zarb-e-Momin). After Operation Brasstacks we did not want to send the wrong signal or create panic. He said: 'We're going to hold it well away from the border.'

Mani Dixit, the trained, blue-blooded diplomat that he was, merely said: 'General, I will convey your message to people back home.'

After I moved to ISI, Dubey was visiting and I was invited to a reception. The DG ISI is unlikely to go to an Indian reception even under the best of circumstances, but I went and Mani Dixit was appreciative. We chatted with his daughter Abha, who was researching on Sindh, and then I had a few minutes one-on-one with Dubey.

The other function was when Nepal sent an invitation for its National Day. The ambassador, that General, was a clever man. There was no one else at the reception, I was the only one there. Just the ambassador of Nepal and the ISI head. The man was so clever that when he found out I was coming, he probably disinvited everyone or postponed it. He just wanted a one-on-one with me. Otherwise no receptions.

Dulat: I served in Nepal three-and-a-half years, under three ambassadors, my only experience in diplomatic service. I made a lot of friends and the key to those friendships was cricket, because I played a lot.

It started modestly. Nepal now has a national cricket team which in 2017 visited Bangladesh. In those days there were five-six cricket clubs. The Indian embassy was one. They had two tournaments here. One was a league, and one was a knockout. I represented the Indian embassy and came into contact with a lot of Nepalese. I made many friends.

In those three-and-a-half years the Indian embassy became a serious cricket team. At the end of it we won the league, we won the knockout, and in our arrogance we took on a combined Nepal team and beat them as well.

Sinha: That's why they called you Big Brother.

Durrani: Beating them was not a good idea. We used to have a polo tournament in Brunei and the American team that came advised us not to beat the Sultan's team. That was the prescription to get invited again and again.

Dulat: Maybe it was not a good idea beating them. As a result, a Nepalese cricket team evolved. Before I left Kathmandu I was invited to play for Nepal; they were going to Bangkok to play in Thailand, there must be some club there. I said I would love to come, but I'm not Nepalese. I'll have to stay out of this.

One became well known here because of cricket. There's a big parade ground known as Tundikhel, where the parades are held, and where cricket used to be played in those days.

There was a game going on, we were playing one of the major clubs in Kathmandu, the Gentlemen's Cricket Club. I was watching from the boundary. The batter had gotten out, and a youngster walked up to me and asked (in Nepali), who's playing. I said Indian Embassy vs GCC. He didn't recognise me and asked, Daulat ki kati ho, meaning, how much did Daulat score. I was tickled.

But the net result was my final ambassador wrote a report on me to Delhi saying I did nothing but play cricket.

Durrani: I got a similar compliment from a famous corps commander. He was asked if I could be taken from the corps for appointment elsewhere. He said, yes, as long as he's available to join the corps team in the coming golf tournament. For him, his brigade commander was of no use.

Sinha: Any anecdote from your MI days?

Durrani: There's one about A.Q. Khan.[17] The DG MI attends certain receptions and I once went to a particular National Day reception. Many cars come, people get out, they go in. Once they come out, the man at the gate announces them. General Durrani Saheb ki gadi le aaye.

On that occasion the valet said, General Saheb aap ek taraf khade ho jaye, I have to talk to you. I said kya hua. He says, what business does A.Q. Khan have to come to all these receptions? Meaning this man should preferably be away from the limelight. He says, Saheb I do my duty, I have never said A.Q. Khan Saheb ki gadi le aaye. I always say, driver Fazalu Khan, gadi le aaye, so that no one knows that A.Q. Khan was here. I'm trying to keep this man as anonymous as possible. This chap comes and takes part in everything.

I appreciated this gesture, but A.Q. Khan loved to be seen and recognised. He may have been applauded at a couple of places, but there were enough people who did not appreciate it. Self-projection was one of his weaknesses, but his contribution to our nuclear programme was substantial if not decisive.

I went to the President Ghulam Ishaq Khan, who was the custodian of our nuclear programme. He got that role from Zia-ul Haq. Z.A. Bhutto as the prime minister was the father of the programme, Zia took charge of it and from him it passed to Ghulam Ishaq Khan. He was the best man to ensure that our programme remained on course, because he knew how to deal with things. If the Americans came, he would not talk to them. If someone else asked, he would explain our need for it.

I said, Sir, A.Q. Khan's appearance on frequent occasions, his public statements, they are not right. The wise old man that he was, he said, yes, I know. Every man has to be accepted as a package. He's useful, he's indispensable for the programme, and this is something we have to live with.

Had I gone anywhere else they would have said, please go and talk to the president. Some would say, lay off. To others, he would say none of their business. He would make sure no one touches the programme, no one fiddles with it, no one even tries to derail it.

Sinha: So your friends weren't scared of the Deep State?

Durrani: On the lighter side: as the head of the ISI, an old friend invited me for a small dinner. Drinks were served. Some guests got scared and said, Good Lord, we came here for a nice evening and the chief spymaster is sitting here. He's going to tell people we were drinking. And some of them were uniformed officers.

My friend assured them, I know this fellow, and he has certain constraints right now, but he's not likely to go around and say that so-and-so drinks. They probably then felt confident that okay, we can get away with it.

People may be scared that those caught drinking are dealt with severely. Regardless of all the prohibition from law, from religion, I do not remember if people who were fond of the tipple were ever harmed. General Zia was surrounded by people who were fond of drinking. It's unbelievable. And these people were scared because I was there.

5

ISI Vs RAW

Aditya Sinha: Which is better, ISI or RAW?

A.S. Dulat: To make a comparison with the RAW may not be fair because the ISI is much older, whereas the RAW is nearly 50 years old, bifurcated from the IB in September 1968. Its creation was a fallout possibly of the '62 and '65 wars, and Mrs Gandhi[1] felt the intelligence from abroad at her level was not receiving sufficient attention.

Asad Durrani: Once an American journalist with poor posture came up to me at a conference, casually posing a question: 'How do you rate RAW?'

It was obviously not so casual a question, and was probably intended to catch me off-guard and provoke me into analysis or say nothing. He was likely to go to the RAW chief and say, look, this is what the other fellow said, and get a response from him.

Instead, almost reflexively I said: 'At least as good as we are.'

The ISI's Afghanistan involvement happened before I took over, but I found absolutely everyone applauding it: friends, old friends, new friends, pseudo-friends. Many came and sang praises that ISI has become capable, it controls everybody, it has a name.

When I had that one-on-one with a member of (Foreign Secretary) Dubey's delegation, he asked: 'What is the ISI's main focus?' At that time our main focus was of course Afghanistan, but I thought I should put South Block to work. So I said: 'India, of course.'

Dulat: I would agree with General Saheb that if you took RAW and IB against the ISI or against Pakistan's agencies, they are as good professionally. There's a lot done by our agencies that people don't get to know about, or should not get to know about. In the intelligence world India produced big names like B.N. Mullik[2] and R.N. Kao[3] and M.K. Narayanan[4] and now Ajit Doval.[5]

Durrani: About ten years ago a ratings website called Smashing Lists came out with, among other lists, the world's ten best spy agencies. Out of the blue. ISI was number one, followed by Mossad, CIA, and all the others.

Of course, at home people felt happy about it. I was asked and I said, I don't know but the criteria for this rating seemed pretty good. One was the number of threats Pakistan faced, both inside and outside, another was the resources available to it. Unlike the days when we got money from Saudi Arabia and America, there's a shoestring budget and so a tight control of money.

The point is not who's one, two, three or four. You do a job well, keep a low profile, no one takes credit, no one blamed, no claims. Like you guys did your Mukti Vahini quietly.

For me, the best way to judge ISI was that during the Soviet occupation of Afghanistan, it got all the help from most of the big players in the West but allowed no interference in its role, organising the resistance. But then the Cold War was over and we had to change our objectives in the region, and the ISI was key to that.

Another accomplishment is that none of our operators ever defected or was 'caught on camera'.

Sinha: What has been the greatest ISI failure against India? I will ask him (Dulat) a similar question.

Durrani: I think my colleague should start.

Dulat: Our biggest failure against Pakistan is that we've not been able to turn around an ISI officer or have an ISI officer working for us. Or not to my knowledge, at a level where it counts.

If you go back to the Cold War, what was the main task of a CIA officer? It was to somehow find a defector. If a CIA guy found a defector then for the rest of his career he didn't need to do anything, because he had done what was supremely required.

On our side I don't think we've even imagined it properly and I don't think we've succeeded.

Sinha: Even if we had a mole inside ISI, nobody would know.

Dulat: Moles are easier to have than defectors.

General Saheb was talking about double agents. Double agents are the next best thing to defectors. If a guy is working for Pakistan and I get hold of him, then I have a chance of getting to where I'm supposed to be. So, not being able to find an ISI defector is our biggest failure.

Durrani: At the operational level, the 1965 war, we could claim we got good information about the other side, how they are assembled for war. But it was a lost effort.

In the 1971 war the ISI was unable to anticipate the attack in East Pakistan.

In my time we predicted that India's military build-up, after the Kashmir uprising, was not intended for war. I can pat my own back for that.

But the biggest failure was when the Kashmir uprising happened we did not know how far it would go. These things usually run their course in six months or a year. When it became lasting, we wondered how to keep a handle on it. We didn't want it to go out of control, which would lead to a war that neither side wanted. Could we micro-manage it? That was our challenge.

ISI's leverage on the Kashmir insurgency turned out less than successful.

In particular, I regret it till today why we did not take Amanullah Gilgiti more seriously. His group led the uprising. He started it, initiated it, spoke about it. I met him when I was at the ISI. He did not seem important at that time. In any case, his third option of independence was unnecessarily muddying the water. And what did independence mean anyway?

Gilgiti, though, was probably the most serious one, focused and connected. Like the rallies at Chakoti. Every year, on our side, October 27 is celebrated as Black Day. Gilgiti was the only person who brought his crowd in, disciplined, sober, serene, conducting the proceedings and the march without commotion. The others were non-serious, they came from here and there, made their speeches and left.

But going back to the evolution of the Kashmir uprising of the 1990s, I think the formation of the Hurriyat[6] to provide a political direction to the resistance was a good idea. Giving up handle on the movement—letting the factions do what they bloody well wanted to—was not.

Dulat: Let me make clear one thing. In public perception not getting Dawood[7] or Hafiz Saeed[8] or Masood Azhar[9] are glaring failures. But if instead of putting out a supari for Dawood, you 'turned' the ISI station chief in Delhi, that in intel would be a much bigger thing.

About the Pakistani angle in Kashmir, they often crow about putting out somebody here, or bumping off somebody there, or forcing someone to form an organisation, or sending out diktats. It's okay, works to an extent.

Kashmir is very painstaking and requires patience. That is where Pakistan has lost out.

Because after a while the feeling was, as General Saheb said, jaane do, let them go. This is on the basis of conversations with Pakistanis over the last ten years, since the Mumbai attack. The general response was that they can talk about Kashmir later, for now they can put it on the backburner.

But it's now 'game on' again in the last three years because of the uncertainty we've created. The status quo mess we create gets Pakistan interested again.

I used to tell Pakistani friends in Track-II, let's discuss your core issue, Kashmir. Even General Saheb would say, there isn't sufficient interest in Kashmir. Forget it for the time being.

It's been like that. It's a typical military reaction, a typical military way of dealing with a problem. That possibly, Sir, is one of the shortcomings in the ISI.

Durrani: That's in our system.

Dulat: You bulldoze your way. The Kashmiri knows how to play different sides.

Sinha: So the intelligence game is won by the Kashmiri even though he is suffering.

Dulat: A fellow I've known for years will tell me one thing and six months later will tell me something else; his perception, his story, everything will change.

In between, he'll bowl General Saheb a googly.

But Kashmir requires time. If you want to understand it or get yourself involved then it requires time, patience, empathy.

Durrani: I agree. I also agree with the point that under the circumstances, Kashmiris or Afghans learn to live with it, which means you have to keep two or three different sides in good humour. And still survive, fighting the Indian army or the US army.

Dulat: About Afghanistan, we always knew it was going to have repercussions for us. If the CIA let loose the ISI in Afghanistan, then you let loose the Hizb,[10] the Lashkar and the Jaish in Kashmir. You may say it is directly linked, but there's an inevitability about it. If the Americans felt the ISI was getting out of control, and they felt it as early as then, then our apprehensions were justified, that this is going to have big-time implications in Kashmir.

Durrani: It's easy to talk about possibilities and scenarios; if you do that, then they will do this. The capability, performance possibilities, conducive situation: many factors come into the picture. It doesn't happen that your people are in Afghanistan and our people will go to Kashmir. It's not a cyber-game in which you can target Jaish-e-Mohammed this side and a RAW-backed group on that side. Does it have ingress? Would locals cooperate with them?

At the same time, if we intend deploying a group I don't think one is waiting for the Indians or Americans to take a step and then, as quid pro quo, do it. We'd probably be doing it already. If not blatantly, at least in some form or other. It's not necessarily tit-for-tat.

Dulat: It was not tit-for-tat, Sir. We already had the tit! Now we were getting the tat.

Durrani: Sometimes you might believe it is so. Sometimes you might do it because if you're not going to do it in Kashmir you're going to somewhere else.

Dulat: So we agree that is when the ISI got a larger-than-life image and that was its heyday?

Durrani: The Kashmir thing?

Dulat: The Afghan thing and then Kashmir.

Durrani: The Afghan thing. Kashmir?

Dulat: Kashmir followed the Afghan thing.

Durrani: When one was looking at Kashmir, it is possible that one was unable to get the whole picture right. But initially, if the potential is suspect, we wait and watch.

Dulat: That's right, that's right.

Durrani: Then we say that because of the problems that you have elsewhere, this is not right time for us to start playing the Sikh card, the Kashmir card, the ULFA card.

Eventually, the idea was that if this is an uprising, it should not lead to a conflict that neither side wants. It can blow up, involve both countries in a war that neither side is bargaining for.

The idea was to keep it on a leash. Whether we could control these things is a different matter altogether. One had a good idea about our limited capability to handle so many big things, and punching above one's weight is not a good idea.

But if the dynamics of that thing was beyond us, that's another matter. The intention of the State was, however, not to continue on this track, and ultimately fly a green flag on Lal Qila (Red Fort).

Indeed, some might have said that—now that the Soviet Union was no more—Zia or Hamid Gul had ambitions beyond Afghanistan! But essentially we were only thinking about trade and cultural links. At that time even projects like 'electricity from Central Asia' looked like a bit over the top. Now with CASSA 100 and CPEC, it seems that some futuristic thinking was always in order.

It sounded fantastic at the time but the only substantial thing I heard was, let's get electricity from Central Asia. I said, what nonsense are you talking, how will we get the lines over the Wakhan corridor? But now, 25 years later, the China-Pakistan Economic Corridor (CPEC) is about that.

Dulat: Returning to the question of professionalism, I had asked those Kashmiris who had seen us and who had been to the other side, which agency has better people or is more professional? The general response was that our guys are generally better. Pakistan has some fine officers but they may not have an Ajit Doval.

Durrani: Thank God.

Dulat: I would say the RAW or the IB could certainly do with a General Asad Durrani.

Sinha: The RAW has had its share of poor leaders.

Dulat: I would always contest that since it would be true of agencies worldwide. There would be outstanding chiefs and some quite ordinary. General Saheb has said his opinion of the CIA was that it is a great organisation but it is a third-rate intelligence agency.[11] If the CIA is third-rate then its chiefs must have been ordinary.

So pedestrian chiefs are everywhere, in the IB, in the ISI.

Sinha: Has the ISI consistently seen strong leadership?

Durrani: Generally we regard the Indian system as more effective. It's institutional. It's not at anyone's whims, like when Tariq Aziz was pulled out of the revenue service and made our National Security Advisor. Or the loyalist who was a security officer but made the IB chief.

The DG ISI may be recommended by the army chief but the appointing authority was the prime minister. Not necessarily because he's somebody's friend. He'll have ideas, flair, know a bit of international relations, management, and the right temperament. Take his time with things. Some who were brusque tried to turn the organisation on its head, but mercifully the organisation is resilient and can withstand temporary shocks.

Dulat: One problem is that unlike some other agencies, we are burdened with not just intelligence collection, but intelligence analysis. I think the ISI is like us in this regard. In both agencies there is too much emphasis on analysis and not enough on collection. Our agencies need to be more hands-on.

Otherwise they are burdened with too much. What is an agency supposed to produce? If you want it to know everything that happens, then you miss out the essentials. What is our focus? Are we looking at Pakistan? Afghanistan? Kashmir, Tamil Nadu, Punjab? Internal security, external security? Counter-intelligence? Counter-terrorism? It's endless.

Another handicap we have is our tenure.

Durrani: Mossad chief has six years.

Dulat: The MI6 chief could serve longer, and after it he gets knighted. I was chief for only 17-18 months, like General Saheb. Just as you're settling in and beginning to understand the whole thing and enjoy it, your time's up. In India now chiefs have two years, but even that is not enough. It should be three years, except that the longer the term, the more people will miss out on being chief. You have to weigh this.

General Saheb said the ISI worked on a shoestring budget. In that case we had no budget at all because we were never funded by the CIA!

There's also the question of keeping a low profile. There was a time in India when you never saw a photograph of an IB chief. Mr Kao was never photographed. Now chiefs becoming public and being in the open is a recent phenomenon. I suppose it's the same around the world.

Sinha: Is it tougher for spychiefs with a strong prime minister?

Dulat: It is tougher, but it's also better. The tasking would be much tougher. The agencies like to create their own tasking. We feel we know it better than anybody else. When the tasking starts coming from the top, how it has to happen and which way we are heading, then it becomes that much more difficult.

It's difficult if you are catering, as General Saheb hinted, to a certain regime, or a certain set-up. With a prime minister as powerful and strong as Modi, the job of the intelligence agencies must be that much tougher. It might be getting simpler but it would not be easy.

There have been, incidentally, prime ministers in India who had no interest in intelligence. I don't think Morarji Desai (1977-79) considered intelligence an asset. P.V. Narasimha Rao (1991-96) was too intelligent and thought it was fraud and chuglibaazi. Even I.K. Gujral (1997-98) was sceptical about intelligence. Prime ministers like Rajiv Gandhi (1984-89) found it fascinating, maybe because he was young. He was absolutely fascinated, and relied so much on the agencies. The story is that the DIB would have coffee and chocolate with him at 10:30 every night.

The prime minister that I served with, A.B. Vajpayee (1998-2004), he liked to listen, he liked to be briefed. He didn't react, but he made you feel important and that what you're telling him he wants to know. He didn't rubbish it. For a person who spoke little and was so really himself, he gave you a patient hearing.

Sinha: Do the IB and the RAW work together well?

Dulat: I'm not saying that we don't work together, we do. The nature of intelligence work is such that inevitably there is a certain degree of jealousy and one-upmanship. But how far do you take that? In America, there have always been problems between the CIA and FBI. Not to say that it doesn't happen elsewhere. It's attributed to how big the CIA became. On the ground that's resented by the other people who're doing the same kind of thing.

Durrani: If in India you are working together, you are one step ahead of us. We hardly see any cooperation between our agencies.

Dulat: Pakistan is one step behind us? I'm glad, there should be something in which they are behind.

Durrani: In Pakistan, cooperation between government departments, civil-military, and generally is far from desirable. It may be because of our history.

Dulat: I grew up in the IB, spent 30 years there and, strangely, hadn't the foggiest idea what happens in the RAW. In the IB we had contempt for the RAW. When asked if I would like to head that organisation, I jumped at it. I was otherwise retiring as number two in the IB; earlier the home secretary offered me one of the para-military forces to head and I said no, I spent my whole life in intelligence, why would I want to move out.

When I went to the RAW they didn't like it. Understandably, they thought I was an outsider. It took a while to settle down and for them to accept that I knew the business. Interestingly, everybody worried that there would be a huge infiltration of the RAW by IB guys. My old friends thought I was still an IB guy in the RAW. So whenever there was a little argument or discussion between the two organisations, IB chiefs would say, arre yaar you're one of us. I'd say, of course, but now I'm heading the RAW and its interests would be uppermost in my mind.

Cabinet Secretary Prabhat Kumar one day asked, Dulat, main dekhta hoon idhar udhar IB wale ko, RAW wale ko bhi dekhta hoon, tumne to dono dekhe hai, tum batao which is better. I said, both are better. I said, the IB's more solid, it comprises basically policemen. Here you have a mix of various kinds, so sometimes there's no gelling together.

Sinha: Esprit de Corps?

Dulat: Yeah, sometimes. But man to man, there are good people in the RAW, so we should not run it down. Working together was so much easier in my time in the RAW because I would call Shyamal[12] up and say, let's sit down and sort it out.

Unfortunately it didn't last long. After us, it was back to square one, the squabbling, etc. There have been periods where it's been good, but not always.

Sinha: Does bureaucratic sloth exist in intelligence agencies?

Dulat: Yes, in two ways. One is the sloth that develops within an organisation. Intelligence agencies in a sense are bureaucratic, but you have to keep clear of bureaucratese. What we do in the agency is not authorised or given in any book. No rules would permit many things that are done. So if you bring bureaucracy into an intelligence organisation, sloth will follow.

The other difficulty is that as an agency you still have to deal with the bureaucracy, which varies from government to government. Like in Modi's government, I don't think that problem exists, because there is only Modi and Doval to deal with. There's no other bureaucracy. Even the other ministers don't count.

Similarly in Vajpayee's government it was basically him and his NSA, Brajesh Mishra. The others didn't count for much.

The defence or foreign ministers didn't interfere in our functioning. When I joined the RAW and went to meet the cabinet secretary, he said, I'm here to help you administratively. Professionally or operationally what you do, I don't want to know. Tell the boss. He seemed almost scared of us.

That kind of response from the bureaucracy is perfect. But it's not what always happens. A home secretary and a cabinet secretary could make things difficult for you. It depends on the in-between man. It's happened from time to time that an NSA has cut off interaction between the prime minister and an agency. Unfortunately, the status of the chief depends on that relationship, and everybody watches you, who you have access to, who you report to.

That's why in Britain they have this wonderful tradition where the chief can ask for time with the prime minister any time.

Sinha: Militaries also have bureaucracies. When you were ISI chief, did you face bureaucratic sloth, or was everyone too afraid of the Deep State?

Durrani: There is a bureaucracy, no doubt about that, one in the military and one in the defence ministry. They have power that the army cannot underestimate. Even when the military is ruling the roost, the ministry can ride roughshod over individuals.

Military bureaucrats are the ones at various headquarters as staff officers, etc. The attitude of these people is better than that of the normal bureaucracy. Not that they won't create problems or write dissenting notes, etc. It's just that the culture has no such thing as a staff officer sitting on a file. The civil bureaucracy is different: it can block a file, the demands won't be cheap. That bureaucracy will not let things happen.

The comparison between the Indian and Pakistani bureaucracies is that ours has its strength and a few weaknesses. The strength is that whether or not anyone is happy, they recognise that they have to do their work. The weakness is it's the military holding Pakistan together. The bureaucracy's ability to keep its political masters in check is limited.

In India it is good: strong, efficient, connected, maintained, functional. It has held together. It has not let politicians run amok. Its problem is the same that the American establishment has. This establishment does not allow anyone to step out of line. If the prime minister is a powerful one like Modi or Vajpayee, yes, but it keeps a check on how much they can do. The bureaucracy can obstruct or facilitate matters.

In the case of America, the establishment's attitude was, we'll see Obama saheb how long you can go through with that.

Dulat: What you're saying is interesting, Sir, because Indian democracy is rated as one of the better ones the world over. I've watched the bureaucracy from 1990 when I returned from Kashmir to 2004, when I left government. What I observed was that the fault lay not with the politician but with the bureaucracy. Of all the great guys that I saw during my 14 years in Delhi, except for a couple of exceptions, the others were just bureaucrats, they didn't stand for anything.

But in the case of Dr Manmohan Singh, he could not go to Pakistan, and while his party did not support him, it was sadly his bureaucracy which did not help. Whenever something went wrong, the fingers were immediately pointed at him.

Durrani: The bureaucracy is not popular anywhere, whether in the US, Germany or here.

Your remark is interesting that politicians are not to be faulted. In our case, we still are not fond of the democratic ways of doing things. Till that happens, not only politicians but sometimes the military leadership too shares the blame for spoiling the bureaucratic culture in Pakistan, making them ineffective, forcing them to give in to their demands. It is the old culture that did not want to be changed.

Dulat: Another significant point that General Saheb has made is the traditional neutrality of the bureaucracy. Where does it exist now? In India it ended with Mrs Gandhi. Maybe in Britain it still exists, but that must be the solitary country, if it exists.

Durrani: Ayub Khan[13] started tinkering with it, but more or less it remained steady.

Dulat: When you say tinkering, how many years after the Brits left did it survive?

Durrani: (Z.A.) Bhutto is when the rot started, Zia-ul-Haq expedited matters. Culture of corruption made it worse. The military bureaucracy too did not remain unaffected.

Sinha: You once mentioned the Soviet system's problem was that it allowed no dissent. But is there dissent in a military system?

Durrani: Our culture has developed in a manner that if you don't like something one would say, tumko zyada pata hai? That is the culture where the boss does not like people with different views.

Once I was part of an exercise with the German army. In the evening we were at the bar with the local command, a sergeant, some officers. Everyone paid for his own drinks. And they all were free to disagree with each other. We are not yet there.

Sinha: Does the RAW man in Islamabad have a tougher time than the ISI man in Delhi?

Durrani: I do not know. In my time—even though Kashmir was on the boil—I do not recall if there were any 'unusual' complaints from either side. But I do understand when they protest that their government was not being as tough as the adversary's.

Dulat: Actually, Sir, it hasn't happened of late thankfully, but some years ago some of our officers were roughed up in Pakistan. They had bad experiences.

Sinha: In the late '80s there was an Uttarakhand IPS officer whose face was bruised. His photo was splashed in the papers.

Dulat: That's right, UP or Uttarakhand cadre. He was roughed up.

Durrani: I was the DG, MI, so I don't remember.

Dulat: I don't remember his name because I don't know if it was his real name or his cover name.

Durrani: Since this is a book about broader subjects, let's say the diplomats, attachés, and cover officers from both sides face a problem. Not giving them a tough time would be exceptional.

Sinha: What about the two agencies and their use of the media?

Durrani: One thing in common between the two are the media wars. They even finance TV channels in the belief that these will work for them. They have no idea how to go about it.
    The first such channel was an Indian one, it was paid.

Dulat: Who paid it? ISI?

Durrani: ISI came to the field much later.

Dulat: He's saying an Indian TV channel was sponsored by an Indian intelligence agency.

Durrani: By RAW. If I remember correctly, 25 million dollars. In those days it was not a small figure.

Sinha: Even today it's not a small figure.

Dulat: But what was this for? Never heard of it.

Durrani: To start a channel to work for RAW. This is what intelligence agencies everywhere believe, that the media must be financed to wage psychological warfare.

Much as I consider the CIA a third-rate service, on this front they manage to persuade the media. It brings journalists around on core issues such as Pakistan bashing, or benefits of a civil nuclear deal.

Once a media organisation establishes credibility, the agencies start on core objectives: micro-managing, choreographing, managing from behind the scenes, steering the type of coverage, etc.

My country on this front has not been impressive. The Americans and British do this the best. Manufacturing facts, creating an environment for when you go to war, these people do it with the help of the media.

Sinha: Why didn't the ISI just sponsor an Indian channel?

Durrani: I believe that a prime minister and the NSC woke up to the idea and said creating assets in India and managing perceptions might not be a bad idea. Whether they came up with the right asset or not, I do not know.

How subtle they are, let me give an example. An article was once published under either a Hindu or Sikh name in the *Nation*, Lahore. I saw that this could not have been written by anyone other than an

ISI officer. The man who was given to publish it did not even change the terminology to Indianise it.

I'm thankful you people didn't say, ha ha ha, is this all that can be done by you idiots, come and learn a lesson from us.

6

The CIA and
Other Agencies

Asad Durrani: I never rated CIA assessments highly. Never. They don't believe they have to carry out good assessments. Because in any case they are going to set the place on fire. Bomb it.

Essentially they rely so much on technology. It's only a facilitator, ultimately the assessment is made by human beings. Like the Indian nuclear tests, I don't know whether it was by design. But in any case their intelligence failed.

Like when no less than Robert Gates[1] came running to India and Pakistan in May 1990. In the wake of the Kashmir uprising earlier that year, India partially mobilised its troops to its border with Pakistan. The ISI assessment was that India did not intend to wage war, as many essential items were left in the cantonments; their government wanted to demonstrate seriousness to its public. So we kept most of our formations in their peace locations. We judged correctly.

The US, however, saw Indian troop movement as well as some cranes moving in and out of our bases and concluded these might be missiles. Gates, however, was scrambled to prevent a possible nuclear war.

The point is, I don't hold them high when it comes to human intelligence (humint) or analysis. I've already mentioned how they got it wrong for both the Gulf wars. They were just providing an excuse for the US military action.

Aditya Sinha: You've mentioned that in the British set-up, the MI6 doesn't do analysis.

A.S. Dulat: It doesn't. But I was talking of the importance of humint. You need people to work for you. If you're banking only on listening in on Hizbul Mujahideen, without context or without getting in the organisation, quite often you'll get disinformation. There is a limit to how much you can get technically. If it gets known. the adversary is warned and can use it against you.

The KGB, CIA, Mossad: they're great names but I agree with General Saheb that CIA assessments have not always proven correct. There's a lot of wishful thinking. You jump to a conclusion and prepare reports. That's not the way intelligence is collected.

For example: I was about to leave Nepal in February 1980. The election had just happened in India, and Mrs Gandhi returned with a majority. Before the election I spoke to some CIA people in Kathmandu and they were convinced that Babu Jagjivan Ram would be the next prime minister. One had a bet with me. I said, no, Mrs Gandhi is coming back, I haven't been in India for four years but I can tell you this.

They often back the wrong horse.

KGB is tougher, but they have their crudeness. They're not the most sophisticated. KGB people have gotten into trouble in various countries.

People say Mossad is the most professional, but I don't know. It is so tight and they're only concerned with their own agendas. It's difficult to say. But there have been some great Mossad chiefs.

Sinha: If Mossad was so great, wouldn't Israel's problems have been sorted out?

Dulat: Problems don't get sorted out if you have a fixed mindset that this is what it is, this is what's right, this is what we know, and this is what's wrong. Then what will you do anyway? It's already done, there's nothing for you to find out or gain. You know it all.

You've got to open your mind also. There have been Mossad chiefs like Efraim Halevy, my contemporary, who was different.

Durrani: There were some credible heads of Mossad. One of them was there in Berlin at the Pugwash Conference, and a predecessor of his. I found that after retirement both of them said openly, so brazenly, that what the Government of Israel had in mind about attacking Iran was insane.

Dulat: Yes, that's right.

Durrani: KGB would not pass those tests I have for intel agencies. Primarily it's in a system where dissent is not appreciated. A subordinate is unlikely to say, Comrade, your assessment is incorrect about this, this is how it happens.

Dulat: Sir, you will find with every agency, the nature of this business is such. KGB's problem was that it was elitist. That's how Putin[2] today rules the world, he's the same stock. These old Cold War warriors are not reconciled to the changes that came about in Russia. That's why Putin is trying to drag it back to the time when the Soviet Union was dominant.

Durrani: I believe the German BND works methodically, seriously. Germans anyway are serious people. But their product is sometimes not up to the mark.

BND is a victim of their own desire to be perfect. Everything has to be done flawlessly, tied up to the last detail.

Sinha: So it loses sight of the big picture?

Durrani: That is what one has learnt over time. You're not going to wait forever for everything to trickle in, and then say we've got everything now, let's come up with a plan. Someone has to say, this is how it seems to be developing, so let's do this. That's the job of a person who is supposed to carry out strategic assessment, strategic analysis, strategic requirements.

That was lacking in the BND. After German reunification, someone said the economy turned out worse than what we expected. Where were you, BND? A department that was supposed to assess this had a chap, and I believe his response was: we had intelligence coming that we were filtering, analysing, and sifting through computer, but it was so much that we had just reached the 1950s and '60s, not the '90s, when the collapse took place.

You don't expect this from any intelligence agency, perhaps saturated with data, 30 years behind on your analysis.

Like this, other agencies have been flat wrong. Later they cook up a rationale. If ultimately the agency cannot provide you strategic or tactical warning in time, then what good is this huge apparatus?

Dulat: Every intelligence agency likes to believe it knows more than everybody else. In professional terms I think the Brits are pretty good. They talk the least, do their job quietly.

Sinha: And they have James Bond.

Durrani: About James Bond I do not know. But the British way of working, like after the 7/7[3] attack, is calm. It doesn't help otherwise.

Sinha: Even after the recent Westminster[4] attack they approached it calmly, methodically.

Durrani: The British reputedly are a hundred years ahead. That is how you become the sole superpower of your era for a couple of centuries. The Americans were more powerful than Britain ever was when they became the sole superpower in 1990-91. More industry, military power, allies, and more threats. No challenge. It was all-powerful.

Ten years later, the decline starts. Nowadays who takes them seriously? Indeed they can bomb a lot; but that is about all they can.

Dulat: The Brits have the advantage of not having to prepare analyses all the time, every day. They're working on something for a long time, taking their time, and you pass on only what is necessary to the executive head. And the chiefs of MI6 and MI5 have access to their prime minister whenever they want.

Durrani: They have a culture, they all work for the Crown.

Sinha: The Americans put out a lot of literature about their agencies but we don't.

Dulat: Mullik Saheb wrote his memoirs.

Sinha: How long ago was that? India and presumably Pakistan have a paucity of literature.

Dulat: I don't know why. We had an IB chief ten years ago, Nehchal Sandhu, who was keen that a history of the Intelligence Bureau be written. But somebody must have said no, it's too early. The usual.

Sinha: Too early! It's the world's oldest intelligence organisation.

Dulat: Archives can't be opened. It's crazy, because if the Americans or Russians or British can talk about their agencies, it's only to their credit. And credibility. In India people don't even know what the IB is. There's confusion between the IB and CBI. They know, as General Saheb said, the local thanedaar, but not what the Special Branch is.

Sinha: The ISI made a splash with *The Bear Trap*.

Durrani: Considering that we have not had an impressive tradition of writing historical accounts, *The Bear Trap*—though of questionable accuracy—was still the right effort. India has a couple of books, but the CIA-sponsored works make atrocious reading.

Sinha: That includes memoirs, or the journalistic accounts?

Durrani: Generally it's bad. Someone spends six months somewhere, then goes back and writes a thick book. After the Soviets withdrew from Afghanistan, Peter Tomsen was appointed the US president's special envoy, so he was there during my ISI period. I never thought of wasting time on him. The US ambassador once asked me, why don't you meet him? I said I had never heard of him, what did he do? Still, I made the effort to meet him. He was unremarkable.

The next one hears of him, he's produced this thick a book (*The Wars of Afghanistan*, 2011), which comprised his six-month or one-year stay, spent going through newspapers. He came into contact with no one. There was even a chapter on me. Even that I might have found flattering except that his book said he was the one running Afghanistan, I was his deputy.

Sinha: How superficial. Still, their organisation vets their writings.

Dulat: The CIA has a section that deals with publicity. They devote considerable time to this.

Durrani: But even for old time's sake I am not motivated to even open the book, considering the trash these people write.

In their system it is the president who picks the CIA chief, and that's how they end up with a lightweight called Woolsey.[5] He also wrote a thick book.[6] And that other chap, he has an uninterrupted record of telling lies. I forget his name. His record of telling lies is unblemished.

Dulat: Panetta?[7]

Durrani: Panetta was a vicious man, but this particular man was the one who obliged on the issue of Iraqi WMDs.[8]

I should admit that we feel that if it is coming from a CIA man, it must be correct. Their pen is backed by a mighty sword. Neither of us has that sort of sword.

7

The Intelligence Dialogues

Aditya Sinha: How does the ISI see these interactions you've been having with Mr Dulat? Does it see RAW as sinister?

Asad Durrani: No one has ever talked to me on this subject, but going by my past experience—in that whatever I said or wrote, never once was I cautioned—all my institutions, civil or military, must have had enough confidence in my ability to hold my own. No surprise there—we have never suffered from paranoia on such matters.
After being liberated from service constraints, I have written joint papers with a former RAW chief and given my assessment on the killing of Osama bin Laden, not quite in line with official versions. No one has ever accused me of indiscretion.

Sinha: What about you, Mr Dulat? Has anyone asked, yeh aap kya kar rahe hain? Or jokingly say, Dulat Saheb toh ISI ka aadmi hain.

A.S. Dulat: It's fanciful, I don't think so. Like General Saheb said, whatever we're doing, we're doing openly. In any case, the RAW would not tell me what to say now. I don't know what is going on in the RAW or IB today. And I have disagreed with people, on television. Even the book hints at it.

Durrani: At this level no one will be blamed. No one will imagine that about Mr Dulat.

Dulat: His advantage is he had the experience of meeting an officer from our side. He had a chief-to-chief meeting. I never had. For me this was absolutely unique, meeting him and then meeting other counterparts from the ISI.

Durrani: This charge of being an ISI agent, whoever it was thrown at I found was not working for us. The ISI had no business to employ that person, he was either so useless or unreliable.

Sinha: That describes us.

Dulat: I'm not in any case of any use!

Durrani: One would not even try to recruit him because he'll probably not be recruited.

But what happens is some people go around saying, do you know who I work for? Just to establish their clout. I've been told, but that chap must be working for you. Not that one would say one way or the other. But, good lord, this is how these things happen!

This particular charge will be laid against someone because of a weakness or unreliability in that person. Otherwise, not everyone who has passed by that gate will be dubbed an ISI or RAW agent.

Sinha: Which RAW chief did you meet when you were ISI chief?

Durrani: It took place in Singapore, some time in 1991. Bajpai[1] headed RAW. We met over two days, exchanged developments. I'm sure the Kashmir uprising was the focus of our meeting, because it had already taken shape when I joined ISI in August 1990. After the so-called Gates Mission, things were getting 'hotter', so, on an initiative by our foreign office, all credit to them, we met around six months later.

Once you meet someone for the first time, you spend most of your time judging the other side, assessing how much they want to reveal or talk about. It's always the second, third or the fourth meeting where you might figure that out, but the first is always a probe.

Nothing earth-shattering took place. We met. I was clear about one thing: the person on the other side of the table was an experienced intelligence hand. He's the chief of the RAW. He must have spent his life in his career. On this side was a person still learning the ropes, and I don't think one can in a year, or the combined time I spent in MI and ISI. I must have been extra careful.

Dulat: This is interesting, General Saheb saying that our chiefs are experienced and good professionals, whereas our view has always been that the ISI is something special. These guys have so much authority and can do what they like. Like it used to be said, it's a state within the state.

Durrani: So Bajpai and I met once, but it was not followed up. If both countries had better sense they would have followed it up correctly. But they can't because of their paranoia. Otherwise Hamid Gul's meeting with A.K. Verma, my meeting, and others,[2] these could be institutionalised. Without having to be announced every time.

But they don't meet, so each time two chiefs meet, it starts afresh. There's no continuity of process. It doesn't happen that after (Musharraf's) four points, you pick up from there.

Dulat: Because it's not institutionalised. If you think intelligence chiefs are too big then take down a level or to the middle level. But let there be meetings, if it is institutionalised then something will flow out of it.

Durrani: In any case, anyone who knows the functioning of the State knows that just because the RAW chief and the ISI chief want to do something does not mean it will happen. The whole establishment gets involved.

Dulat: I agree with you entirely, Sir. I'm only interrupting you to say, please give the ISI chief and the RAW chief a chance. A fair chance in which they should believe. It's easy for us to believe because we are now out of this. But if you have an ISI chief and a RAW chief who believe, then things can happen, even small things.

Durrani: That chance won't be given for the simple reason that when I met my counterpart I did not know him and I don't think he knew me well. Our conclusion was, we will keep at it. But he was not allowed. In my case someone merely had to say, haan bhai karte raho. There was a deafening silence instead.

Dulat: Now it seems there's no meeting, nothing.

Durrani: Are you sure there are no meetings now?

Sinha: Are the current RAW and ISI chiefs meeting?

Dulat: Who knows? We should not know.

Durrani: This is the right answer. If they are really meeting seriously, then we should not know.

Dulat: I certainly don't know. I also don't know when they last met. General Saheb has met, Ehsan Saheb has met.

Sinha: You didn't meet General Mahmud?[3]

Dulat: No, I've not met.

Durrani: When I met Bajpai only five-six of our people knew. And for many years, I denied it—even after B. Raman had written about it in his book. Then a time came when I decided to say yes, I met the RAW chief.

Dulat: It's something I always wanted to do. I've more than made up. Pakistani friends have helped, and I'm the only RAW chief who's been to Pakistan, not once but four times. I've been on Pakistan TV. Our friend Ejaz Haider put me on TV and later had tea with me. He said: thank you, for me this is the greatest thing because nobody in Pakistan has had the RAW chief on TV.

Durrani: Someone who knew I never watch TV rang me up when I was sitting doing something else, not necessarily more productive. 'Quickly, quickly, switch on that channel,' he said, and Mr Dulat was there. I just caught him say, yes, of course I have a friend in Pakistan, and he took my name.

Sinha: In your book you said the best intelligence organisation because of its influence is the ISI.

Dulat: I maintain that. General Saheb was kind to pay tribute to the RAW but the fact is what we think of the other side is not always accurate, no matter how many books are written about it. When he and I talk, we're talking facts, if we're honest. Otherwise it is just an assessment, and the rest is hearsay.

Sinha: How have the Track-II meetings of former intelligence chiefs been going? Is there acrimony?

Dulat: In our Track-II my experience is that when there have been meetings without diplomats, we seem to make more headway.

When the University of Ottawa started a military-to-military dialogue (between India and Pakistan) it went well. General Durrani suggested they have a similar dialogue of retired intelligence officers, and it's going all right. At least there's no bickering. It's pleasant though we may not agree on everything.

I've attended many such sessions since 2008, and of all the sessions, the ones between the intelligence officers are the most pleasant. Foreign service officers take themselves so seriously that they seem to be still at the Agra summit[4] or Islamabad, etc. They forget this is Track-II and that they are no longer ambassadors or foreign secretaries.

The other day someone made a long presentation. I said why do we need presentations? We're all talking here as friends. Nothing wrong with a presentation but it seems you've come prepared for something.

There are times when the mood is better, and times when it's not that great. I'll tell you this time[5] it was not so bad. From the General's or the Pakistani side, though, I got the feeling they think it's worse than before. Things are slipping.

Durrani: I agree. When we started this dialogue many sessions were sanguine: no fireworks. I even worried we weren't talking about things provocative enough. But that's the way intelligence people work. Hard-boiled, cold-blooded assessment, no blame games; one understands what it's about.

Lately, not only in this dialogue but also in a different Track-II session, it is different because of the situation, especially in Kashmir. That necessitated one of our colleagues to give a background, substantially and in a particular sequence, to focus the discussion. That was the reason for the presentation.

If this time there were heated discussions it was because Kashmir is bad, getting worse. It may lead to consequences that have nothing to do with Kashmir per se, but will affect the India-Pakistan relationship, regardless of what we want. So, certain aggressive and defensive opinions come to the fore.

Dulat: I'd like to take this up with the General. Sir, you'd recall when we met in September 2016, there was more to talk about or bitch about. Kashmir was pretty hot at that point of time: in July, August, September, October. Those four months were bad. In September, we were still in the thick of things in Kashmir. Your side legitimately had more to rake up and ask what we were doing.

Things have cooled down in Kashmir. In any case, things cool down in winter. The reason this heat gets generated is that in Pakistan there's this perception that's getting stronger all the time, that as long as Modi is prime minister nothing will happen.

Durrani: My difference here is that in September 2016 it wasn't because of the Pakistani side. Right now, things are quiet. But Uri and the so-called surgical strike happened, which have vitiated the atmosphere more than ever.

The concern in Pakistan is that this is likely to erupt again. Even if we keep out of it, there would be a spillover in the form of more Uris and more surgical strikes. Maybe that's why people were not as cool as our Indian colleagues expected.

Dulat: It was cool enough, Sir. No one gets excited. But this time you had over-imagined Kashmir. Kashmir has always been there, it never goes away. There are times when things are absolutely normal or cool but those are exceptional.

That's why I've always maintained, not only with our Pakistani friends but even our Indian friends, why don't we acknowledge that Kashmir is the core issue? Let's talk Kashmir. What is it that we're afraid of, or ashamed of, in Kashmir?

Amongst this group, the reaction is 'okay'.

Durrani: What about your colleagues back home, for example?

Dulat: If you bring diplomats into it then, 'Oh My God, don't mention the K-word!'

These guys understand it. One advantage is both CD (Sahay)[6] and KM (Singh)[7] have worked in Kashmir. They may not agree with me but in meetings they agree that we need to talk Kashmir.

Sinha: Mr Dulat, you were in an event in London recently[8] with another former ISI chief, General Ehsan-ul-Haq. How did that go?

Dulat: It was great fun. Aamir Gauri, who runs a think-tank called South Asia Forum for the Future, called up about six months ago and asked if I would go to London and talk. I said, I'm always prepared to go to London, but talk to whom? Originally, Sir, he said, are you all right with General Asad Durrani? I said perfect, there's no one better. Next time he called to confirm, he said General Ehsan will be there. I said okay.

The function was on October 6 at the London School of Economics (LSE). The hall that could accommodate about 300 was packed: students, staff, academics, journalists and diplomats.

He called us for dinner the night before, and I said, good, Ehsan Saheb and I can get on the same page so that we are talking to each other rather than at each other. The subject he told me was intelligence cooperation. The function was headlined something like 'Does intelligence do any good?' or 'Is intelligence any good?'

But General Ehsan decided to talk about the India-Pakistan relationship. He said it's a 70-year-old relationship, we need to talk that. He had Kashmir on his mind, basically. I said, Sir, the subject is intelligence. He said, no, no, so much has happened, India-Pakistan-Kashmir. I said, okay. He said, if you don't mind I will speak first. I said, I would like you to speak first so that I can react.

He started with Kashmir, human rights and what happened in Kashmir, and the India-Pakistan relationship. I reacted to that, and agreed with a lot of what he said and disagreed with some of it, but it was lively banter and in good humour.

I got him back to intelligence. Actually I wanted to credit him and Sahay, without naming Sahay, so I said: 'You and your friend did a good job when you were talking to each other, that's what comes out of intelligence cooperation. In 2003 we had a ceasefire, both of you did what your masters wanted.' I added the story that we provided intelligence which may have saved Musharraf's life. 'Congratulations,' I said, 'great work done.'

People were tickled that these two spooks had such easy conversation. There was a question-answer session, and we tried to answer everything. At one point Ehsan Saheb was in a fix. A couple of Baloch boys were there and asked awkward questions. He tried to skirt the question, I don't blame him. Finally the moderator said: 'General, are you going to answer that question or not?' He told her: 'I'm not a politician, these are things for politicians to answer.' He dealt with it fine, but they did embarrass him.

That apart, it went off beautifully, and afterwards we went to a pub next door where the media was at us. It was mostly the Pakistan media, and one group were talking in Punjabi. I answered their questions in Punjabi. They were tickled.

Sinha: Did that talk come up for discussion in the current dialogue?

Durrani: On my prompting, this round was kicked off with an account of the London meet. I thought it was an important high-profile event that had taken place. Second, it would start our process on a pleasant note. Later on one knows what is coming. Maybe third, my vested interest. Dulat Saheb always says Boss first, this time you're not going to get away with it. He switched bosses and started calling Ehsan the boss, but at least he had to talk first.

Ehsan does a good job and is better suited to represent our point of view. He's more recent on many things, since he headed the ISI ten years after me. Then he was Chairman, Joint Chiefs of Staff, dealing with such issues in a broader context.

Dulat: Ehsan is a nice guy, but the two of us have a chemistry that allows us to be more candid.

Durrani: It's true, it's true. I'm happy that my interlocutor is honest. I try to be as honest as possible, and when I cannot I will probably say so.

My problem is with those under peer pressure. Always looking over their shoulders at their compatriots, thinking, ghar jaa kar kya bolenge.

Dulat: It's not just peer pressure, Sir.

Durrani: Everyone limits themselves. In this group I have been fair, I don't think there is pressure, I don't restrict myself. In a public forum like LSE, it's possible that I might hedge my bets on certain things. Even there, one would probably be more frank than many colleagues.

Dulat: That's the whole fun of it. This business of hush-hush and, what you said, guys with horns stabbing each other in the back has its limitations. If one were to be more open and to cooperate, then the sky's the limit.

Sinha: What is the equation between General Ehsan and Mr Sahay now?

Durrani: They met back then because it was required by their bosses, it probably worked out well. Neither has carried a positive or negative burden from that time. Each speaks independently. But there can still be backslapping, they are not inhibited. Which is all right.

Sinha: They share a comfort level?

Durrani: They would probably say the same things elsewhere, it's not because they are Ehsan or CD. In our case, I may say something frankly if Mr Dulat is there; if some others are there I would not care. I'm liberated to that extent.

Dulat: The trick is your comfort level with the other person. I try my best to treat it lightly, crack jokes. Why so serious about these things? It takes weight off the other guy, that I'm not here to belittle him or Pakistan. We're here to have fun, that's the reason we got together to talk.

Durrani: This attitude helps us get somewhere.

Dulat: We might have a dig at each other but we laugh and it's all in good humour.

III

KASHMIR

These six chapters go to the very heart of the problem between India and Pakistan: the issue of Jammu and Kashmir. The bilateral relationship is frozen in a status quo, and Dulat and Durrani each have their own interpretation of what 'status quo' means to each country, and what makes it attractive to their respective establishments. They discuss the sustained attempt to tackle peace in the 'composite dialogue'; the telling way in which the ISI treated one of the earliest advocates of Kashmiri independence; the unmet Kashmiri expectations during Narendra Modi's prime ministership; and the enigma of Farooq Abdullah. Both men agree that the only way forward for Kashmiris is to 'take what you can get', instead of looking for a total resolution all at once.

Setting the scene

After an eight-month gap, the project is resumed in Bangkok in February 2017. From my room on the 12th floor we have a magnificent view of the Chao Phraya river as well as the southern skyline of the city. Strong coffee gets the General and Mr Dulat to recount amusing anecdotes during their foreign postings.

8

Status Quo

Asad Durrani: For as long as I can remember India has been considered a status quo power. Which for Pakistan meant no movement on Kashmir, frankly. We weren't at that time thinking anything more than Kashmir. You may have added something about POK being yours, it was merely as a bargaining chip; but I felt that whenever the need arose we would say, let's settle down and sort it out. No one took it seriously. Pakistan was the one that wanted to change the status quo because it was not happy with the state of affairs in Kashmir.

I arrived at the conclusion that composite dialogue that concluded in 1998 was an excellent framework to resolve or manage India-Pakistan conflicts. Its formula was good, its algorithm excellent, essentially saying that by discussing less intractable issues we could create an environment of confidence. Then we could start on difficult issues like security and Kashmir. At a later stage we could bring in 'terrorism'.

This composite dialogue worked out, after many initial hiccups, when your foreign minister came to Islamabad in 2006 to sign a 'milestone agreement'. It made plenty of sense, and there was plenty of excitement. I was among those invited to be at the Marriott Hotel for the announcement. I flew in from Europe. The expectation was that the two sides would agree to kick-start the peace process by facilitating the Kashmiri leaders from both sides of the LoC to interact.

Some of us were hanging around outside the hall, quipping that they were going to start a bus, but what if the odd bus got blown up? Suddenly people emerged and said, yes a bus will run. I said, looks a bit risky but a great symbol to kick off the process.

It was supposed to be only symbolic. Substantial things were to happen on other tracks, the easier ones. And when nothing happened, even on the simplest issues, that is when I concluded that India was serious about maintaining the status quo.

My argument is this. India believes that if the status quo was disrupted, the dynamics of change might be difficult to control. If the situation went below a certain threshold, it would not only harm Pakistan but also India. Similarly, an upward trend was not in India's interests. Pakistanis might become more confident, more cocky; Kashmiris more vocal, more violent, and they might feel that in a new situation they could achieve something. So even if it was not comfortable with the existing situation, India must have concluded that it was better to contain any upward trend.

India is comfortable, Pakistan has problems. India is doing well, going places, being wooed by the world, 70 to 80 billion-dollar trade with China. Why upset the apple cart?

It seemed like sound reasoning. Also, a number a people outside the subcontinent but with an eye on India got the same impression. 'This is the message we get,' such people said.

India is thus not just status quo but a strictly status quo power. It will do everything to preserve that and not even move in a direction from which it may benefit, because to do so means giving up on old friends with whom you're comfortable. The-devil-you-know argument.

I can then understand why Delhi did not respond to Musharraf's[1] initiatives. If you don't like something you respond by saying, thank you, we'll study it, you'll get our response in due course. The studied silence indicated to me that Delhi had no desire to respond.

In diplomatic terms Delhi told us to get lost, go climb a pole, we'll handle it our way.

A.S. Dulat: We've always had this argument about the stalemate. What is the status quo if there is nothing between India and Pakistan? Even coming and going is a problem. If relations were better, we would be having these conversations in Delhi and Lahore, every weekend.

I've always been of the belief that the status quo is nothing, and we need to move forward. Actually, if the status quo helps anyone, it helps Pakistan.

Let me give a concrete example of this status quo business. Let's take Kashmir today. It has been stuck with the status quo since 2012. But today the status quo favours Pakistan because this BJP-PDP[2] coalition has let down the Kashmiri in many ways. Mehbooba knows it but she's stuck, and both she and Pakistan know discontent is growing in Kashmir.

For the first time since the movement started, militancy is pretty much indigenous in the Valley. The boys have grievances or feel discriminated or feel hopeless. It's just 20-30 boys but that's bad enough. The whole population is willing to walk behind them. These are disturbing things for us, so how does the status quo help?

But yes, at this point of time, it helps Pakistan. But in the big picture the status quo can never help.

Durrani: A year or two ago Mr Dulat began saying the status quo suits Pakistan more, because there is a problem in Kashmir. I didn't comprehend his reasoning nor did I go into its depth until the turmoil after Burhan Wani's killing.[3] Then I started toying with the idea that because of what is happening in the Valley, Pakistan should simply sit back and 'watch the fun'. Perhaps India would be forced to change its original policy, its old threats, its old approaches. And then we might have a new status quo.

One could say that at this point of time, the status quo is not unfavourable to Pakistan. Pakistan could be comfortable with the unrest except that Kashmiris died. Also, if it inevitably goes on and even if you want no part in it, there would be fallout on this side of the Line of Control. Still, we can not only live with it, but also get on with other things. I sometimes say our relationship has achieved strategic stability.

Dulat: Now why would a stable stalemate be positive?

If we could write a paper on intelligence together and if at every meeting we've advocated together that the intelligence chiefs must meet, it is not status quo. I've gone beyond that to propose that the station chiefs in both capitals should be open posts.

We used to have this routine of preventing the All Party Hurriyat Conference from going to tea at the Pakistan High Commission in Delhi. Then, when President Farooq Leghari visited in 1995, Narasimha Rao said stop this nonsense. Anyone who wants to go should be allowed. Anyone who wants to travel abroad, let him go. Vajpayee took it further by actually facilitating Hurriyat travel to Pakistan.

So there was forward movement. Then it stopped, and we are now moving backwards. That's why we are where we are today. The mood in Delhi is that there's no need to talk to the Hurriyat. There's no need even to talk to Farooq Abdullah, though there is nobody more knowledgeable about Kashmir and Delhi and the world than Farooq Abdullah. So he goes off to South Africa or Dubai or wherever and holidays with his family.

It's a no-win for both sides.

Durrani: The status quo does not mean that there is no meeting, no movement, no going and coming. In fact, you can have all that so long as you ensure no change in the political arrangement. No change in the stakes that can provide incentive for further change. Nothing like, this bus started running so something else must happen; for then the bus is stopped in its tracks.

To the extent that when Musharraf spoke of a four-point formula that he thought was reasonable and partly aligned to the other side's view, one found a reluctance (in India) to formalise it. Because today we may say LoC is irrelevant for trade, tomorrow they may want a European Union-type arrangement. That's when I said strategic stalemate is India's objective.

I believed it so because improving relations with Pakistan, even if not limited to Kashmir, meant peace but also meant compromises on certain policies, because it's give-and-take. Therefore the saying: the price for peace is at times higher than the price of conflict.

Conflict is manageable, there will be occasional firing across the border, and people may die. But the price of peace may entail accepting the old division of Kashmir or arrangement with Pakistan, changing the former Indus Water Treaty, etc. That might trigger other dynamics.

Dulat: I agree that even the things which look simplest don't get done. The four-point formula that I keep harping on is something that came from Pakistan and was accepted by the Kashmiris. We did not have too much objection, so it seemed most doable. And yet, when the back-channel got on to it, they just kept on talking. All we needed to do was sit down with the four or six points that Musharraf had laid on the table, and eliminate whatever we didn't like. But we didn't. Nonetheless, Dr Manmohan Singh did say while demitting office that the deal was almost done. Done but not done. How typical of Indo-Pak relations.

The window of 2006-07 closed before Musharraf went, and after he disappeared we said, if only he had been around so much could have happened. The same fellow we bitched about as the villain of Kargil. Musharraf had to say let's forget Kargil and move on, I made a mistake.

Musharraf repeatedly said whatever is acceptable to Kashmir and Kashmiris will be acceptable to Pakistan. His four-point formula was in keeping with this statement.

Aditya Sinha: Twenty years from now, will we have the same status quo?

Durrani: I do not know which term to use but usually, when it looks negative it is status quo, and post-nuclear tests it was strategic stability. We often discussed it internally, our ministry of defence even published my views in a journal.

The crux of it was that strategic stability exists, at all levels. It's not static, stability is also dynamic. Once it's upset by, let's say, the requisition of a fantastic technology by India's defence, like ballistic missile defence, BMDs, Pakistan would try to restore it by something like tactical nuclear weapons. It just reconveys a status quo-like situation.

Twenty years from now, chances are we'll have a different type of stability. There would be developments in 20 years that we do not know, so much can happen even next year. But the 'new normal' will not be the status quo of 1980s or '90s.

On the other hand, if I look back, 20 years ago we had these same problems: Kashmir, India-Pakistan friction, Afghanistan. The narrative is more or less the same, the pressures continue.

Sinha: Twenty years from now things may look a bit different but will essentially stay the same.

Durrani: Status quo means a stability of a particular kind. The more we change the more we remain the same.

Dulat: Twenty years from now, Omar Abdullah[4] might still be the chief minister in J&K. That's the way I look at it. Seriously.

Sinha: You don't get much more status quo than the Abdullah family.

Durrani: Twenty years from now, Omar Abdullah is, let's say, a member of the Kashmir Muslim Conference.

Dulat: He can be a member of anything, Sir. Omar Abdullah is Omar Abdullah. He is now not yet 50, so 20 years from now he'll still be in his 60s. Perfect age.

Durrani: Who can say with certainty that it will not happen?

Dulat: Nobody. But if you ask me, this is the most likely. Also, he will be chief minister after Mehbooba.

Durrani: That is reasonable. Look at a bigger rivalry, United States and Russia. Twenty years back, the Soviet Union collapsed, the US was the sole surviving superpower, ruling the roost. Today we again have the two biggest powers that count: the US and a toss-up between Russia alone or Russia-China. Europe is no longer the sort of US ally it used to be. There is a situation in which various poles are balancing out. It does not look stable but it is sustainable.

But why get stuck on 'status quo'? I only lightly mentioned it, and in the context of Kashmir. Now I see it as a status quo of compulsion, which leaves the alternatives, policies, strategies a bit risky and that's why you stick to it.

Sinha: Will SAARC exist 20 years from now?

Durrani: I didn't know SAARC existed or that it meant anything at all. It means less than 'no first use' of Indian nuclear policy, which is merely to score brownie points. SAARC, if anything, has provided a platform where you can get together on the side to exchange some words.

Dulat: Not even a 'walk in the woods'.[5] There's an interesting correspondence between Kennedy and Khrushchev in which the Russian talked about a bridge across a river. He said, tell people there is a bridge across the river. And if people start believing there is a bridge, then even if there's no bridge it'll serve the purpose. Quite fascinating.

Durrani: In the time before Pakistan demonstrated it had a nuclear bomb, if people suspected or believed we had nuclear capability then it served our purpose. So I agree, but in this case there is a deeper meaning.

Dulat: They meant they must help create a bridge across the river. People should believe there is a bridge. In India-Pakistan relations that is necessary. People should believe that there is a bridge, if you don't like the word 'hope', Sir.

When Musharraf came to Delhi in April 2005 to watch cricket, around that time we had a few friends and family out on the lawn and a cousin of mine arrived with a Pakistani friend. He was a businessman in Lahore or Karachi. I said, welcome, have a drink. When he was leaving he said, I could have been in Lahore or Karachi. There's no difference between there and here.

The Punjab-to-Punjab relationship is like that. So the people-to-people relationship is important, and the belief—I won't say hope—is important.

Ironically, I must admit that back in my IB years I used to think of people-to-people contact as a lot of bullshit. I'd say, Pakistan is screwing us in Kashmir, how is people-to-people contact going to help? But since then one has seen a lot. One has experienced a lot.

Durrani: There is the context of assessment. Once an assessment is made, a leader gives people hope things will improve. That is his job.

Dulat: Another thing: India is a huge country unlike Pakistan, which is Punjab plus a little bit here and there. And in India, when you move out of Delhi then who bothers about Pakistan? Those who do talk, the intellectual in Calcutta or the south, they're for better relations with Pakistan. It is this wretched Delhi with its north Indian or Punjabi culture where we're always ready for a scrap and believe nothing can happen. But go to Kolkata or to Hyderabad or Chennai or Bangalore, you find they are different.

Durrani: Understandable. They are detached, and some may not be aware what exactly the problem in Kashmir is. However, we are referring to that larger environment in which both countries find certain pitfalls or impediments to moving forward. Whenever things do not seem to be moving very much is 'status quo', though let me avoid this phrase.

Dulat: Kashmir keeps coming up in bits and pieces, but you were mentioning Burhan Wani.

Durrani: Once this phase of the uprising took place, I asked people who are involved in the Kashmir issue, not officially but otherwise, some of them old Kashmir hands: Will things be different? Yes, it looks different, people are angry. Instead of talking of fighting, they are talking of embracing shahadat. 'Martyrdom cults', someone said unkindly.

If it's going to be unusual then the Indians will adopt unusual ways of handling it. Regardless of what India does, it will continue to manage on most occasions, it can contain whatever happens, it can suppress Kashmiris, appease them, accommodate them. It has happened, it will continue. If it continues 20 years from now Omar Abdullah might be the chief minister, but the problem keeps festering. But Kashmir uprising is only 28 years or so, there are things that have gone on for 50, 60, 70 years.

We also have an example, though not as severe, in Balochistan. In the last 70 years, five uprisings. Few people are involved, mainly 5,000-10,000 angry youth, but it's a vast area so they are dispersed. It's not united. We manage to contain it each time and have limited it to five or six districts out of 34. For most Balochis Pakistan remains the least bad option.

Despite their weaknesses and despite our ability to contain the unrest, the problem will continue. It is not only a problem of 5,000 people. Others who may not have taken that path and may still believe in Pakistan have grievances that aren't less. There are inherent structural deficits in the politics and economics, all complex, so they will continue. It indicates that a problem is resolved by many short-term and long-term astute measures.

Similarly, things will keep happening in Kashmir.

Sinha: So during the next 20 years there will be more Burhan Wanis?

Durrani: Assuming there is nothing more than containment, crackdown, political management, hanging on to the policy that Kashmir hamara hai.

Kashmir has blown up so many times, not because we were doing something. This time it has blown up for one reason, next time for another reason. Because Kashmir is complex and needs something other than simple management by a Kashmir expert.

Dulat: There's no expert, Sir. The question of Kashmir 20 or 50 years down the line is going nowhere, leaving Kashmir where it is. But if we don't change our way of thinking on Kashmir then there can be more Burhan Wanis. Because frankly our problem is that we haven't been honest with Kashmir.

Sinha: Kashmiris fear demographic change in the Valley, which is what hardliners want. If in the next 20 years that begins to happen, will it not change the ground situation, and thus the status quo?

Durrani: Changing status quo through a 'dhamaka' event, like a bus yatra or an Uri, is one way. I am suggesting something more nuanced and gestures that are more substantial.

For example: Both of us talking, it's not a 'shosha' to distract people but something for discussion. Maybe after a year or so the same thing would be discussed more seriously. That would be a change of the status quo for the better.

On Kashmir one has often talked about sending out a feeler. We know the type of noise it will create on both sides, so it must not be done officially. Unofficially it has already been done. Away from the spotlight people talk about the dangers or disasters of an independent Kashmir. A TV channel discussed what would happen and its implications. Would Pakistan suffer more or India? Such discussions break the mould.

India got divided into India and Pakistan. Pakistan got divided into Pakistan and Bangladesh. If before any of this happened someone had said, break up India, that chap would have lost his head. But at some stage it happened.

So the idea is to start a discussion like that of Quebec. You want independence, go ahead and vote for it. We want to change the status quo and improve it; but at the same time we don't want to question our articles of faith. That status quo will not be broken but will worsen, as it has within six months. Another status quo was created, another quasi-stable relationship reached. The next time something happens, it will worsen.

We're looking for a development that will raise the bar.

Dulat: Sir, we can play these wargames, but who knows what will happen. There are people in Delhi who believe Pakistan will inevitably break up, which is a lot of rubbish.

Durrani: So let's consider the implication of Pakistan breaking up. Discuss karo, bhai. Good for us or bad for us.

Dulat: Oh no, much worse for us.

Durrani: Let them discuss it, and after that if it is not good for us, if it's not going to be better for us then...

Dulat: That's precisely why a smart politician like Vajpayee went to Minar-e-Pakistan, against all advice.

Durrani: Hamid Gul used to talk about India being too big for us and that we should do everything to break it up. We just laughed, but in that no one was saying it will not happen, and someone said if it happens it will be good. Informally people speak of breaking the monster.

Dulat: There are also people who believe in Akhand Bharat.

Durrani: I don't mind discussing Akhand Bharat. We have come this far but we have no solution.

Dulat: As Aditya would say, these are all academic discussions.

Durrani: We can consider moving to a confederation, and then to a united India. How can we reverse the cycle? At least discuss it. Europeans have been doing so for a long time. It took half a century to achieve the 'united Europe' imagined by Churchill.

Sinha: Europe became a union, and now it's coming apart again.

Durrani: Yes. There's no such thing that is final. No borders can be redrawn? Borders get redrawn all the time.

Dulat: Dr Manmohan Singh spoke of breakfast in Amritsar, lunch in Lahore and dinner in Kabul. Was he dreaming?

Durrani: One can talk about this when this discussion takes place.

Dulat: That's why as a gesture from India, the easiest thing for our prime minister is to ring up the Pakistani prime minister and say come lunch with me at Hyderabad House. It only takes 35 minutes from Lahore to Delhi.

Durrani: Yes, we can also go. And while they're having their lunch we know a few people who would rather have a...

Dulat: Why not, Sir, why not.

9

The Core K-word

Aditya Sinha: In the end, it comes down to Kashmir.

A.S. Dulat: Rhetoric apart, there are a couple of realities in Kashmir. The Kashmiri accepts it's not going anywhere, India won't let go; and that beyond a point, Pakistan cannot help. Pakistan is a friend and a good fallback. It's been tried through invasion or raiders or war but Pakistan has not been able to claim Kashmir and will not be able to.

But something needs to happen, something positive on the ground. Otherwise, K-word or no K-word, we come back: Kashmir is an issue, in dispute, it is a problem. We don't accept it as a dispute or problem, but the fact is there is an issue. The story's not over. Common sense says that for everybody's sake we try and move forward, however gradually.

What do I have in Kashmir? I'm not a Kashmiri, I'm not related to anyone. But I keep talking to the Kashmiri so that he believes that not everybody in Delhi is unwilling to listen. It is important to keep that sentiment alive. In my years in government only Home Secretary K. Padmanabhaiah would entertain Kashmiris. Otherwise there is no one. So I disagree with my own Indian friends. We should face this K-word or K-factor up front.

Sinha: Does that include Pakistan's role?

Dulat: We saw the Kashmir development in 1989-90 as inspired, monitored and supported by Pakistan. Interestingly, as General Saheb said, and as Kashmiris also told us, it became bigger than Pakistan imagined or bargained for or prepared for. Certain things went out of control. It just carried on. That's why in the end—and also because of events like 9/11—when it fizzled out then once again Pakistan was blamed for not understanding Kashmiri sensibility.

Durrani: On Kashmir I defer to my friend because his knowledge and experience are more.

Dulat: That's very kind, Sir.

Durrani: He knows the ground, the people; he served there, has been in and out. I can't even cross the border. But I did serve in [so-called] 'Azad' Kashmir for many years.

Sinha: If India admitted Kashmir is the core issue, would it be a breakthrough in bilateral relations?

Dulat: I don't know. Depends on how Pakistan would react.

Durrani: On a couple of occasions I have heard Indians say they consider Kashmir the core issue. The first was Salman Haider, a co-author of 'composite dialogue'. I don't remember exactly but he said something like, yes it may be the core issue.

In a composite dialogue, the core issue need not be discussed at the beginning, but only as the peace process goes along. The initial focus is on improving the environment. Only then is it time to talk about the difficult issue: Kashmir. And later, terrorism. Some in India will concede that Kashmir is a major problem without calling it 'core issue'; at the same time, however, they say that Pakistan believes the core issue must be discussed at the beginning.

The composite dialogue was for me learning about making peace. Earlier one had only learned and taught how to make war. I tried to see if the lessons of military strategy were applicable. Enough people agreed, including Salman Haider.

'You and Shamsad (our foreign secretary) absolutely got to the core of our operations strategy,' I told him. Operations strategy has two prongs: one is the battle, the other is the manoeuvre. You fight somewhere, create the right environment for the manoeuvre or break-out. It should be in such a manner that it creates a favourable environment for the battle. It's a cycle of battle and manoeuvre. 'You seem to have done it,' I said.

This composite dialogue was the manoeuvre, and it was essentially creating a favourable environment for the battle, which was the resolution of Kashmir. A civilian version of the battle for Kashmir.

I saw that the concept might fit. I admired that these people thought of moving on eight talking tracks. In military strategy you sometimes launch an offensive and see which front makes progress. The one that creates an environment for your main battle, and not where you might not have made progress due to enemy resistance.

Yes, Salman said, whenever we worked on the evolution of composite dialogue, people spoke of Liddell-Hart's strategy of 'expanding torrents'.[1] You start little streams, others join in, and the whole thing expands.

On intractable issues, unless you've gone through the crust you don't get to the core. I've said this at home, that to get to the core issue you must negotiate through the peripherals.

Sinha: Do you believe it, Mr Dulat?

Dulat: It's a laborious way of going about things. Kashmir needs to be dealt with more directly.

There are bureaucrats who have never been to Srinagar but pontificate on Kashmir.

We say that 2001-08 was good for Kashmir and that because Pakistan had to live with the burden of 26/11 for five-six years, it didn't raise Kashmir. 26/11 further embarrassed Pakistan at Track-II meetings. Some Pakistanis said, 'If even now we did not learn, we are doomed.' I used to needle some Pakistani diplomat or other at larger, broader gatherings, that's what's happened to your core issue, yaar? Let's talk Kashmir. Pakistan was comfortable with it not being on the agenda. Now we've gone and messed it up.

Durrani: Even after the setbacks of Kargil, the nuclear tests, after Musharraf's Agra visit, I assumed that we would return to the composite dialogue. Sensible people had worked meticulously to make it robust.

Then I found Kashmir-related development in the meantime, which surprised me as I thought Kashmir will take a backseat till the environment improved. Both Indian and Pakistani decision-makers, however, wanted a symbolic gesture on Kashmir and they came up with the bus that would run between both parts of Kashmir. I hoped this symbolic bus would take care of hotter things, Kashmiris would be involved, and then Islamabad and Delhi would get on with mundane affairs, cultural exchanges, and the political settlement of other disagreements. But even on the easiest things, visa or culture, etc.: no progress. The only development was on the thorniest matter, Kashmir, and that was a bus.

I said there must be a reason why India won't move even on the smallest problems. It led to another earth-shattering conclusion: India does not want the status quo to be rocked because it is favourable.

With even Musharraf's initiative that was popular in India and Kashmir, no response coming, I'm convinced that India would not risk any change in the stable relationship between the two countries, as it might create a dynamic that goes out of control. India's objective seemed to be: 'Zameen junbad na jumbad Gul Mohammed' (the earth may shake but Gul Mohammed will not).

My thinking was shaken.

It was also shaken after the Wani episode. Things were so difficult for the Indian side that I used to read panic on the faces of various Indian interlocutors at these meetings. They looked worried. Mr Dulat said something will happen.

It happened and didn't seem to be too bad for us. It has been tactically handled for containment. For an actual breakthrough you need something else: something that's difficult, takes time, requires compromises. It usually doesn't happen. So for us the best thing is to sit back and watch.

Sinha: Pre-Partition India—where were Kashmiris going to work, migrating to? Where were their cultural, business, political links? With modern India or Pakistan?

Durrani: Good question. Statistics can probably give an answer. Many Kashmiris came over a period of time: Iqbal and Nawaz Sharif and Salman Taseer or his father and others. The main artery was Srinagar-Muzaffarabad. Even today that road is trafficable.

Dulat: I don't think the question is significant. Yes, General Saheb is right, most Kashmiris who left the Valley in those days naturally gravitated towards Sialkot or Islamabad. But that is true of the Punjabi also. Very few Punjabis went to Delhi. The most cosmopolitan city in the region that everyone went to was Lahore. If you played tennis in the Lahore gymkhana, or if you went to Government College, Lahore, it was the ultimate.

Many years later when I had to go to college my mother asked, 'Don't you think he should join St Stephen's College?' My father responded, 'What is St Stephen's College?' He was a product of Government College, Lahore, so he felt Delhi University could never match Punjab University.

So I don't think that is relevant.

If you look historically, Kashmir's linkage is more with Iran and Central Asia than the Arabian side. In Srinagar there is now a new class of Richie Richs, like we have in Delhi and other cities. Guys who've made good money, the upper middle class, like to travel to Dubai and do their shopping. Even sanitaryware is from Dubai.

Of course, Kashmiris would like to be part of India's growth story, even if it implies going to Bangalore or Bombay or Goa, etc. But what they ultimately aspire for is growth in the Valley itself. If there is an IT revolution in the south then why not here?

Kashmir is still one of our more affluent states. You don't see many beggars in Srinagar. Most Kashmiris own a house. They eat good gosht, few eat beef; only the rural folk can't afford mutton so eat beef.

What hurts him is being treated differently from the rest of the country.

Durrani: The Pakistan government's per capita investment in Kashmir is the maximum in the country. No other region received that kind of money. It can be seen on ground. The infrastructure there till about the 1990s was better than the rest of the country. People have to be won over, so let's make roads. Kashmiris desire education more than anyone else in Pakistan. Children walking to school is a common sight. At 7 a.m. I was shivering and saw Kashmiri kids walking in short-sleeves, bags on back.

Perhaps Kashmiris on the other side felt they were not being looked after as well as on the Pakistani side.

Dulat: I don't think so. You mentioned POK. I deliberately haven't talked about that Kashmir. I don't know it well, so it's better to keep shut. But I know there are problems that side also. It's not correct that the grass is greener on that side, because Kashmiris have told me on various occasions, jaane dijiye inko. Allow him to go across and see for himself, he would return immediately disillusioned.

We have Kashmiri boys left back in Pakistan. Some of them married, took up businesses, settled. They're all right. But quite a few would like to return. Salahuddin is not young, but he may like to return and succeed Geelani Saheb. He has from time to time indicated political ambitions.

Durrani: Best would be getting Kashmiris involved, be it in Track-II or formal meetings. Ask a few from that side, a few from this side. Even if initially inhibited they are capable of telling you off. Delhi, you are the devil; and Islamabad, you have not been our best friend. We might then hear their sentiments. Otherwise you're quoting Kashmiris in India who have no other way but to be part of India, saying, inko jaa kar dekhne toh de doosri taraf.

Sinha: General Saheb spoke of a bandwidth of stable stalemate: that above this bandwidth, better India-Pakistan relations might worsen things in Kashmir for India.

Dulat: On the contrary, the better the relationship, the happier the Kashmiri is. His fear is that whenever there is India-Pakistan tension, he will be at the receiving end.

The only Kashmiri leader who didn't react to this earlier was Farooq Abdullah. Now, he has said repeatedly that there is no other way but to have good relations with Pakistan. He understands. The question is, what is the way out? You can say Kashmir is key or core or Pakistan's unfinished agenda, but the point is to move forward from the status quo.

Durrani: India has made symbolic compromises in the past like the bus. The establishment's paranoia is that an upturn will make Kashmiris confident. It will encourage them to blow the lid on the pot of their sentiment, the simmering that was handled technically will boil over.

How good would Kashmiris feel in a Pakistan-India patch-up? Some of them rightly believe that once our relations improve, on the Pakistani side Kashmir goes on the backburner. We're doing trade, why bring up this contentious issue? The K-word becomes an irritation for the political leadership: phir Kashmir? Badi mushkil se kiya.

Dulat: We hear this from Kashmiris as well. India remembers Kashmir only when there's a problem. Mirwaiz has said this, others too.

I've believed that if the Kashmiri is happier, the fallback position you provide would diminish and hopefully over a period of time disappear. If the Kashmiri is happy then why does he need Pakistan? He needs it when he's in trouble.

Durrani: An improvement in Kashmir will also mean greater Pakistani influence. Geography, history, religion, and sixty years of oppression and second-class treatment; even today security forces are there.

Things are now taken care of thanks to your good management, but I don't see happiness on the Kashmiri face. Those who have a passport, who travel out, who are enlightened, who are allowed at all these Chao Phrayas and elsewhere: they look all right but the moment they get a chance they say, we still have checkposts.

Pakistan is comfortable with that, perhaps. If it continues, the backlash will be against India. Let them face it for some time. We, in any case, won't be able to do much. The Pakistan factor is not necessarily always good for Kashmiris or Muslims.

Dulat: The boss's observation that an improvement in Kashmir will imply increased Pakistani influence is something I never looked at. Would that actually play?

But from the Kashmiri point of view, the Indian point of view and the point of view of peace, some forward movement should keep happening. General Saheb talked about the bus that started. Start trains, start coming and going, send apple trucks back and forth, make life easier. Let there be peace on the LoC, where life is tough because of constant shelling. A lot of locals are in wheelchairs, maimed for life. If nothing else, people on the border could be reassured of peace. You can understand if people in Srinagar feel insecure whenever tension grows, how insecure people on the border feel.

Kashmiri friends asked me many times: ab jung toh nahin hone wala hai?

Durrani: My assessment on India-Pakistan, Kashmir, on the ground reality, the possibilities, etc., does not talk about hopes or wishes. I just continue looking at the facts on ground. Very seldom I move from a realistic or pragmatic approach. On two occasions I made an exception.

One was Amritsar.[2] It is not that Pakistan has not been criticised before, but it was embarrassed against all norms. Pakistan can internally say it is bothered by this thing. But once it happens on Indian soil, this South Asian hospitality, diplomatic norms were violated by Modi, Ashraf Ghani (whom I call a non-Afghan), saying things that embarrass their own people back home.

Second, with all that is happening in Kashmir, post-Wani, when the Kashmiri leadership, the Mehboobas, etc. sit back and feel helpless, and do not even symbolically answer the pain of their own people, then the battle is lost. Finito.

Dulat: That's why, Sir, India and Pakistan together could do a lot in Kashmir. As we could do in Afghanistan as well. I say this about Kashmir because we know the Kashmiris better than you will know them. They're a part of our country, we deal with them every day. They listen to you, they're afraid of you, but we know them better.

Durrani: On a hard-boiled, cold-blooded, hard-nosed assessment alone I can tell you now: I don't see that happening.

Dulat: No, no, I can't disagree with you on everything.

Durrani: On this, if you think it will change, do let me know.

Dulat: I don't know if it will change. But if we were to change, we could change so much.

Durrani: We could.

Dulat: Both in Kashmir and in Afghanistan.

Durrani: So the moral of the story is India and Pakistan should hand over this management to us. Should this go down in the book?

Dulat: There is a Kashmiri, better not mention his name because last time I got grief for mentioning names, he knows, like most Kashmiris know, they know more than both of us know, Sir. They know that we meet at these Track-II meetings, also because of the book and the photographs, the whiskey and all. They enjoy all this.

This Kashmiri says to me, aap jab Durrani Saheb se milte ho toh humme bhi le chaliye. Hum teeno faisla kara sakte hain.

Sinha: When will General Saheb be able to visit Kashmir?

Dulat: Whenever I can visit Murree he can visit Srinagar!

Durrani: For him to go to Murree is no big deal.

Dulat: It's in a lighter vein because I once asked him if could go to Murree and drink beer. He said, no, I'll give you Murree vodka in Islamabad.

10
Amanullah Gilgiti's Dreams of Independence

Aditya Sinha: Have you ever met Salahuddin[1] or Amanullah?

Asad Durrani: Amanullah, yes. When the uprising began, we were just marking time to see what happens. Amanullah was an early resistance fighter. His idea of the third option, independence, was not bad. But it put off many Pakistanis, especially the establishment. Its support was, well, to describe it as weak is not doing justice because some didn't like him at all. I admired some of the things he did and said; for instance, his religious commitment to his October 27 visits to the LoC. And how well-organised it always was.

Amanullah had reason to be upset with us. So overwhelming was our desire that Kashmir accede to Pakistan, towards Sardar Qayyum,[2] the slogan 'Kashmir banega Pakistan', to the Jamaat-e-Islami,[3] that these got our political support. We tried to tell him, haan bhai, Amanullah, you are right, and that fellow is also right. But Amanullah was short-changed and he knew it, and he was right. I later realised our mistake, but by then it was too late for me personally to do anything.

Sinha: He was not the ISI's favourite?

Durrani: He certainly was not the ISI's favourite. Not the ISI's favourite, not Pakistan's favourite.

We had no business to make value judgments. Pragmatically we should have asked which country would lose more if Kashmir became independent. My own assessment was India would lose more because India had more. If after having been in India for 60-70 years they still want independence, that sentiment must count for something.

If independent they would keep good relations with India, I'm sure of that. They would reach out to China for various reasons. But Kashmir's heart would be with its western neighbour.

That's why if someone talks of independence then we have no business getting in the way. So Amanullah was not handled well by us.

A.S. Dulat: Independence is not an acceptable option in Pakistan.

Durrani: India gives it a special status of 370.[4] We like to believe they are another type of state, with a president and prime minister. Okay, they have the same currency and same administrative structure, etc. But if they decide on independence, enough would say: why not? We always claimed the Kashmiris' heart is with us, so an independent Kashmir should gravitate towards us. I have no problem with independence.

Dulat: But the establishment has.

Durrani: The establishment is, at best, careful. Some stupidly say that an independent Kashmir would be disastrous.

Dulat: There you are.

Sinha: What is the logic of disaster?

Durrani: Paranoia.

Dulat: Paranoia and whether the Kashmiri is reliable. Can he be trusted?

Durrani: Some do talk of the Kashmiri's unreliability but it's typically a Pakistani or sub-continental or universal trait not to believe that anyone other than yourself could be reliable. In Pakistan, Punjabis cast aspersion on Pushtuns, Balochis and lately on Mohajirs; Punjabis say we are the largest community but we were also the most reliable for the British and Mughal empires. Since they—and the Pushtuns— acted as mercenaries, why should they be considered 'more reliable'?

None of them think an independent Kashmir would be for the better. They are more worried about what would happen to Mangla Dam. Its water would come through another country, they argue.

The worst argument from a sensible person: If Kashmir would become independent it would get more foreign support and troops; America, Germany, Japan, all would be there. They'll give money because Kashmir is strategically important. They'd like to establish bases, as they have in Afghanistan. Pakistan and India will both have less influence, and powerful Westerners will take over Kashmir.

That is why I suggest to our various Track-IIs to discuss the independence option. Wargame the different scenarios. If a large section, even a majority, of Kashmiris would take independence if given a choice, then let them have it.

Dulat: I once discussed independence with Yasin Malik,[5] because he said: 'Aapke saath kya baat karenge, hum toh azadi chahte hain.'

'If you could get independence then I would wave the Kashmiri flag with you,' I told him. The hard reality is that Kashmir will not get independence. India will never countenance it.

Pakistan is also nervous and it is clear in Amanullah's case. He was part of the first resistance, or revolutionaries, of the JKLF. He was involved in the Ravindra Mhatre[6] murder case in England. The Brits didn't have enough evidence so he was deported. He then went to Brussels and finally even Belgium threw him out. Then he came to Pakistan hoping he would be acknowledged as the ultimate

Kashmiri leader, as big as Sheikh Saheb. Interestingly, all these revolutionaries, including Amanullah Khan, had a background in the National Conference.

Amanullah originally belonged to Gilgit. He lived a while in Kupwara and then shifted abroad. But in the Valley he was general-secretary of the Plebiscite Front, working closely with Mirza Afzal Beg[7] while Sheikh Saheb was under arrest. The JKLF boys had a similar background.

When he came to Pakistan post-1982, during General Zia's time, he was reduced to an ideologue because there were no takers for independence. He sat at home, organised marches and in due course, as the Kashmiris say, he became Uncleji. It's a sad end to his story. His daughter is very bright, married to Sajjad Lone.

Durrani: The third option is saleable in Pakistan. Nawaz Sharif, without forethought, spoke of it during a visit to Iran in his first tenure. Ghulam Ishaq Khan said the UN Security Council resolution gave us a locus standi in the matter and should not be given up, but we could explore other options. It is saleable, except there will be hue and cry.

Sinha: But Amanullah could not sell it.

Dulat: Amanullah could not sell it, even Yasin Malik could not sell it.

Durrani: They can't sell it.

Dulat: That's how the Hizbul Mujahideen came about.

Sinha: You said he was the first wave of resistance, and he could not sell it.

Durrani: No Kashmiri leader will be able to sell it. Properly orchestrated, one can win over many Pakistanis. The problem is that Pakistanis are not smart. And the Indian Deep State will not let that happen.

Dulat: The point you do not mention, Sir, is there aren't many people like you with the confidence to sell this proposal. You mentioned Mangla Dam; but more than that it's the Kashmiri, how will you deal with him?

Durrani: Yes, yes, I've already granted that some will not look at it other than in a narrow perspective. They will say: You also? You want Pakistan to suffer? You want to lose Kashmir?

That criticism scares most. That's why, if properly explained, those favouring independence can go up from five per cent to ten. A tsunami can develop, I'm sure. But who will orchestrate it?

Sinha: Amanullah Khan's son-in-law is very much a part of the J&K government.

Dulat: He is half BJP.

Durrani: True. I think lack of smartness, lack of wisdom.

Dulat: Lack of belief.

Durrani: Lack of confidence.

Dulat: Lack of confidence. That is why when the movement started it got out of even Pakistani control. Immediately you drew the Jamaat in because you needed more reliable foot soldiers.

There was a debate in Kashmir in late 1989 on whether the Jamaat should join in or not. Geelani[8] Saheb is on record having referred to these boys as terrorists. Then he was summoned to a meeting in Kathmandu, and things changed.

Durrani: Movements are usually hijacked by better organised parties.

Dulat: Quite right.

Durrani: Like the Iranian revolution was triggered by the Tudeh Party, a communist group, but then hijacked by the clergy led by (Ayatollah) Khomeini. The Egyptian Arab Spring was started by the people but after a pause taken over by the army. Afghanistan's problem began with infighting among the communist factions—the Khalqis, the Parchamis, etc.—but when the Soviets invaded, the ground was captured by the mujahideen and their Islamic supporters who were nowhere close to the communists. Now we have those who collaborated with the Soviets installed in Kabul with American help.

In Kashmir, Amanullah and others led the resistance, but the Jamaat was better organised and had more influence on our side. It's a universal phenomenon that once a movement starts, the initiators are jettisoned in due course. They are ideologues, may have the good of the people at heart, but rarely the ability to steer it through.

11

Kashmir: The Modi Years

Aditya Sinha: General Saheb has repeatedly referred to the fallout of Burhan Wani's death in 2016. The summer of 2017, however, was different; it was relatively peaceful. Was this your expectation?

A.S. Dulat: Burhan Wani's killing was only a catalyst. After all, who was Burhan Wani? A good-looking lad whose photos were on Facebook. Some even say he was a CID source, but only God knows the truth.

It goes back to the December 2014 elections whose result satisfied nobody. The BJP dreamt of Mission 44,[1] and my friend 'Pompy' Gill was managing the BJP campaign in Srinagar. He said five-six seats definitely but hoped for eight. They didn't get a single seat.

It frustrated the BJP, and also the PDP because it too dreamt of 45 seats. They got 28. Mufti Saheb could have done with three-four seats more to be a stronger chief minister. He was vulnerable and had no option but to go along with the BJP.

He invited me to his oath-taking on March 1. It was still cold. BJP bigwigs were on stage, hugging. The moment the prime minister left, his entourage left: Advani, Murali Manohar Joshi, Amit Shah, the RSS guy Ram Madhav, the whole lot. Mufti Saheb made the mistake of calling the press and thanking the separatists and Pakistan.

Immediately in Delhi people said, arre yaar yeh kisko bana diya chief minister? Yeh toh Pakistani hai. The journalist Jyoti Malhotra called me: 'Please give me a balanced view.' I felt sorry for Mufti Saheb. As J&K chief minister he had to say something. What good is calling him a Pakistani? He's been Indian all his life, he was in the Congress for many years.

After that Mufti got nothing.

Mufti underestimated Modi, overestimated himself, and found himself in a fix. But having long been a politician with thick skin, he managed things. Most disappointing, though, was that nothing came as relief for the September 2014 floods, in which people died, property was destroyed. The Kashmiri thought the PDP-BJP alliance would bring something, but nothing happened.

This drift continued. Mufti Saheb died a broken man. That's why Mehbooba took three months to take oath of office. And Mufti Saheb's funeral in Bijbehara saw just 3,000-3,500 people.

Asad Durrani: Thank you for saying this. We are counting on the mistakes you people make.

Dulat: Worse was to follow. Once Mehbooba became chief minister she came under greater pressure. The RSS-types spoke of special camps for sainiks and for the Pandits, etc., and every now and then dropped hints that Article 370 was unnecessary.

The Kashmiri felt that he was being taken for granted, and that in his own land he might be reduced to a minority. Then where does he go? That is the real fear. It has never been as conspicuous as now. Therefore, even Geelani Saheb, who remained a loyal buddy of Mufti Saheb, is in two minds: is Mehbooba okay or not? But there is no other option.

I was in Srinagar in June 2016 and everybody said things were looking good, tourism was at its peak, flights coming, no rooms available. Yet I could sense something was going to give. There was a whisper, dekhte hain, Eid ke baad kya hota hain. We met somewhere, Sir, in London, and I said something is going to happen in Kashmir. And it did.

It's difficult to predict Kashmir because it can change overnight, as it did with Burhan Wani's killing. But it is apparent that the Kashmiri is sick and tired, and wants peace. Therefore, this stone-pelting, these protests, could go on indefinitely.

To the security forces' credit, they did a good job in 2017 neutralising big names in militancy or terrorism. Militants have been picked up or knocked off, or they've come overground. Still, strange things keep happening, like this chopping off of women's hair. They say it's a ghost.

On the ground the situation may look normal to somebody from Delhi, but things are not all right in Kashmir.

That's why the appointment of the special representative is welcome. Whatever the reason for it. At least we will start talking to people we have stopped talking to.

In Kashmir we have a chief minister who was silent for a long time. This appointment gave her heart, and she welcomed it: 'This is what you wanted, things will improve now,' she told her people.

Dr Farooq Abdullah also said it's good except that we also need to talk to Pakistan. Omar had some reservations. Ghulam Nabi said, why have you taken three years to do this? Chidambaram, who's a regular commentator now on Kashmir after having been home minister, said this is an acknowledgement that the government's muscular policy has not worked. But he also welcomed it.

Sinha: What is the reaction in Pakistan to the events of 2016?

Durrani: There was consensus in Pakistan that in the post-Wani developments it should neither interfere nor be seen to be involved. Some schadenfreude (feeling pleased with the adversary's plight) was understandable, but after Uri and the so-called surgical strike, we realized that sitting back and doing nothing was not an option. We would inevitably get involved. I'm sure the concern now is what to do if the events of 2016 follow a course that Delhi is bent upon steering.

Dulat: There were indications in the six-eight months post-Burhan Wani, as General Saheb puts it, of separatists and the mainstream in Kashmir coming together. Remarks or statements from both sides indicated this, and it was the best thing that could happen, for Kashmiris need to think together.

But post-UP elections[2] there was no more commonality. This suited both the Government of India, which didn't want to talk to separatists, and the Government of Pakistan, which would like the separatists to remain on their side.

Sinha: Their limited aim is keeping the Hurriyat on their side?

Dulat: Yeah. The Hurriyat is the Pakistani team. India has its team, Pakistan its team, and the Kashmiris are in between.

Sinha: General Saheb, do you agree with this assessment?

Durrani: The best that can happen and seems possible is to make Kashmir the bridge. The two of us would love to work not for independence or reunification, but to provide a sense of comfort to the people.

When we get permission we don't even have to talk about it. Neither side has to say this is about terrorism or a solution to Kashmir. But how to convert this process into reality?

Dulat: I couldn't agree more. Kashmir should be the bridge, it's the right starting point. I have always maintained that if we have to talk, let's talk Kashmir. If you move forward on Kashmir, then you are automatically moving forward on terrorism. When we complain about terrorism, we are talking about Kashmir without saying so, that is where terrorism is.

That is the way to go about it, but I don't see it happening.

The crucial thing is don't rub the Kashmiri nose in the ground any further, don't give him a sense of defeat. That is when the Kashmiri starts to pelt stones.

Take Siachen, for instance. I'm tired of talking about it because of the deflection. It won't happen unless there's some forward movement on Kashmir.

A.S. Dulat (standing, centre) playing club cricket in Chandigarh with Kapil Dev's coach, D.P. Azad, to his right in 1973.

Bishan Singh Bedi, arguably India's greatest spinner and an old friend of A.S. Dulat, who visited the Dulats' residence in 2018.

With the General in good humour at one of their many Track-II meetings, in Istanbul in 2016.

Receiving the President's Police Medal from Prime Minister P.V. Narasimha Rao.

With Prime Minister Atal Bihari Vajpayee at the RAW headquarters in 2000.

With wife Paran, CIA chief George Tenet and his wife Stephanie at the Taj Mahal in Agra in May 2000.

With Director Louis Freeh at the FBI headquarters, working out counter-terrorism cooperation, in September 2000.

With Captain Amarinder Singh at the launch of *Kashmir: The Vajpayee Years* in Chandigarh in 2015.

Taking a stroll with the General in Kathmandu in March 2017.

With former ISI chief Ehsan ul Haq at the London School of Economics in October 2017.

With Dr Farooq Abdullah at the Dulats' 40th wedding anniversary in December 2006 at New Delhi's Ashoka Hotel.

Escorting the Prince of Wales to the Sisters of Charity in Calcutta along with Mother Teresa in November 1980.

With Ambassador Shahryar Khan, former foreign secretary of Pakistan, in New Delhi in 2015. Apart from their Track-II meetings, they shared a common passion for cricket.

With the legendary late Ashwini Kumar of the Imperial Police, and P.A. Rosha, icons of the service, at a lunch at the Dulats' residence in New Delhi.

Speaking at the Henry Jackson Society at the Parliament House in the UK in October 2017.

With media icon Barkha Dutt at the Hindu Lit for Life in Chennai in January 2016.

With Barkha Dutt, then Vice President of India Hamid Ansari and former J&K chief minister Farooq Abdullah at the launch of *Kashmir: The Vajpayee Years* in New Delhi in July 2015.

At one of the India-Pakistan Track-II Chao Phraya Dialogues in Bangkok. The participants include Pakistani politician Sherry Rehman, Pakistani lawyer and activist Asma Jehangir, Indian political leaders Hardeep Singh Puri and Baijayant Panda, among others.

Sinha: What if Modi were to announce that he would scrap Article 370?

Durrani: I'm not impressed by sudden moves that aren't well thought through or sustainable. Indeed, the media has a rollicking time thereafter. Later, when the bubble bursts, one may have to come up with another gimmick.

Dulat: Yes, 370 is talked about from time to time, maybe not in serious quarters. If it happened one could anticipate celebrations in India, but it would negatively impact Kashmir. It is now a meaningless thing, some say it's just theatre because what's left of 370? Nothing. It's been gutted to the extent that nothing is left. And why would you want to remove this last symbol?

Sinha: Demonetisation did nothing for black money, but it made people believe Modi is tough.

Dulat: I hope 370 isn't scrapped because it will give the Kashmiri reason to say, see this keeps happening to us. It's being debated in Srinagar: if it happens what do we do?

Sinha: General Saheb, how do you see the appointment of former IB chief Dineshwar Sharma as a special representative to talk to Kashmiris?

Durrani: If you want endorsement from Pakistan, appoint a person like Mr Dulat. This man can handle the genuine grievances of Kashmiris. If it's an establishment man it won't make much difference except temporarily calm tempers. He will not establish the sort of change that could excite Pakistan.

But they've appointed someone. Let's see.

Who am I to say good or bad? No excitement on my part. Our foreign office said the right thing, which is what the foreign offices do. Why stick your neck out and endorse something that may turn out badly for the Kashmiris and for us?

Sinha: What do you think was the motivation to do this at this time?

Durrani: I think it was yet another gimmick, because Tillerson[3] was coming to the region. In Pakistan, on such occasions, we would usually get hold of a few people to sustain the illusion of cooperation. In the good old days the Indians had a marvellous plan. A few weeks before an American visited they would create a hostile environment so that on arrival he was on the defensive. India's not a small country that has to present itself in a good manner.

Now there is a nexus between India, the United States and Israel, with the Kabul regime playing the poodle. The bloc they target is Pakistan-China, with scuttling CPEC (China-Pakistan Economic Corridor) as their immediate aim.

India wanted to tell Tillerson not to worry about Kashmir. You don't even have to raise it, we've appointed a competent man—like your AfPak envoys—to take care of it. Tillerson in any case would have agreed; even if he had mentioned it he probably would have said, look, Kashmir continues to present a problem. He was not going to make much noise, but even that was pre-empted.

Dulat: Let's say it's because of Tillerson. As you know I'm an optimist. I know Dineshwar, we've been colleagues and also colleagues in Kashmir. He's a simple, straight, uncomplicated fellow who feels for Kashmir. He's a good listener, not a guy who likes to blab.

Sinha: But Mr Doval would have appointed him, though Rajnath Singh announced it. So he would do as Mr Doval wants, isn't it?

Dulat: Quite right. So we welcome it all the same. I told General Saheb, let's give it a chance for six months.

Durrani: Indeed, it is his chance to take.

Sinha: General Saheb said something about the Kashmir issue going on for the next 200 years.

Durrani: No, no, no. That was not the point. I meant that even if it goes on indefinitely, it does not mean we should do nothing in Kashmir.

Dulat: Quite right.

Durrani: Building roads, infrastructure, democratic representation there. That is what I meant.

Dulat: I'm all for it. I'll get blacklisted in Delhi but I say that Kashmir before anything else in Pakistan. We don't have much explaining to do. Yes, now and then things are not as they should be, as in 2016-17.

But when we talk to our Pakistani friends I would like to ask them some questions: Why are you doing this? Why don't you understand Kashmir a little better?

Sinha: This book comes out in the summer of 2018. What scenario do you see in Kashmir then?

Dulat: Difficult to say. There's the Pakistan factor. If we start talking to the Kashmiris, we also need to talk to Pakistan. Ultimately, when we reach some civility with the Kashmiris, then they should be allowed to talk to Pakistan. This has happened in the past.

What happens in the summer depends on what happens in the winter first. Usually, once the J&K government shifts to Jammu,[4] there's comparative peace. But the six months of 2017-18 winter are crucial.

When the government shifts to Jammu the action also shifts there. To the army camps, the paramilitary, the J&K police. Jammu is bad enough, but lately we've had incidents in Punjab, which borders Jammu. We had an incident in Gurdaspur and one in Pathankot which gave me the heebie-jeebies. Suppose there's an incident down the Grand Trunk Road, in Jalandhar or Ambala, almost touching Delhi.

So let's watch the winter, how it goes.

General Saheb said that in bad times, if you're talking it helps. Some argue that even when we are talking or start talking, something goes wrong. It may go wrong, but in the long term it will benefit us. Give it a little while, give it traction.

Durrani: You don't need rocket science to know what should be done. Sometimes it would help to stick one's neck out and say this is likely to happen. The syndrome is known: unrest starts in some form and the State's first reaction is crackdown. It panics that if it waits, the unrest may spread. The first instrument used is a military one. Then, regardless of what people say, the situation is contained and you're willing to talk and address their grievances. But once it's over, the reaction is usually that there's no need to for anything more. Let's get on with something else.

The State can use force, sometimes brutally and regardless of its consequences. The unrest can make a tactical withdrawal or be battered. But inevitably there is a resurgence. He's right, it could be six months or six years later.

Whether it is Kashmir or Balochistan, it will resurge. If the resistance is potent, it bounces back more violently. Like Kashmir, post-Burhan Wani. The episode may have been triggered by something less significant than 10 or 20 years ago, but the eruptions are wilder, more serious.

The Afghan mujahideen were harmless, focused on resisting foreign occupation. Some went on to become the Taliban; a little more radical and you have al Qaeda. If al Qaeda is put down, you have Da'esh. That is the pattern.

Call me cynical or nihilist but I feel it is realism to say there will be no meaningful talks on Kashmir between India and Pakistan for the foreseeable future.

Dulat: If this interlocutor works then ultimately the Kashmiris will want a political interaction. Dineshwar Sharma can't decide that.

We forget Kashmir is not a military problem. General Saheb is absolutely right, when there's upheaval, the first reaction is, let's put this down and then we'll see. That's okay but let's not forget this is a political matter. In Kashmir it's an emotive issue.

Don't disturb the Kashmiri psyche by saying unnecessary things, like the army chief did after this appointment, that it won't affect military operations. Everyone knows it won't stop. But why must you state this? When you do, it means Dineshwar Sharma is of no consequence.

Similarly, when we agree to talk to Kashmiris, this is a set line, we'll talk within the Constitution. You have to be daft to think that the Union Home Minister or the Prime Minister...

Sinha: Or the President of India.

Dulat: ...can talk outside the Constitution. Prof. Butt[5] said this to me, yeh aap baatein kyon karte ho? It's rubbing salt into the Kashmiri wound instead of saying, come, what do you want to talk about, we have an open mind.

That's what Advani, who in NDA-I was considered a hawk, said. You ask these Hurriyat guys who had two rounds of talks with him and they say, Advaniji was reasonable. The first Hurriyat demand as always was for the release of some of their jailed colleagues. Advaniji said, all right, give us a list. And then: What else do you want? Prof. Butt said, Sir, we'll come back with a roadmap. In May 2004 they were to produce a roadmap, but the BJP lost the election. But even if the BJP had won that roadmap would not have been put on the table because it's only in the mind. Very little beyond the status quo can be said except accommodation and honourable peace.

What I'm saying is that the obvious need not be said if it offends someone. The Kashmiri understands very well his limitations and what is feasible.

12

The Unloved Dr Farooq Abdullah

A.S. Dulat: When we talk of Kashmir, I'm confident that General Saheb and myself could co-opt Farooq Abdullah and the three of us could sit down together. A lot on Kashmir could be done. If, for some reason, Farooq alone is not acceptable, then co-opt two persons: Farooq and a separatist like Prof. Ghani. Two of us and two Kashmiris. We could trigger some excitement. All it requires is reasonableness.

It's been on my mind. Farooq has not been to Pakistan in a long time. He needs to go there for his own fact-finding mission.

Asad Durrani: What a coincidence. Soon after the 1990 uprising, in a meeting with Gilgiti and others, there was a suggestion to invite Farooq Abdullah. The establishment people were opposed to this idea and I'm not sure how it would have played out.

I met him only once, during the Tehelka conference in London. He tried his best to avoid me, but after my talk he wasn't unhappy. I believe he made positive noises post-Burhan Wani. Do say hello to him for me.

Dulat: Everyone tells me that Farooq is my friend, and I am flattered, but the reason I suggest Farooq is that he is one Kashmiri who understands not only Kashmir but New Delhi well. He is the best bridge between Delhi and Srinagar. Now he's reached a stage where he needs to understand Pakistan, and if he did, and he already knows Delhi, then it would help. His involvement would help a great deal in moving forward.

His views are well known but he has been saying repeatedly that you cannot have a solution, which he's never earlier said, without Pakistan. New wisdom has dawned.

Durrani: If it happens after this book is out, we will have reason to feel gratified. The point is, here is an idea. It's not been attempted. It needs no funding. It might be better in a book than either of us going and suggesting it to our NSAs.

Dulat: You can take it for granted that Delhi will never appoint Farooq as interlocutor on Kashmir. The only way it can happen is if he goes to Pakistan, and Pakistan is convinced that Farooq is the right interlocutor. The proposal then comes from Pakistan: from the prime minister, or the army chief, or the ISI chief, or the NSA, etc. That's how it could happen.

Durrani: True. Tarika yahi hota hai. The way of making something happen is that it must look like the other person's idea.

Dulat: I'm reminded of 2002, after Farooq lost the (assembly) election. He suddenly decided to go to Pakistan, and the NCP minister Praful Patel would accompany him. He called the press to his place in Delhi and announced it. I was taken by surprise, and I asked, have you spoken to the PM? He said the two of them would now go and meet the prime minister. All Vajpayee said was, 'Have some food.'

So, such an invitation has to come from Pakistan, because it won't come from Delhi.

When Farooq fought and won the by-election in Srinagar (in April 2017) there was widespread feeling that the Government of India didn't want Farooq in Parliament. It's ironic because the Government of Pakistan also doesn't want Farooq in Parliament. This is the message from the separatists, which implies Pakistan. It echoes their political thinking: 'Why Farooq? He's unreliable. What has he done? What is this family, this dynasty? They're pro-India. Sheikh Saheb used to do the same.'

Ironically, the main lesson that Farooq learnt was when his father, Sheikh Abdullah, made peace with Mrs Gandhi in 1975. His great father, after spending 23 years in jail, found it necessary to make peace with Delhi, then he must always stay on the right side of Delhi. At the beginning he spent a year and a half trying to defy Delhi and received a rude shock in 1984 with his dismissal.

Other politicians might think Farooq is a joker, they might think anything of Farooq, but Farooq cannot be ignored, his very presence cannot be ignored. Looking ahead to the 2019 election, he would have a role in Opposition unity.

I also believe Farooq would make an outstanding foreign minister.

Aditya Sinha: Not in this government.

Dulat: No, not in any government, even his own. People don't take him seriously, that is the unfortunate part.

Durrani: We can make him deputy prime minister. We can say though he may have come from your side, he's ours. So we make him deputy PM. Farooq will have a problem accepting the offer, and the Pakistanis would have delivered a masterstroke.

But who is going to bell the cat?

Sinha: No one wants to rock the boat.

Dulat: Mufti was to be given a Padma Shri posthumously, but Mehbooba, etc. turned it down. Padma Shris have been awarded to

Kuka Parrey's counterinsurgents. But Farooq Abdullah, for all the services he's rendered India, hasn't got recognition.

Durrani: Farooq has got nothing?

Dulat: Nothing.

Durrani: Serves him right.

13

Take What You Can Get

———

Asad Durrani: On Kashmir, there's the old recipe. One is realistic to know what is at stake for both countries. This issue of conflict is a conflicting issue: we're always saying resolve the issue, find a final solution, for us it's a core issue, etc.

But it can be turned around. It is best resolved by making Kashmir the focus of the two countries' cooperation. 'From Conflict to Cooperation' might be a reasonable slogan.

A.S. Dulat: Absolutely, absolutely.

Durrani: So this is our recipe: don't look at independence, don't look at 370, and don't look at the LoC.

Aditya Sinha: What would be the first step towards this cooperation in Kashmir?

Durrani: We don't have to reinvent it. People before us, wiser people, have found a way by starting at the people's level. Simple movement, a little trade, let them be involved in these matters while Delhi and Islamabad take a backseat.

Once the people feel comfortable they might themselves say: 'We don't want to be the main issue between you two countries, which might lead to war, etc. We're all right as we are. No change in status, nothing big. The two countries, you'd be better off following our example.'

But the approach has to be indirect. Instead of saying we want a divided or jointly administered Kashmir, or any other formula that has been talked of, I'd suggest an indirect and incremental approach, starting with little steps, like bus and trade, etc.

Dulat: Confidence-building measures.

Durrani: Continue without saying what you want at the end. When it comes to conflict resolution, it has to be an evolutionary process.

And everyone must always remember the conventional wisdom: you don't always get what you want.

Sinha: So then, taking what you can get makes the most sense.

Durrani: In 2000, Ehud Barak offered a package to Yasser Arafat.[1] Barak, a former defence minister and a highly decorated soldier, may not have been the greatest Israeli prime minister in history, but what he offered on the surface of it looked good. If you looked deeply you might have found weaknesses. But it had that wisdom, that spirit.

God knows I'm not an expert on the Prophet's accepting the Treaty of Hudaybiyyah.[2] I just read about it. Maybe it was intended to teach us all the need to compromise and the criticality of timing.

When the Palestinians objected to various provisions in the package, it was that they could only compromise if Israel agreed to all concessions. It was a mistake. The summit failed.

Take whatever you can. You never have to say it is over. Khatam, chhutti. You take it, improve your position, and after a decent interval of five, eight or ten years you come back and ask, but what about the return of the refugees?

In Kashmir's case, this may be how you discuss the solution.

Dulat: The story is that before Sheikh Abdullah went ahead with the Afzal Beg accord in 1975, he sent Dr Farooq Abdullah to Pakistan. Dr Farooq went and met Z.A. Bhutto, who is supposed to have told him: 'At this point we can do nothing to help you. So, take what you can get. If you're offered peace and power in Kashmir, take it.'

There was also a story in Kashmir that Yasin Malik was advised by the Americans to do business with Delhi. When Yasin said that Delhi was unreasonable, they said: 'You should take what you can get.' They said it was not the final arrangement, but if something is on offer, grab it.

Call it the semifinal or quarterfinal; and who knows what may happen?

'Take what you can get, that's good enough,' this is the essence of what Dr Farooq Abdullah repeatedly advocates. In Kashmir, you can't change anything. What is theirs is theirs, what is ours is ours. There's no point in pretending. We have to settle on the Line of Control. This can be done in various ways, and maybe not as crudely as Farooq puts it. But that was also the essence of Musharraf's four-part formula: LoC-plus. The LoC cosmetically dressed up so that both sides won, neither lost. That's where forward movement lies.

Pakistan is sitting pretty as the situation in Kashmir suits them. Delhi seems to think that we're all right, there's no problem in Kashmir.

Durrani: Bhutto's advice was so good. I don't know how these things keep getting missed; do we want all or nothing? Is it just take it or leave it? When we want all or nothing, we are likely to get nothing. But also, whoever asked you to take it or leave it was also likely testing your nerve. So, as Bhutto said: 'Take what you can get.'

IV

KABUKI

These seven chapters go into the meat of the India-Pakistan relationship itself, and the personalities who have come to define it. These include not just General Pervez Musharraf and the politicians of his country, but also Prime Minister Narendra Modi and Ajit Doval, for whom the Pakistanis have strong feelings; and the section of Indian government that Pakistanis regard as its most hawkish. Lest we forget, there are also positives in our countries' history with one another.

Setting the scene

Kathmandu, March 26, 2017: We spend the day in a noisy lobby of our hotel, off to a side but still not escaping the general hub-bub of the ebb and flow of guests as they come and depart. We go out for lunch to Thamel, but the thick smog of the Nepalese capital, comprising pollution and the dust that hasn't settled from the devastating earthquake two years earlier, makes it difficult to see where we all are actually headed.

14

India and Pakistan: 'Almost' Friends

A.S. Dulat: One day in 1980 or '81, I was summoned by a senior IB colleague, Vinod Kaul. He sat downstairs from me in our RK Puram office in Delhi. Kaul was from my cadre (Rajasthan) and much senior to me; I was recently promoted to deputy director. He was a top analyst in certain subjects, including Pakistan. He sat me down and said: 'You know these Pakistanis well, can you help us?'

I was taken aback. 'Sir, you've got it wrong,' I said. 'I know no Pakistani. In fact, I stay far away from Pakistanis.'

'Your car number was noted at the Pakistan counsellor's, where there was a cocktail,' he said. 'You were there.'

No, I told him, I hadn't attended any such function. He told me to think it over. Then: 'Your parents are also good friends with Pakistanis?' Yes, I said. That part was true.

I thought perhaps my car had been stolen from my Kidwai Nagar residence. I went home and asked my wife if she had loaned it to anyone, because it was noted at a Pakistani function. She hadn't. What's the address, she asked.

'Oh my God,' I said. In Vasant Vihar, near where the Pakistani gentleman stayed, there was a nursing home where my brother-in-law was admitted after an accident. So our car must have been parked nearby and the number noted.

Then there was the second part of Kaul's queries, about my parents. They lived in Sagar Apartments, on Tilak Marg in Delhi, right next to Pakistan House. My parents loved to play bridge—as did two successive envoys. So they used to play bridge together, mostly at my parents' place, sometimes at the Gymkhana Club.

The first of the envoys was Syed Fida Hassan, appointed ambassador in 1976. He was my father's old friend as both were Punjab cadre and both had been posted in Sialkot together. The moment he arrived in Delhi he began looking for old friends and found my father living next door.

The gentleman following him was Abdul Sattar, who was passionate about bridge and would land up at Sagar Apartments. So for about six years my parents continuously interacted with Pakistani envoys. For them, they were all the same Punjab.

Aditya Sinha: Bridge was their bridge. Any other prominent players at their gathering?

Dulat: A prominent Indian diplomat, Samar Sen (popularly known as Tinoo Sen), an old ICS who got shot in the shoulder while he was our high commissioner in Dhaka. He was bindaas, a unique bureaucrat who didn't own anything after years of service. Sattar Saheb once called him 'fakir'. He lived as a paying guest, didn't own a car, went around in a taxi. Some years later he heard I was involved with Kashmir, so he called me to the club and asked: 'Are you one of those bloody hawks? All right then, we can talk like gentlemen.'

Asad Durrani: This reminds me of a Lalu[1] story. He visited Pakistan (in 2003) and created an impact because of his awami ways and his talking the language of the people. Passing through a market he would pick up a potato and say, 'Lalu ke haath mein alu.' People went wild.

What impressed me was when we had a television discussion involving three Pakistanis and Lalu. One of us was aggressive, saying, 'I do not know what the Indian policy on Kashmir is.' The wise

Lalu did not utter a word. He knew if he spoke about policy the atmosphere would sour. But the man insisted. Finally, very, very slowly, Lalu said: 'Indian policy is Kashmir is an integral part.' The man on our side lost all steam.

Lalu's reluctance to answer indicated a hard-boiled politician who wanted to convey a message of peace and cooperation. Why would he want to talk about official policy if it would complicate things?

Dulat: But, Sir, what is the basic problem between India and Pakistan? Your high commissioner was in Chandigarh and said the trouble with India and Pakistan is misunderstanding. What is the misunderstanding when there is no understanding!

There is distrust, more distrust and most distrust.

Durrani: It may be true, difficult to say. Is it Partition? Is it the history of 1,000 years? Is it that we started off so badly and continued to get complicated? Is it that the establishments' approach is not amenable to breakthroughs or dramatic reversals? Is it that we've gone in different directions and now find that changing direction will produce dynamics that are difficult to manage?

I used to find this too philosophical. But over a period of time, you evolve hypotheses or principles. Don't have big designs, keep achievable targets, and let time pass and we'll see what happens.

But going step by step, tactically, managing things, you're actually just drifting. You will not control the elements required to achieve a particular sublime objective.

There are many things that will come in the way of peace with India. A particular bigger step was agreeing to the composite dialogue framework.

You took a step and suffered a setback. You managed it, and after four-five years, Vajpayee says, give peace another chance. Moving in fits and starts, momentum is never built. We never get to a stage where we can say from these four points we can take this point and it will make a difference, it will make the process durable, if not entrench it.

Sinha: What do you see as the problem?

Dulat: Going back a thousand or 10,000 years is going too far in history. Partition has played a part, it left wounds. There are people in Punjab's border areas who have not forgotten Partition. Whenever there is talk of better relations with Pakistan there are people who say, better relations with whom?

The other thing is that it has to do with where power lies. Like I mentioned, outside Delhi there is little hostility towards Pakistan. Delhi is hostile, even to the people who live there. Being the centre of power is not easy to deal with.

The basic problem has been distrust. It has grown over the years because Partition happened and Pakistan was not happy with Kashmir going to India, the invasion of Kashmir, and its bifurcation. We had Operation Gibraltar, the war of '65, then the '71 war. It's remained like that. There's always been some amount of hostility. I think it is only post '75, when Sheikh Abdullah made peace with New Delhi or with Mrs Gandhi, that things calmed down. Mrs Gandhi was tough and could have taken a position on peace, but after the '71 war Pakistan was of no great consequence to her.

Morarji Desai, Chandra Shekhar and Gujral Saheb were well-meaning but none of them lasted long enough, like Mani Dixit, and so on the Indian side there hasn't been anyone big enough to take a call on moving forward and shaking hands till we came to Vajpayee. He thought differently, had stature, authority, and he always felt that this madness has to end, this permanent confrontation with Pakistan is meaningless. Manmohan Singh tried to replicate Pandit Nehru, who made efforts but couldn't clinch the deal.

Sinha: Which Indian leader is larger-than-life in the Pakistani mind?

Durrani: There were a few. The first one was Desai. I believe some forces from outside the region—Americans can always be counted upon to be behind such acts—wanted him to create some difficulties for ZAB because he wouldn't give up the nuclear path. Not only that he refused, but also made it very clear that getting the outside powers in regional disputes was courting disaster. Then there was Chandra Shekhar, who in the few months that he was prime minister also took a long view of our bilateral relations. Listening to him on a variety of subjects was sheer pleasure.

Gujral was intellectually well endowed and probably the brain behind the composite dialogue initiative. If sub-regionalisation was the fulcrum of the Gujral Doctrine, I think it can form the bedrock of a renewed initiative. But like Chandra Shekhar, he too led a minority government and did not have the time and power to turn things around.

Vajpayee was the only one who could and did to an extent. Manmohan Singh had his heart in the right place but did not have the resolve to stand up to his detractors. All of them, however, ultimately failed to override the entrenched India establishment.

Dulat: No, Sir, no-no-no-no-no-no. Here I disagree totally. Vajpayee was never overwhelmed by the establishment; he was the establishment. Nobody questioned him, even in meetings.

The only time that Advani[2] sulked was during IC-814.[3] He was reportedly against releasing the terrorists and hijackers. He did it smartly, by absenting himself from the meeting when this decision was taken. Yet he never said a word against Vajpayee.

Durrani: But Vajpayee ultimately didn't work out. That's what I'm saying.

Dulat: That nothing happens no matter who's the Prime Minister of India is a cynical view to take. This whole project is about looking at things positively. General Saheb is on record with regard to people like Morarji Desai and Chandra Shekhar and Gujral Saheb because he's a great admirer of the Gujral Doctrine.

Vajpayee and Dr Manmohan Singh both did their best. Vajpayee was not that young, he was cautious and he moved slowly, but he kept moving. He took the bus to Lahore,[4] and despite Kargil[5] invited Musharraf to Agra.[6] Unfortunately, it ended in a fiasco, and Vajpayee came back from Agra extremely disappointed. Despite that he went to Pakistan again for the 2004 SAARC summit. His NSA Brajesh Mishra told me clearly to keep working on Kashmir while he worked on Pakistan, so that the two streams would merge somewhere. In Vajpayee's mind he was at it all the time, and he probably thought he had time. He didn't expect to step down in 2004.

Durrani: Vajpayee's initiative continued to benefit India because one and all blamed us for Kargil, which was anyway a foolish operation; it came after the bus to Lahore. Who was going to credit Musharraf?

Dulat: You're right, Sir. One thing after another, and yet after Kargil we still called Musharraf to Agra.

Durrani: Yes, after Kargil. It created an environment against Musharraf. Once Agra was over, people called it an honest-to-good idea. Musharraf regained ground, and not only in Pakistan. Some respected Indians blamed Advani for scuttling the summit.

But about Vajpayee, embarrassed as he was by Kargil…

Sinha: And the Parliament attack.

Durrani: Yes, Parliament. But in Kathmandu, when Musharraf walked up to him and extended his hand, you could see Vajpayee's hesitation. People called it a great gesture but the Prime Minister of India visibly didn't like it. He looked as if a military man ruling a smaller country walked up to him and he was now expected to act graciously!

Still, he had the good of the region at heart. He was no doubt asked, why do you continue to make these gestures towards Pakistan? He said, we never know what USA was up to in this region. For a man of few words, this single sentence was enough.

Some didn't get it, on either side, that cosying up to the US has never been a good idea.

Dulat: When Manmohan Singh became prime minister, everything had been presented on a platter, it was just a question of taking it forward. The good man tried his best; he didn't just want it, he craved it. He wanted to go to Pakistan, it was an emotional thing. As an economist and a world leader in his own right, he wanted to leave behind a legacy. As he and the Pakistani side have each said, a deal was almost done.

Unfortunately, the Congress was not supportive, his bureaucracy—he had a principal secretary, an NSA and others—did not seem supportive. He cut a lonely figure. I don't think Sonia Gandhi ever opposed the idea, but just kept aloof.

I agree with General Saheb that often deals are almost done but not done. That's the sad part. But why wasn't it? It should have been completed by 2007, we had that window of opportunity when Musharraf was still in control.

Durrani: But 'almost' does not make it happen. In Pakistan, Naseerullah Babar, God bless his soul, as interior minister in Benazir's second government 'almost' did an operation against militants in Karachi but then the government fell (in 1996). Similarly, we 'almost' achieved a breakthrough when Sheikh Abdullah was in Pakistan (in 1964), but Nehru died. And of course, had Musharraf not got into domestic trouble in 2007, a deal on Kashmir had 'almost' been clinched.

These 'almosts' have happened many times. A mathematician once said, if something 'almost' didn't happen then there was a 100 per cent chance that it would not.

Dulat: Dr Manmohan Singh all the time had Pakistan and Kashmir on his mind. It's unfortunate that he had his limitations. I agree with General Saheb that the Indian establishment, as he calls it, or the Indian bureaucracy is very powerful, there are no two ways about it. But having said that, our bureaucrats are risk-averse. They are so smart they also look for what the politicians want. Nowadays the bureaucracy is totally sold on Modiji.

Yet politics and leadership are a key to this whole thing. With Vajpayee's bus to Lahore, there was a euphoria in Delhi that now all our problems with Pakistan are over, settled, khalaas.

Durrani: Institutions should be stronger than the individuals, and India is 'generally' well served by its institutions holding together, evolving consensus on national policies, and digging their heals to protect them. Downside, however, is that this leads to the 'permanent establishment', the bureaucracy, assuming the role of 'godfathers' of the policy. They get so attached to whatever they have sired that even a change for the good, or to keep up with the 'zeitgeist' (the spirit of time) becomes nearly impossible. That may explain why despite public and political yearnings on both sides, even the flimsy visa regime could not be liberated. Even declared concessions like senior citizens would be exempted, or such-and-such category could get a visa on arrival, had no chance to be implemented. The chap at immigration would simply say, bhai mujhe toh letter abhi tak aayaa nahin hai.

After Musharraf's takeover, Mani Dixit was asked in what direction relations were now headed. He replied that history showed that when the military had the reins of power in Pakistan, Indo-Pak relations looked up.

There's a reason for that. The military has enough on its plate internally. Once you have the levers of power, you would like to keep the eastern front as quiet as possible, as well as send out a good message. So there's a pragmatic reason. Institutionally, the military in Pakistan is not anti-India. It shows that when the generals talk to one another, they don't have to act tough, they say we can manage relations, I'm not inhibited by any political force.

India's advantage is the capacity or capability of the state. You have Modi and Doval vs Janjua[7] and Nawaz Sharif.

Sinha: A doubles match.

Durrani: No match! Take Narasimha Rao and Nawaz Sharif. It was my time, I said, problem for us. Narasimha Rao had spent 50 years in the corridors of power, had a good understanding; and on our side was a first-time prime minister whose experience was limited to thana and kacheheri. He believed he could turn India-Pakistan relations around.

He was bound to fail. Narasimha Rao knew how to handle him. He sat quietly on Nawaz Sharif's overture for six months. That's how it's played. That's how it was played years later on Musharraf's initiatives. When Narasimha Rao did not respond for six months, Mian Saheb said, hmph, jawab hi nahin aata, now what do we do?

When your gang has this advantage, why does it blame Pakistan for the deterioration in relations? Our gang does not know how to make use of developments in Kashmir, or for that matter, any development. Whatever happens these days is by default, it saves Pakistan perhaps, and not by the mistakes of your team, which is obsessed with giving no relief to Pakistan or changing the relationship.

Sinha: You seem to be cynical about your own political leadership.

Durrani: The India-Pakistan relationship was best played by Zia-ul-Haq, in my assessment.

Dulat: With which of our prime ministers?

Durrani: Rajiv Gandhi.

Zia went on regardless of the difficulties on the western front, because he understood that the eastern front had to be kept quiet. One wished that our prime ministers had taken this into account. Musharraf had the right idea but was impatient.

After Uri[8] happened, a correspondent from *Outlook* called and asked what I thought would happen. I said: 'Nawaz Sharif would be the last man standing for rapprochement. Mercifully, Modi will not give him a chance.'

The more interesting point is one that Dulat Saheb keeps making about leadership: if one has not done it in the beginning of their tenure, they won't get a chance to do it at all. I don't like politicians at all, they may come up with something at the last moment that has no chance, just to save face. It will be an initiative they wanted to take but could not, and before going just want to have a legacy that they were among the greatest leaders.

In the five years of Zardari's presidency, he did not have the courage to sign the pipeline project with Iran. No international law prevented him from doing so. A few days before leaving office, he finally did, probably for posterity. No one was fooled.

If Manmohan Singh at the fag end of his tenure said he had almost clinched a deal with Pakistan, then he belonged to this category. On a personal level, I found Manmohan Singh clean, efficient. While I moved from MI to ISI in 1990, I was looking at India, seeing its economy was collapsing, stock market was down. A big country like India was unravelling. We were feeling better after a long time.

Sinha: They were celebrating.

Durrani: The election happened soon after I took over. Narasimha Rao appoints Manmohan Singh as the finance minister and India turns around. This coincided with a reverse in our system because a new democratic order took over which wasn't up to maintaining the momentum of the previous three decades of GDP growth of 6 per cent or more. The politicians were euphoric at finally getting power and exercised their policies.

I gave Benazir the benefit of the doubt that her team was new and didn't know how to go about things, so their policies suffered. Then Mian Saheb came in and his policies were no less disastrous. His team was a little more experienced, so they could stabilise the economy a bit. But his political management, which mattered more than a few economic reforms, didn't work out well.

Sinha: Are politicians less keen about the national interest and more about image management?

Durrani: In the long run the national interest can be served by things that we believe should be done or that Dulat Saheb says should be done. But in the short term, or for their political tenure or for their image management, these people did well for themselves. For themselves.

On the macro front I agree with people like Vajpayee, Brajesh Mishra and Amarjit Singh Dulat. They were on the right track, could sustain it. But what if it was not sustained when the government changes? The Pakistan army can be blamed for many things, but it did do a few things honestly and with vision.

Like restoring civilian government in 1988, that it would be Benazir and Nawaz Sharif, etc. A new republic is set up, now it's up to you people, you will run the policies. Please keep the Opposition on board. I have witnessed this personally. If after making your 5 per cent difference or improvement, if the Opposition comes to government and reverses it or does not sustain it, then we'll have a problem.

No civilian government was prepared to accept that they would have a common minimum agenda with the Opposition to sustain such issues.

Dulat: I'm not talking about politicians necessarily agreeing or disagreeing or there being a summit. Generally when we talk about diplomatic relations, the first barometer is: are the foreign secretaries meeting or not meeting? Fine, why shouldn't the foreign secretaries meet, it's their job to meet.

Durrani: That's my point, in countries like India or America where the establishment is strong, leaders like Obama or Trump, or Vajpayee or Modi, may come and make a difference in nuance, in atmospherics, and can even bring about a cosmetic change. But the policies remain the same.

Another development that is even more serious is that over time, when advice on how to go about things was not followed, the committed peace-lovers or the peaceniks or the peace lobby turn into hawks. They had long believed in working for peace and when they see the whole thing scuttled, they would say to hell with it.

Dulat: That's why it requires a lot of patience.

Durrani: Yeah, that's right, patience, over a period of time.

Dulat: Limitless patience.

Durrani: Who are those people who have limitless patience?

Dulat: Ultimately, you have to invest in trust.

Durrani: And stop talking of the mindset. The international community, world media, our own media, our own neo-liberals, they all say: let's address the mindset. They've been let down so many times, either making peace or negotiating territory, or more rights, that they become disillusioned.

The worst advice is to address the mindset, madrassa bandh karo. They haven't even been to a madrassa. I've not gone through a madrassa, and I once believed in our alliance with the US. I've analysed the peace process with India. I never had to go to a madrassa to conclude that gimmicks for peace won't work.

15

Lonely Pervez Musharraf

———◆———

A.S. Dulat: General Saheb said he would explain how Kargil happened, just after Vajpayee had been to Lahore. So why did it happen, Sir?

Asad Durrani: It was Musharraf's obsession for a long time. Pakistan had an advantage in the Kargil sector before the '65 war, dominating a particular vital supply line. These were lost in '71 when some dominating heights were captured by India.

Dulat: You're suggesting that it had to do with Siachen.

Durrani: That road to Leh was critical for India. In both the '65 and '71 wars, India pre-empted. Since the territory is secluded, India easily took the Kargil heights.

After the '65 war the arrangement was to return the captured territory by each side, whether it was Chamb or Kargil or Rajasthan. etc. I'm a veteran of both the wars, and during the '71 war I was in the desert, but soon after the war I was in the Kashmir sector and got to know the deal that was made. The deal was that Pakistan would keep the Chamb salient, and the new Line of Actual Control was drawn so that most of the Kargil heights were on the Indian side.

Musharraf was obsessed about taking them back.

As a two-star DGMO he suggested doing so during Benazir Bhutto's second tenure. 'Prime Minister, we can do that,' so he said. She replied, 'Maybe you can, but politically it won't be sustainable.'

When he became the army chief, he said that after carrying out nuclear tests Pakistan was in a better position for the operation. Hostilities would not escalate, post-nuclearisation, he felt. But, he said, I can assure you that we will take the Kargil heights back. What can the Indians do?

In many ways this nuclearisation theory was a flawed assessment, but he built his premise on 'nuclear immunity': that after going nuclear, we could get away with plenty of things. The part he got wrong, of course, was that if you do these things it may not escalate to nuclear war but you would be accused of being reckless, unwise. That you are risking a nuclear confrontation in the belief that 95 per cent of the time it will not happen. But what about the other 5 per cent?

Dulat: What are these Kargil heights you're talking of, Sir? Did he not have Siachen on his mind?

Durrani: I'll come to Siachen. This reaction must have surprised him. He admits he did not foresee this reaction.

Dulat: Which reaction?

Durrani: How the rest of the world reacted to his irresponsibility.

He probably misjudged India's strong reaction too. Vajpayee was going for early elections, so leaving it at that would have cost him dearly.

It misfired and the heights had to be vacated. Only a few people were privy to the plan. Nawaz Sharif knew a bit, not the whole thing, but he had given the go-ahead, so he had to take political responsibility. I give him the benefit of the doubt, that he did not know the plan's extent; he may have thought that just a small area would be taken.

The Siachen connection was an afterthought. When asked why he did it, his response was that otherwise the Indians would have done another Siachen. In '84 they took the Siachen Glacier while we were looking the other way. According to Musharraf, Indians were planning another ingress, and so he pre-empted them.

The Siachen move was confirmed by one of your generals, Chibber,[1] who in 2000 came to Islamabad and said, 'You Pakistanis wanted to go and occupy Siachen but I got there first.'

Dulat: That's what he said at the time that it happened also.

Durrani: I didn't believe Musharraf's rationale. I wrongly connected the new post-nuclear situation with his earlier efforts.

Dulat: Earlier you said Nawaz Sharif is a dimwit who should never have gone to Washington. He had no option, he was summoned to Washington.

Durrani: An old friend kept me abreast of the developments. I was retired and living in Rawalpindi, where the defence ministry is. Defence secretary General Iftikhar[2] Ali Khan served with me when I was NDC commandant. Now he's no more. Whenever I rang up, Ifti was one of the few people who always found time and said, come over, let's have a chat.

You say we had no option, but I understood that Pakistan had its options. One was, having said these were irregulars, and since they do not hold ground, quietly vacate the heights. And since we were talking to China, who said: 'Are we not your friends? You've made your point, now withdraw.'

And then, since Vajpayee had called Nawaz Sharif and said: 'Kya kar rahe ho bhai? I've an interim government and an election to fight. Why don't you take them back?'

He could have claimed to have responded: 'Achha aap kehte ho toh le jata hoon, varna pata nahin humne aapko kya kar lena tha.'

The worst option was to go on July 4 and say, 'Meri jaan chhudao.' If the idea was to 'oblige' Clinton when the latter asked him to withdraw from the Kargil heights—and thus expect the American President to save his government just in case Sharif ran afoul with the military—Mian Saheb was deluding himself.

During Nawaz Sharif's visit to Washington, DC, I met Musharraf. I said, 'Theek hai, jaane ki kya zaroorat thi?' But he was silent because the pressure had probably already got to him.

Aditya Sinha: During the Kargil war, the government released a tape of a conversation between General Musharraf and General Aziz, intercepted by RAW. Mr Dulat in his book says he was not in favour but his chief was. What was your reaction as a professional or as a former soldier?

Durrani: Your high commissioner in Islamabad, G. Parthasarathy, sent me copies of the tape and the transcript. Once I read and heard them, I was not amused.

Dulat: If you were the RAW chief and the tape came to you, how would you have dealt with it?

Sinha: Were you not surprised that the Indians were recording your army chief's conversations?

Durrani: Our army chief acted unwisely: talking on an open line. The Indians were doing their job.

Dulat: When it landed on my chief's desk, he got excited and took it straightaway to the prime minister and they decided it should be made public, to tell the world, especially the Americans, that we have tapes. I said, Sir, why did you make this public? The channel which we were listening into would now be closed down.

Durrani: That point is correct, as far as intelligence is concerned. We would have said now that we've heard it, how much capital can we get by making it public? Or shall we keep quiet and see if something more would follow? I didn't even know what channels, I thought it was some open bloody channel.

Dulat: It was an open channel. But the point is that there was a line between Musharraf and Aziz that was used and we listened into. It might have been used again.

Durrani: True, if it was a special line then making it public was a blunder. But we know each other's capability to intercept, especially if the line is less than absolutely secure. I would agree, unless you have milked the cow dry, don't expose it.

Dulat: What the boss is saying is that we listen in to a lot of stuff but we don't tell you.

Durrani: Yes, it must not be made public, but that is why you don't use telephone, email, messaging, Skype, which nowadays they say is secure, or Whatsapp, which also they say is secure, for confidential information.

Sinha: Didn't Musharraf say that Mian Saheb will not hold up?

Dulat: He was calling from Beijing and he asked Aziz how things were back home. Aziz said, haan, haan bilkul theek hain. The exciting part was that Musharraf then says, I hope these politicians haven't panicked. That was the crux.

Durrani: G. Parthasarathy, as I have already mentioned, sent me a transcript and a copy of that tape. He simply said, for your information. But on the health, or ill-health, of the overall operation, it had no effect.

Sinha: You don't sound impressed with Musharraf.

Durrani: I have nothing personal against Musharraf. During service he was respectful. He was commissioned four years after me, in my formation; I was then a captain. After taking over he offered me a good assignment as ambassador to Saudi Arabia.

When I found his policies to be disastrous I started publicly criticising them. We've had our militants, extremists, hardliners and fundamentalists, but the current phase of militancy in Pakistan started because Musharraf sent the army to South Waziristan in 2004. However, to his credit, no one ever threatened me for criticising him.

Sinha: Mr Dulat's book states that Musharraf could have clinched a peace deal with India.

Durrani: He's probably looked at it closely, being on that side, more objectively. Musharraf wanted to improve relations but his methodology was defective. You do not start bombarding India, or Delhi, with proposals. One week you make one, the next you make another. This tsunami of proposals from Islamabad—if I was in Delhi I would say, no need to react. We'll see what happens. We'll wait till he makes another that's more favourable to India.

Or, coming from him is there a design? Will they gain more and trap us? So you give it time.

The methodology should also be different. It should not be done through the media, because even if it looked good to India, it might be reluctant to let Pakistan take the credit for the 'ground-breaking' initiative.

Dulat: Why India did not react, I agree, Sir. We wasted that window of 2006-07. Khurshid Mahmud Kasuri has written a book, Sati Lambah has also said we almost did it. What is the point of that? I also almost did many things.

I don't know Musharraf, though I would have loved an interaction. My admiration of him comes from what I saw in the context of Kashmir. Without hesitation or doubt, in the last 25 years there hasn't been a Pakistani leader more positive or reasonable on Kashmir than Musharraf. His repeatedly saying that whatever is acceptable to Kashmiris is acceptable to Pakistan—that was good for India. We should have taken that and built on it, but again we dragged our feet.

Musharraf was hemmed in by American pressure because of 9/11. But whatever it was, he told the separatists to fall in line or become redundant, and that if they had political ambitions to fight elections, then to get on with it. Today Pakistan is trying desperately to get the Hurriyat together; Musharraf made no such effort. When he found that Geelani was an obstacle, he even said, at some meeting, 'Get out of the way, old man.'

He was definitely forward-looking. If you ask a Kashmiri today, Geelani Saheb apart, he will say if anything is doable then it is the four-point formula.

As for Musharraf the general, the army chief, the president—I don't know anything other than what the Americans said, that he's a good guy, English-speaking, whiskey-drinking. We can do business with him.

Durrani: Musharraf's in Dubai, whenever you go...

Dulat: Sir, I'll need an introduction.

Durrani: He'll be happy to meet you. Ehsan can facilitate it. In my case, he's not happy with me the last ten years. I went to town criticising his flagship project, the 'devolution' policy that was supposed to take governance to people's doorsteps. The concept was fine but the way he and Tanveer Naqvi went about it was a recipe for disaster. It was my first big interaction with the media, and he did not like criticism coming from a former military man. I was supposed to be part of his constituency. So he won't be happy with my reference.

Sinha: Why didn't Nawaz Sharif sack Musharraf immediately after Kargil?

Durrani: Sacking Musharraf was something he wanted to do. He in due course did so.

Dulat: That was much later.

Durrani: I'm sure some saner advisors were holding him back. Musharraf's predecessor, Jehangir Karamat, had resigned—or was made to resign—just a year before. A naval chief had been sacked soon after Sharif became the prime minister. Riding roughshod over an institution like the military was never a good idea. With our history, a more deliberate course must have been recommended. But, of course, Mian Saheb could only wait long enough.

In September Nawaz Sharif concluded that he would be uncomfortable with Musharraf continuing in the powerful post. One way of making Musharraf irrelevant without sacking him was to promote him to be the chairman of the joint chiefs of staff. This is a post that commands one PA and one orderly. An emissary was sent with the offer but Musharraf turned it down. Nawaz Sharif then offered to keep him as the army chief and also promote him as chairman. Musharraf says, that I can do.

It became clear to Musharraf that he would be sacked at the first opportunity, so he developed a contingency plan.

In August, Musharraf and I had a one-on-one. Musharraf invited me to his office and said the government was bent upon publicly blaming the army for the Kargil fiasco. Fine, I said, so what? He said he just wanted my opinion on what would happen.

I said, if I know Nawaz Sharif, he would continue to be uncomfortable with you, as he was with Baig, with Asif Nawaz, and even with Jehangir Karamat, who was a laid-back army chief, professionally sound and who did not throw his weight around. Even after the 1998 Indian nuclear tests Karamat said merely, prime minister, this is the army's view, you have to consider the political and economic fallout. But with him also it did not work out; three months before he was to retire, he resigned rather than take a second more of the acrimony.

So I told Musharraf it won't work out with you. He'll look for an opportunity to get rid of you. But this is not the right environment for a political coup; 'even banana republics nowadays have a facade of democracy,' I remember saying. So go ahead and think of the next step. That's where I left. It was clear that Musharraf could not launch a coup unless there was a grave provocation.

That rationale was soon thereafter provided by Nawaz Sharif, when he sacked him on October 12. It was not just the decision but the way that it was carried out. Arre, the army chief is in the air and you announce he's sacked and order his aircraft to fly to Amritsar or elsewhere. It was a distasteful way of doing things but rather typical of Mian Saheb. It turned out to be pretty costly.

Dulat: What surprises me is that the Generals closest to him during the coup, who helped him and were considered loyal to Musharraf, dumped him once he left power.

Durrani: In fact, it was Musharraf who dumped the 'co-conspirators'. Aziz got off lightly, given the 4th star, but outside the army; Mahmood was sacked; Osmani, Commander 5 Corps, who might have facilitated Musharraf's plane's landing in Karachi, eased out in due course.

Dulat: Mahmood was sacked because of the Americans.

Durrani: Yes, the Americans.

Dulat: Aziz benefited in every way, but he had no good word for Musharraf. Why?

Durrani: This is the way of the world. Zia-ul-Haq also jettisoned people like Fazle Haq, who said 'ikatthe aaye the, ikatthe jayenge', and Chishti, who he hypocritically used to call his 'Murshad' (guru). Zia was too clever for that. To continue with kingmakers is to ensure that they will take you down in due course. New people come in, serve their purpose, and get thrown out.

Dulat: That is the sad thing about whom you are serving, that there is no loyalty.

Durrani: Few people are loyal.

Dulat: Even less have a regard for loyalty.

Durrani: The really loyal person may not be loyal to a personality but to a movement, a coup. Or they do it for the country.

Dulat: Sir, when we talk of loyalty we talk of personal loyalty, but these things don't last. The only General who still speaks well of Musharraf is General Ehsan. And Sikander[3] is okay with him.

Durrani: Ehsan was close to Musharraf. He was unhappy with a few policies but he's not one of those who, when out, start bad-mouthing the once benefactor. There is another who benefited almost as much as Ehsan. He had retired and was brought in as federal minister. Once he served his purpose…

Dulat: Out is out.

Durrani: Out is out. But he does not spare Musharraf. There are two-three of them who do not spare Musharraf. I understand both views. One, you benefited and don't speak; the other, if you believe something went wrong then nothing should stop you from giving an insider view.

Dulat: Yet despite Kargil, Vajpayee still called Musharraf to Agra. Sir, you must know quite a lot about the Agra summit.

Durrani: Not enough except what I've heard from you.

Dulat: This may be mere conjecture because I was not involved, but I think it was a marvellous operation.

Durrani: Really? Achha.

Dulat: It was. Vajpayee's NDA cabinet was one of exceptional talent with exceptional people. Not all of them but even the younger lot like Arun Jaitley and Pramod Mahajan. It had bigwigs, though: Vajpayee, Advani, Jaswant Singh, Yashwant Sinha and, most underrated of all, George Fernandes.

George was a great player and a good defence minister. He fitted in perfectly with Brajesh Mishra, and like Brajesh Mishra and Vajpayee, he would not utter a word in a meeting. But if you went to him, he would talk frankly one-to-one. Whenever Vajpayee was in trouble he used George.

The way Agra played out was remarkable. My knowledge is based on two things. One, what Brajesh Mishra came back and told me, which showed his frustration. Much more was what Qazi Ashraf said. He told me things in greater detail, both as high commissioner and then when I met him in 2014.

Brajesh Mishra ran a parallel foreign office out of the PMO, and he planned this. If you recall, the idea to invite Musharraf came from Advani. Brajesh Mishra had a direct line with Qazi and he encouraged Qazi to befriend Advani—through George Fernandes. He probably told to call George to set it up. He ran this operation.

Qazi and Advani became buddies. Advani proposed the Agra summit. Then he asked Qazi, are you happy now, which Qazi was.

I later asked Qazi, what went wrong with your friend in Agra? He said the Advani of Agra was different from the Advani of Delhi. The chemistry had gone wrong in the meeting with Musharraf.

The lacuna in this plan was that the Pakistanis, particularly Qazi, were not adequately briefed to take care of Advani in Agra. That is where one's ego comes in, that he can manage it all. All the eggs were in the Vajpayee basket, so Advani felt offended, and the summit failed.

Sinha: Even within the government there has to be a lot of politicking before it can make peace with Pakistan.

Dulat: This was not an ordinary move. It was exceptional, expected by no one. This is after Kargil, after the coup, after Musharraf appointed himself President—as soon as it was announced, an invitation was sent. So some kind of politicking was required for it to happen.

Sinha: So it has to be like this. For there'll always be a Kargil or a Bombay just behind us.

Dulat: After Bombay nothing happened.

Sinha: General Saheb, have you seen this kind of manoeuvre to get something going with India?

Durrani: Two-three points that are more significant than the summit itself. One is that if you went and briefed the foreign minister or the deputy prime minister, your boss would get upset.

Dulat: I don't know if he would get upset, but he had no relationship with Advani or Jaswant Singh. The IC-814 hijack provided an opportunity to shift Jaswant Singh to finance and Yashwant Sinha was brought in his place. The moment Yashwant joined, Brajesh Mishra told me to go brief him on Kashmir.

Durrani: This can happen in our system but most of the time if I went and briefed someone, no one would be too bothered. The DG ISI, DG MI, must have something. We trust him. If he meets Najibullah's intelligence chief without anyone knowing, okay, he takes this decision, let's see what happens. That is probably where we may take credit for our system being more trusting. Your bureaucracy is more efficient and is known to be tough.

Sinha: All you're saying, Sir, is that in Pakistan the military is supreme.

Dulat: You've got this wrong. This PMO was relaxed, it was wonderful to work there. Brajesh Mishra never told me, don't meet Advani. On the contrary, Dr Manmohan Singh called up just before the 2002 (assembly) elections and said, can you come across and give me your assessment on Kashmir. I said, certainly Sir, I'll just inform my boss. Brajesh said, yes, yes, Manmohan Singh has spoken to me, please go ahead and brief him. I went and had a long chat with Dr Manmohan Singh, at the end of which I said, Sir, I have good news for you. You're going to do extremely well in Jammu. He was kicked, and said, can I go tell Madam?

It's not as if I was choked up in the PMO. I had freedom, it was probably my weakness that if the boss didn't think it important to meet these people, why should I.

Durrani: I'll take (Sinha's) remark in good spirit, that at least the military system is not suspicious or paranoid.

The Advani thing surprised me. The deputy prime minister, a famous man and an experienced person who let such an important thing be scuttled or subverted or not supported, simply because he wasn't getting enough attention? India-Pakistan relations can be endangered because of that—is what I've understood.

Musharraf spoke to me before and I had hoped he would tell me something about the preparations, diplomatic and other, but he didn't tell me anything. I got the impression he was going ad hoc, that was his personality. He probably thought he can go talk to the Indians and after some time they'll be eating out of his hands. That sort of conceit he's had for a long time.

He went, and like Mr Dulat says, it was subverted by Advani and others. The breakfast meeting where Ashraf Jehangir Qazi invited editors was telecast before the summit, that was not very wise. In an important visit you don't convey your messages through the media. If at all something is to be said it is that we'll do our best.

After the summit, when people saw that nothing happened, Vajpayee, an experienced, highly respected man, did not see off Musharraf. He did not come out to the car. In our culture this is unusual. Zia-ul-Haq would think of getting rid of someone, but would walk him to the car and open the door. That was his style. The prime minister not accompanying the visiting president to the car looked bad.

Vajpayee shook hands and went off, and Musharraf's few steps to the car seemed to have lasted an eternity. Oh god, I could see from his body language that the man was hoping that no one would see him or take his photograph.

16

Modi's Surprise Moves

A.S. Dulat: As surprising as it may sound, Modi did more in his first two years for India-Pakistan relations than his predecessor. It's a different, instinctive diplomacy in which the foreign office has little role. It fully flows out of the PMO, and so happens easily. Modi has no problem overcoming the frictions and reservations that diplomats have. Even the foreign minister is often not in the loop.

Aditya Sinha: It's a good way to short-circuit internal friction.

Dulat: Not that Sushma would be an obstruction because she's one of the better ministers in this government.

Modi's record shows he had the imagination to invite Mian Saheb for his swearing-in. That it was messed up by the foreign secretary[1] is unfortunate. And after that, as things seemed to reach a dead end, whether in Kathmandu[2] or New York,[3] he finally landed up, extempore, in Lahore.[4]

We were together on December 21, Sir, hoping that something would happen.

Asad Durrani: Yes.

Dulat: Lo and behold on the 25th he was in Lahore.

The other positive thing is that the NSAs are in close contact. I'm told they talk to each other. Unfortunately, despite everybody's intentions, the relationship has reached a dead end fast. I get the feeling that we're only marking time.

Unfortunately, the politics is too mixed up, unlike with Manmohan Singh and Vajpayee, who kept it in the background. Yes, politics comes into the picture, in what you get out of it. Every prime minister is political, but we don't have to make it so crude.

Sinha: What is Modi's Pakistan policy?

Dulat: Frankly I don't know. There is no Pakistan policy.

Durrani: Doval is his Pakistan policy.

Dulat: Yeah, but you know, Doval and Modi are the same thing. After all he's his NSA and he wouldn't do anything different.

It's more opportunism. He went to Lahore, but those were better days. Everyone said the chemistry between Mian Saheb and Modi was good, perhaps because Mian Saheb went out of his way; his political instincts maybe tell him that better relations with India would help him politically and as a businessman. If relations improve, so does trade, business prospects and many other things. He would be more confident in Punjab and Pakistan.

At one point of time, Modi was going along with that. Till Pathankot happened. Then he could sort of live with Pathankot. But after Uri, Modi's feeling was, we tried you guys and you failed us, every now and then there's a Pathankot or an Uri, so how can we do business?

Mufti Saheb's absence from the political scene has also affected the larger political scenario. His daughter Mehbooba has been a disaster.

Sinha: General Saheb, you said Modi did not cut a good figure across our region. Please elaborate.

Durrani: The reaction in Pakistan to Modi's election was that it served India right. Let Modi take care of India, destroy its image, and possibly destroy its inner balance.

I've not been impressed by his antics. What did he mean crash-landing after giving Pakistan an earful in Afghanistan? He comes to Raiwind to attend Nawaz Sharif's granddaughter's wedding, and his drama and tamasha merely created spectacular confusion. People were shell-shocked and just stood there.

I prefer someone like Vajpayee who did not deliver but his approach was right. A person who manages the relationship well will not keep you on tenterhooks. Not that there is any intention to equate Vajpayee with Modi. World of difference. We would be happy if someone like Vajpayee was prime minister in Pakistan. Poet, philosopher, he could have been a good prime minister for us.

Dulat: Does Pakistan prefer Dr Manmohan Singh or Narendra Modi? There's a contradiction because somewhere General Saheb has said that a hardliner in India may be in Pakistan's interest. That's why I believe Pakistan is happy if Kashmir is in a mess.

A lot of people think Modi is the greatest thing to happen to India. I've earlier said that Vajpayee was an exceptional prime minister, and he led an exceptional government. But Modi doesn't have much of a cabinet. There's Modi, and the next guy is a mile away. The only one Modi holds close is Doval.

Even his home minister, a decent person who is keen to do something in Kashmir, is quite helpless.

Durrani: Rajnath?

Dulat: Rajnath.

Vajpayee, who was head and shoulders above Modi, still had to deal with Advani. Modi is on his own trip. He doesn't even bother about the RSS at times.

Sinha: But their worldview is one. So what exactly has Modi accomplished?

Dulat: People say he needs more time, 15 years.

This brings me to another point. General Saheb's or Pakistan's problem may not be what happened in 2016[5] as with the government in Delhi. As a hard-nosed intelligence officer he said that whether he liked Modi or not, this was still a good opportunity for India and Pakistan to move forward. He felt that it is a BJP Hindu government with which Pakistan can do business.

Like the argument in India that we need a military government back in power in Pakistan. Advani used to say that if there is to be forward movement there has to be a BJP government. Now Modi's is the perfect BJP government. It won't get better than this. More Hindu, or more numbers. You might disagree, but in 2019 Modi won't get as many seats in Parliament. The BJP will take a very long time to get as many seats again.

Durrani: The ISI's preference is because hardliners can take hard decisions.

This reminds me of an episode, the end of 1997, before the '98 election that the BJP won. I published an article in the *News*, Islamabad, 'Who's afraid of the Indiana wolf', on how we need not worry about the BJP coming to power because it might turn out to be good for us. If nothing else, the illusion of India being a secular-led country would go.

After a few weeks there was an explosion in Coimbatore, where Advani was to address a meeting. It probably added to the BJP's support base, not very big in south India. After this explosion, a paper in Switzerland picked up my piece and linked it to the Coimbatore blast, saying that since Durrani says a BJP win would be good for them, the ISI may be behind the blast.

They got elected, and I said I hope they carry out a nuclear test because that will give us a golden opportunity to do the same.

The Vajpayee government gave us the impression that a Muslim-baiter in power in India would not necessarily be a bad thing. This party may be able to take decisions the Congress was unable to.

Sinha: When the US invaded Iraq, people said it can't get worse. Now they call George W. Bush a moderate. If Yogi Adityanath becomes prime minister, you will say Modi bada shareef aadmi tha.

Dulat: We still say it, Modi is a very decent man. The point is if he shook up the system, he'd create an opportunity.

During Dr Manmohan Singh's early days, when I had just left the PMO, I told a Hurriyat leader, why don't you carry on with what we were doing? He laughed: 'You want us to do business with him? Our problem is with Hindu India.'

That's why Dr Manmohan Singh got the wrong end of the stick. Vajpayee left it all for him on a platter, but the BJP would not leave him be. He was more afraid of the BJP than 10 Janpath, as many presume. The BJP was always all over him.

Durrani: In Obama's eight years he never took the risk in Afghanistan, on Pakistan, in Libya, in the Middle East. So his legacy is failure, other than Cuba and Iran. Similarly, if Modi later finds failure is staring in his face externally and then wants to extend a hand, no one will take it seriously. They will wonder: lame duck? Outgoing?

Dulat: I beg to differ. Modi is no Obama, who was a fine American president, intellectually and otherwise. It's not easy for a black man in the United States. I don't think these guys here even had that kind of imagination.

Durrani: Obama was intellectually well-endowed, I agree. So was Carter. All these intellectual big-wigs, their intellect led nowhere. Reagan was no intellectual, much like this Donald Duck or whatever his name is. Trump is a big duck, but may turn out to be smart ultimately. Reagan turned out to be the most successful American president of the 20th century. He knew nothing but he selected 12 good people and things turned out all right. For America, they did.

Modi is a showman. He likes theatrics. He likes to keep people guessing. He knows that after reading the riot act to Pakistan in Dhaka[6] and Kabul,[7] if he crashlands in Lahore, people will be wonderstruck and say, here is the man of the moment. Here is a man we can do business with. But he has no intention of doing good for the region; his only thought is of creating an impact back home. He's smart.

With Mian Saheb it is not the chemistry that works because Mian Saheb does not work chemically. He works at best instinctively or probably driven by business and financial consideration. He understands how to survive politically at home; but on international relations he has the acumen of a camel.

Sinha: A duck, a camel, and Modi is?

Durrani: A fox. Modi is smart. Absolutely. So is Doval. How do we think about Doval and Janjua? Doval was a good intelligence operator, a good thinker; a cunning mind, but that's not the point. Janjua? Run of the mill soldier. I don't think he's learnt more about relations with India after commanding corps and divisions and the Southern Command. I have met him just a couple of times and my conclusion is, no; he could not get the better of Doval.

On both fronts, prime minister and NSA, you have had a huge advantage.

Sinha: Mr Dulat is saying Modi can do it, you're saying Modi won't. Why not?

Durrani: I am fed up talking the same thing the last 20-30 years. When I look at Modi and his team, and what one knows of people like Doval, the political environment in India, I feel they can't. Yes, there are people like Vajpayee who knew how to manage it by cooling the situation with Kashmiriyat-Jamhooriyat-Insaaniyat. But these people are not cut out for it. They're not likely to do it.

Sinha: So Modi can't dilute his tough guy image?

Dulat: That is one problem, that he has a certain image and would not like to dilute it. It was to his advantage in moving forward. I would agree with General Saheb that as time goes by it looks more unlikely that anything will happen.

The other thing is that for all politicians worldwide, unless they do things in the first six months or year, then it's unlikely they'll do anything the rest of their tenure. Also, Modi's guys are obsessed with elections and move from election to election.

Sinha: So you agree with General Saheb?

Dulat: It's not likely to happen, no.

You had asked how it looked when we were halfway through Modi's tenure. It didn't look good. Even his admirers wondered what had happened.

I used to feel uncomfortable that whenever I went to a social get-together in Delhi, I found that 18 of the 20 people would be pro-Modi. It was difficult to even inquire about him. Two years later I found it changed dramatically.

Harish Khare wrote that the last election was won on Hindutva. Along with Hindutva, the upper middle class thought it was doing well and that with Modi it would do better. That hasn't happened.

Sinha: Modi has a year left. How does Pakistan see his prospects?

Durrani: First, he's likely to get a second term. Second, whether or not he remains, my old thesis is that its management can be different but the relationship remains the same. Sometimes a bit calmer as in Vajpayee's or even Manmohan Singh's time. Third, the environment in India is such that even the public would say there was no point in making another gesture.

Sinha: General Saheb says that even if Modi does not return in 2019, things won't change. Do you think Modi will be back?

Dulat: Modi probably will but he'll find the going much tougher. The Congress and other Opposition will give him a run for his money. But then who knows the Indian voter, he's fooled everybody most of the time. Modi could be surprised.

Sinha: Could there then be a 'reset' of India-Pakistan relations?

Dulat: I don't totally agree with General Saheb. He said it's always the same, the actors don't matter much. But there's clearly a world of difference between Vajpayee and Modi. Vajpayee was a towering personality, a philosopher, and unfortunately he became prime minister too late, when he was a cautious old man. Still, he was a shrewd politician and could choreograph things his way. When he said things they made an impression.

17

The Doval Doctrine

A.S. Dulat: Ajit Doval keeps coming up in our intel dialogue. For the Pakistanis, he's the devil incarnate.

Asad Durrani: I don't want to put it like that. Maybe some in the Pakistani press do give that impression. In the business he's just another person doing his duty, probably doing it well. But what has he done to deserve a mention in our book? Even if one mentioned him negatively.

I met Doval a couple of times, even before I met Mr Dulat. The first time was in Muscat, Oman, at an India-Pakistan Track-II in 2005, organised by the International Institute of Strategic Studies. Recently liberated from service he sat there quietly.

They seated three of us with intelligence backgrounds together, and by chance our microphones weren't wired. Doval had just stepped out. I made a crack that we weren't wired to the same system as our monitoring was being done elsewhere, and Mr Doval has gone to activate our channels. There was a good amount of laughter.

He was also at the Tehelka meet I mentioned. Quiet, observing, difficult to read. Ultimately he also spoke, and that is where one could assess that his experience in Pakistan affected him in a different way. He's no Mani Shankar Aiyar.[1]

Dulat: He was part of our intel dialogue and attended the first few sessions.

I've known Ajit for a long time. He's been a colleague and good friend too. When he joined this group I told Peter, I now see hope in this process because we have here a gentleman who is going to go places. Everyone looked around and realised I was talking about Ajit. He has gone places but he hasn't helped the process, and then he just opted out.

As far as his capabilities go, he's one of our outstanding operational guys. He's a field man.

The trouble, though, with people who are so much into themselves, is that they're lonesome and they stay aloof. In *A Legacy of Spies*[2] there's a relevant line that says, the trouble with spooks is that they find it difficult to invest in trust.

These high-profile guys who keep to themselves have a problem of trust. Ajit is a guy who won't trust anybody. In our business it is, in any case, not easy to trust. He's not the only one, incidentally. Other big names in Indian intelligence have been similarly lonely.

Aditya Sinha: You never hear in the Indian press about the Pakistani NSA, General Janjua, in the way Doval is mentioned in the Pakistani media.

Durrani: Sometimes when the press finds a target, it benefits the person. He hasn't changed policy. He's just a little more hardline but it's still what I believe has been Indian policy for a long time. He shouts more, like Trump does, a lot of hot air. He provides that masala.

We're talking more of the substance of the relationship, not of people who froth at the mouth. One met him later in this intel dialogue once or twice. He spoke with a swagger, so I thought he has gained confidence. I didn't know he was going to join Modi as his NSA, and that he was cross-examining me like an NSA-designate.

The upshot is he's just doing what his boss wants done. Maybe more muscularly, more vocally.

Sinha: You've talked about Mr Dulat's hands-on experience. The NSA is another gentleman with a lot of hands-on experience...

Dulat: More than I.

Sinha: ...though his approach is different. So is it experience or is it outlook?

Durrani: That's a good point. People have experience but how does it affect them?

When it comes to Palestine, we in Pakistan, the Arab world and the Muslim world have similar reactions. Yet we do not all believe that you must take the sword and book to non-believers.

So your hands-on experience in Pakistan can be different. In Ajit Doval's case it probably affected him in a way where he felt, 'Oh God, this country must be dealt with an iron fist.' And Mr Dulat after working in Kashmir may have concluded that there were other approaches.

Sinha: General Saheb, how did it go when a group of former Pakistan high commissioners met Doval[3] in Delhi in 2016?

Durrani: Six high commissioners had an invitation from the Aspen Centre, Sati Lambah[4] was the moving force. They considered their most substantial meeting was when they called on the NSA. Ajit Doval treated them indifferently, saying: 'We are watching you. If something good does not come out of our investigation, and if we find a link between Pathankot and Mumbai and a state structure, there will be consequences.'

When the meeting finished he did not shake hands with a group that is highly regarded in both countries. Just walked away. The message was conveyed.

Dulat: Sir, you obviously got it from somebody at that meeting. What I heard in Delhi was the contrary; the high commissioners were pleasantly surprised that he was nice and soft despite his reputation of being tough as nails.

Durrani: He softly put across the message that India didn't want good relations, thank you for coming.

Dulat: Yes, if something like that was said, it's uncalled for. Let me say there are understandable reservations perhaps about Ajit Doval in Pakistan.

Durrani: Here it was not about reservations, it's the account of the participants.

Sinha: You said his name came up in the intel dialogue. What happened?

Dulat: He comes up in every meeting because of the things written about him. That Doval's shadow looms over the place. I don't know how far that's true. I've had very little interaction with Ajit since he's become NSA.

Durrani: In this particular meeting,[5] we talked about the present environment and whether it is possible to reach out to the dispensation in Delhi. My point was, no, let's not even try.

Dulat: I had once stuck my neck out a few meetings ago. I said this dialogue thing isn't going anywhere, I have an idea, why don't you invite Ajit Doval to Lahore or Islamabad? My gut feeling tells me he would love to go. Maybe that could be a beginning.

Durrani: I raised the first objection.

Dulat: Ehsan agreed and said yes, that should not be difficult. On our side, K.M. Singh said why not also a meeting with the army chief? And Ehsan's response was, yes, possibly.

Having suggested this, I was sceptical. Ajit in present circumstances is not easily going to get an invite. He hasn't got one.

The two NSAs have a relationship. I'm told they talk on the phone but they haven't met for a long time. So that relationship is not going anywhere. Would you agree, Sir?

Durrani: My two objections are, first, this invitation would not go down well in Pakistan. More importantly, suppose he rebuffs us and says, why should I. It's possible that he then goes around saying despite all I have said and done about Pakistan, these guys still come crawling on their knees. He's capable of that.

Sinha: That's a bit much.

Dulat: Actually, the question of his accepting the invitation was raised. It was checked and the response was, yes, Ajit would be quite happy. As I thought. Yet the invite never came.

Sinha: So the NSA is the key person to breaking the India-Pakistan stalemate?

Dulat: That depends on the NSA system, which in India is only three prime ministers old. The way it's evolving, the NSA is a key figure. This particular one is Modi's henchman. He's the number two, much like Brajesh Mishra was to Vajpayee. But that was a more sophisticated relationship, nobody talked about it.

Durrani: Let's say Modi and Ajit Doval are work in progress. We do not know where it will go. Till now the signals are mixed, but if one believes they are more into theatrics then it's not likely to go anywhere.

Dulat: There's no doubt that signals are mixed. I'm sure it would confuse you; it confuses us in Delhi. I see it like this, that there is a keenness, almost an anxiety, to succeed. To prove that Modi's visit to Raiwind was not for nothing.

Sinha: What is the dynamic between the two NSAs?

Dulat: General Saheb will know better, but from whatever one hears the chemistry is good.

Sinha: That's puzzling.

Dulat: Not if it's a question of one's sense of importance. They get along fine, no problem, each is just a phone call away. They call each other, see each other. It's a good relationship. But they're not taking advantage of it, and both sides are to blame. If there is something good going, forget the prime ministers for the time being, why haven't they capitalised on it?

Pakistan has not paid sufficient attention to Ajit Doval. When everything else closes there is a great window of opportunity and that is Ajit Doval. He would grab an opportunity if it shows him coming in better, bigger light.

Durrani: Well, I don't feel comfortable thinking Doval is the person. If it was up to me, I would not even talk about him. However, he matters nowadays, as Modi matters. I agree he is smart and would not miss an opportunity for another spectacle. Win Modi or himself brownie points. But I'm not counting on him to turn around the relationship and make it stable. Next time he's in Lahore or Islamabad, it will be for all the right reasons for India, but all the wrong reasons for the long-term relationship, and without wishing us any benefit.

Dulat: I think that's one of the problems in the relationship right now, and I'm a little handicapped because, as I said, he's been a colleague, a friend, so I don't want to put too much into it, but I think, in the Pakistan mind, where it matters, Doval remains a problem unfortunately.

Sinha: Sounds like deep distrust.

Dulat: That's what I'm saying. It's unfortunate. You said you wouldn't even bother to think about him, somebody could say the same about Henry Kissinger. Also, he's not necessarily a hardliner.

Durrani: Who?

Dulat: Ajit Doval. He toes Modi's line. He also toed Mani Dixit's line. He at one point toed [M.K.] Narayanan's line ... I'll tell you something. He is convinced that Modi is the greatest thing that has happened to India. That I can vouch for.

Durrani: So in future we have to work on Doval and not Modi?

Dulat: Doval would enjoy this. That's why I keep saying get him to Lahore. He loves Pakistan!

18

The Hardliners

Aditya Sinha: You said Indian foreign office was radically anti-Pakistan. Please elaborate.

Asad Durrani: That was based on having dealt with Indian diplomats in Islamabad and other places. At the Pugwash Conference in Delhi in February 2004 the Indian foreign secretary hosted a dinner and I met a few people. Talks were taking place and the environment was all right, but I listened to the way some of the junior diplomats spoke. One of the minions threatened us that all would change if we didn't improve our behaviour.

Tavleen Singh wrote a piece saying the foreign office seemed programmed for Paki-bashing. That confirmed my feeling. Over time one understands the stance of organisations and institutions. I believe that institutions develop a culture of their own, and South Block[1] is hawkish on Pakistan.

A.S. Dulat: Diplomats tend to have fixed mindsets. It might be the baggage of Partition, or the foreign office files, but I wouldn't say it's across the board. There are some on both sides, particularly those posted in each other's capitals, who have been outstanding.

Most of our diplomats have been understanding and reasonable. Our high commissioners in Islamabad, you would agree, have tried to reach out and make friends and do their best.

What happens in Delhi is slightly different. Satyabrata Pal, who served in Islamabad, is pro-Pakistan because he's not anti-Pakistan. He has an open mind. There are others as well. You've mentioned Mani Dixit, Shiv Shankar Menon and Sati Lambah. The last few high commissioners, T.C.A. Raghavan and, before him, Sharat Sabharwal, have all done an outstanding job.

But I agree there are people with fixed mindsets, and I'm sure there would also be some on the Pakistani side.

Each successive Pakistan high commissioner in Delhi seems to be better than the last. For an Indian high commissioner, Islamabad is not as comfortable as Delhi is for a Pakistan high commissioner. He is able to get around, has lots of friends. In Pakistan there is more hostility. Also, if you call the Pakistan high commissioner names, immediately there is a tougher tit-for-tat.

It's sad because it is a waste of time. We need to be more positive, to move forward. There is no point nit-picking that this is wrong, that is wrong.

Let me also say the generals are most comfortable with one another.

Durrani: A foreign office has to keep a stance in keeping with the country's declared policy. So it's careful. It tries not only to maintain the country's stance but reinforce it as well.

Let's take another foreign office. In the US, with whom our relations go up and down, the CIA and the Pentagon, but especially the CIA, act as good cops, saying we have to hang in there, this is our policy, Congress is tough. The State Department, on the other hand, keeps a straight face, stiff upper lip, speaks the minimum—all to give the message that you'd better be careful. It may be the nature of the relationship, but it is also their job. Not to be caught off-guard later on having said something off-policy.

Dulat: Absolutely correct. Diplomats tend to be cautious. They have a knack for spending hours producing nothing.

Sinha: Perhaps the foreign office is always on record, while faujis and spooks are off the record.

Dulat: That's possibly true, but not the only reason. It's a mentality in the foreign office. You're not going to concede an inch. There are umpteen stories of obstruction by diplomats. Even Agra. No one knows what really happened there. Musharraf said it was Vivek Katju who stalled it.

Sinha: He's hawkish.

Durrani: He's bound to be. We never had any doubt about him, especially in the IPA rounds. He speaks softly, he's pleasant to talk to, but things he says reflect both his mindset and his message.

Coming back to the quality of diplomats, I agree that your high commissioners who come are top of the line, they return and become foreign secretary.

Sinha: Mr Dulat said Pakistanis are tougher on Indian high commissioners than Indians on Pakistan high commissioners. Do you agree?

Durrani: It's absolutely possible.

Dulat: It is a fact.

Durrani: You can't take it out on anyone else. You see someone on our turf, you pressure him.

Dulat: The ISI has more manpower in Islamabad to chase the Indian high commissioner around than the IB has in Delhi.

Durrani: That is a reflection of their quality. After retirement many speak and write openly, and are known on Track-II, except Riaz Khokhar, who's at times considered difficult. There was once an informal exchange planned between Dr Mubashir Hassan, now in his 90s, who only leaves Lahore for Delhi, never Islamabad; and Maharaj Krishna Rasgotra, an icon in Indian diplomacy. Mubashir Hassan had recommended two names for his next visit, Riaz Khokhar's and mine. Rasgotra said there'll be a problem with both names, and we didn't go.

Except for him, everyone else is well regarded, like Aziz Khan, the darling of the Delhi crowd, or Niaz Naik, known as the father of Track-II. After retirement, they pleaded for a forward, positive move.

Every high commissioner is better than the last because his job is to manage the relationship, not to threaten.

Sinha: Riaz Khokhar, who is considered most hawkish, was in Delhi a 'Page 3' personality.

Dulat: He had a remarkable combination of high commissioner and deputy high commissioner, a gentleman by the name of Kakakhel.

Durrani: Shafqat Kakakhel.

Dulat: He was a great player in Delhi, seen everywhere.

Durrani: Certainly considered a good diplomat. He was a colleague when I was defence attaché in Germany. Well-essayed, positive or pro-good relationship, but as a deputy high commissioner if he had to do his duty he must have done it.

Dulat: He did more than his duty!

Durrani: Are you suggesting he went around and met the 'softer' targets?

Sinha: You said that no matter how proactive a diplomat, they were unable to overcome the establishment.

Durrani: Mani Dixit had the good of the region at heart but didn't live long enough to do the things he had undertaken. When we met at Pugwash in 2004 he said, I'm now with the Congress, and though it's unlikely to win it will do better than before. The Congress won and he became NSA. He said, now things will look up, and our response was in any case likely to be good because of Musharraf. His passing away was a setback to the relationship.

Shiv Shankar Menon had his heart in it during his time in Islamabad and was quite popular there. When he was going back to be foreign secretary he said, now leave it to me, let me see what I can do.

Sinha: This UN general assembly (2017) India and Pakistan had a lot of exchanges, holding up photos, etc. It's odd we attack each other on the world stage every year.

Dulat: Not every year, but this year we're back in action.

Sinha: What purpose does it serve?

Dulat: It's a level of whining, a bigger stage, worldwide publicity. We thump the table and say, this is what these guys are up to, and they thump even harder and say, look at what these guys are up to. This happens when you don't want to look each other in the eye and sit down and talk. This is an outcome of not talking. It happens also in Geneva, which doesn't get much publicity. When we're talking then these things don't happen; it's just frustration and theatre.

I said to my Pakistani friends, when you talk of the suffering of Kashmiris or of human rights excesses, even I would tolerate it in support of the Kashmiris. But when you talk of a 5,000-year war or of UN resolutions, then who's listening? Even Kashmiris say, the Pakistanis are no longer serious about us, because these things have long been forgotten. Why do you raise this again? When I met General Ehsan in London I said, why do you want to use this word dispute? Because if we go back to the Shimla summit, Bhutto and Mrs Gandhi decided that whatever issues there are, most of all Kashmir, would be settled bilaterally. This is another reason for not going to the UN.

Sinha: But the key is that when you're not talking, these things happen.

Dulat: Sir, let me ask you. Why is it much easier when you and I talk, or when our group meets, than when diplomats meet? I'm asking of Pakistan really, not that our diplomats are any better. Why are diplomats more hawkish than military or intelligence men? It puzzles me.

Durrani: The diplomat minces his or her words all career long, hiding words, soft-pedalling things, because that's the job. He wanted to kill the other man but was taught not to; and he was taught that if he had to send someone to hell, as the saying goes, say so in a manner that the man may look forward to his trip.

People like us during our career believed in the muscular approach, kinetic use, nuclear bomb, etc. Once free, one can say we know the price. We know what we've done. Continuing is pointless.

Dulat: That's the thing. We know the price.

Durrani: When diplomats cannot solve the problem, we go to the frontline, we suffer the price of the war. For diplomats words have been their tool. That's why the verbal exchanges.

We have exchanged not only words, but also other assets. Having done that, we do not have any desire to continue doing something for the sake of it. That's why we believe in taking a calmer view.

Dulat: Whenever the Pakistani diplomats react, are they answerable to the ISI or GHQ? Do they get briefed by them?

Durrani: None of that, but what I initially said probably fits. Your diplomats are usually more aggressive.

Dulat: Ours?

Durrani: South Block is called the GHQ of India, but actually it is more hardline than that.

Dulat: In these Track-IIs, why do you get the most aggressive ones?

Durrani: From our side?

Dulat: From both sides.

Durrani: Yes, but from our side you might be thinking of Aziz Khan, Riaz Mohammed Khan. They're not the aggressive guys. You have no idea of how aggressive others are.

Dulat: Riaz Khokhar I don't know well enough. But I've known Aziz Saheb for a long time. He's always struck me as a fine person, a gentleman, and reasonable. But of late, for instance in our meeting[2] he was aggressive. Now what does it come out of? There has to be some explanation.

Durrani: When things continue to remain frozen despite our desires, some of the best among us become hawkish.

Dulat: I've never seen Aziz Saheb talk so long in a meeting, with so much elaboration. He's usually a man of few words. This time each intervention of his was long. I was sitting next to him, thinking, is this the same Aziz Khan?

Sinha: Must be the shrinking of the peace lobby, as General Saheb said.

Durrani: He has believed in this.

Dulat: All our diplomats who were high commissioners in Islamabad have been good with people.

Durrani: Not all of them. Look at G. Parthasarathy. He was here when Kargil happened. But he goes back...

Dulat: I think Partha is still reasonable, he just likes to have his last word.

Durrani: But is there any former high commissioner who is more hardline than Partha?

Dulat: They haven't been on Track-II, so I wouldn't know. Somebody like Sabharwal, everyone says is a gentleman.

Durrani: Sabharwal is not that bad.

Dulat: Satyabrata Pal.

Durrani: I'm sure he's a good man.

Dulat: Excellent man. We've been on TV together and I haven't found anybody more reasonable on Pakistan. T.C.A. Raghavan, again a reasonable person.

Durrani: That's why I said the only person I found who after going back didn't go overboard. There are a couple I know who after retirement, well, they can command a division.

19

BB, Mian Saheb and Abbasi

Aditya Sinha: Do you feel democracy has not worked well in Pakistan?

Asad Durrani: That goes without saying. Democracy is not only about elections, though it's a step in the right direction. I will quote an army chief who was known to want to keep holding the reins. When Aslam Baig, during Benazir's first tenure, heard rumblings from all sides that, look this is not working, the civilian government is not getting its act together, he made a statement. It was an unusual statement for any army chief, meant not just as a message down the ranks but also for public consumption. He said: 'Qaum ne apni direction chun li hain. It's the democratic way. Anyone trying to come in the way would not come out looking good.'

If it did not work, it is possibly because Pakistan did not have India's strength in institutional consensus and way of working. Your institutional conclusion may not be good for Pakistan or the region, but it's a consensus. In our case, so-and-so's the boss, he wants to lead the way in his own way, and the institution sometimes gives an opinion, and sometimes just falls in line.

A.S. Dulat: Does religion play a role? How important is it? Does it affect or impact?

Durrani: I'm sure it does, but not in the way that some people believe. Take Zia-ul-Haq, whom I knew. One of the most religious on our side who usually didn't wade into domestic politics to his own advantage. But in international relations, especially with India, I don't think religion played a part. People just use this to rationalise a particular policy.

Dulat: This is the advantage of a dictator. He's answerable to nobody. He may be religious but if he's practical or pragmatic then he does the right things and nobody questions him. Whereas we favour the democratic way because we've had no other way. I feel that problems, or what you call domestic compulsion, is making things difficult for Prime Minister Modi. I don't know what he thinks, but the fact is he has started-and-stopped, started-and-stopped twice. It means there is something troubling him, for he is a problem-solver.

Sinha: Isn't he riding a tiger he can't get off?

Dulat: Isn't that the impression you get? Don't you think so?

Durrani: That's true. If you ride a tiger you have that problem. But of the military dictators Ayub Khan, Zia-ul-Haq and Musharraf, the most religious-minded was Zia. When it came to the relationship between our two countries, each of them had their own way.

Dulat: Musharraf was the best, the most reasonable with us.

Durrani: Yes, I mean, okay. In the dealings of these three dictators, and also the civilian heads of government, religion did not play a role.

Dulat: Not even at the back of anybody's mind?

Durrani: No, no. If Zia-ul-Haq decided to improve relations, there was no opposition. If Musharraf decided so, despite his highly secular or suspect credentials, no one in the country opposed him.

Sinha: Personally speaking, which is your favourite politician in Pakistan?

Dulat: I don't know Pakistan that well but I would say my favourite politician there was BB.

Durrani: I see.

Dulat: She had charisma. She was good-looking, forward-looking, and I felt sad when she was killed because she had a future. It's one of those 'ifs', you can say nothing would have happened, possibly. But there was no doubt she could carry people with her like nobody else in Pakistan.

I was in Karachi in 2011. There was a dinner, and it was outside, hot, and I sat with someone from the Bhutto family. He was a little older than me and he was letting loose, abusing the political system and politicians in Pakistan. He said, Pakistan has had only one politician, Zulfikar Ali Bhutto. He was a politician, a leader, a statesman. The rest are all ruffians.

These are two interesting parallels. Many believe that Rajiv Gandhi in 1991 would have made a better prime minister in his second term. Likewise, if Benazir had come back things may have been different in Pakistan. Whether she had the stature to contribute to India-Pakistan relations, I don't know.

Durrani: You must know that Pakistan considers Z.A. Bhutto the architect of the Bangladesh disaster. The ultimate responsibility rests with Yahya Khan, the man in charge. But Bhutto did subvert many attempts by Yahya and Mujib to accommodate the interests of both the wings—and indeed he could become the prime minister only if the more populous eastern wing was jettisoned.

Leave aside his acumen, intelligence, his grasp and his knowledge, even his close colleagues considered him a fascist. He tolerated no dissent. Close associates like Mubashir Hassan, Meraj Muhammad Khan, Mustafa Khar and J.A. Rahim fell out of favour because in his eyes no one could be big enough. Also, he would drink and play billiards throughout the night after a meeting, but in the morning could immediately dictate a perfect telegram.

I've known BB personally, serving her in both tenures. She twice did me a good turn. When she became prime minister there was a myth or narrative around her and her suffering at a young age. Her father was hanged, she was exiled: fairy tales don't get better. She returned and with the help of the downtrodden won back her father's throne. The dictator was taken care of by the hand of Allah. Excitement.

But she never did anything for the poor. Not one thing that could have politically helped her even 5 per cent. The first time probably only the husband was corrupt, the second time she herself was involved in corruption, as revealed by close associates.

The second time she believed nothing could stop her; she had divine blessings and all the important players on her side. Punjab could be ruled by allies. She was infatuated with the US, though it never came to her help despite her pleas twice-thrice.

She had learnt her lesson and was never going to fight the military again. She thought she would have survived her first term had she kept good relations with the army though, and I was witness, the army had nothing to do with it. Well, not nothing, it was happy when she was ousted. But it didn't create the situation for her dismissal by Ghulam Ishaq Khan, the President.

I may not have been infatuated with politicians generally, but their share of loot pales compared to what BB, Zardari and the Sharifs skimmed off the national exchequer.

When Rajiv visited,[1] I attended the state banquet though as DG MI, I usually wasn't invited to many. The decorum was poor as the usual sobriety was replaced by a bazaariya variety programme. BB did not believe protocol applied to her. Similarly, when the German president visited I attended the banquet thrown by President Leghari as I was then the ambassador to Germany. She walked in with her two children, as if it were a family affair. Maybe the Americans do things like this.

Rajiv wasn't kind to her. At the joint press conference he was asked about Kashmir, and he replied that they'd held elections there and what were we talking about? BB had no idea how to respond to that. What he said suited Indian policy, but her inexperience disqualified her from a reasonable response. His visit did her no good. People muttered: Was she aware enough? Did she want to give a response? Was it just a cosy relationship and did it matter to her? These questions were asked.

Dulat: BB was my favourite but as far as India is concerned, Vajpayee and Mian Saheb had a special relationship. Vajpayee had a lot of regard for him and his whole India-Pakistan plan hinged on Nawaz Sharif. He was disappointed and upset when the coup happened. Then again in the last days of UPA-2, when the Pakistan election was held in 2013, our high commissioner Sharat Sabharwal was given an extension.

Durrani: Sabharwal was given an extension?

Dulat: Yes. Sabharwal was on extension because he had a good relationship with Nawaz Sharif and the UPA hoped that Nawaz Sharif would become prime minister. Nawaz Sharif has been a favourite on our side.

Durrani: I know and can understand why he is. The man, from the day he came to power, is only a call, a whistle away. He never learnt his lesson.

Dulat: BB?

Durrani: No, BB on India-Pakistan was neither wishy-washy nor extreme. But in Mian Saheb's case, all efforts were made to persuade him to attend Modi's coronation. Later, one thought his number two would have been better. But, theek hai. He was treated badly and read the riot act.

Modi's crashlanding in Raiwind after bad-mouthing Pakistan both in Dhaka and in Kabul. Anyone else would have thought, what the hell is this circus. Mian Saheb still responded.

You people keep saying it was a great gesture by Modi. No. Mian Saheb actually showed more commitment. Because of his naiveté, everyone took it for granted that he would continue to do so.

Dulat: From India we saw Nawaz Sharif as a better bet in moving forward. I don't agree with the Pakistani way of seeing it. But yes, when he came for Modi's swearing-in, he should have been treated better.

Durrani: The only point on which I was happy with Mian Saheb was when he ordered the nuclear tests. I absolutely publicly supported it. He took the right decision, a brave one, though he probably understands nothing about the role of nuclear weapons or nuclear capability. He took the decision against the wishes of his own constituency, the business community, and withstood the pressure of the five-ten calls from Clinton. That I appreciated publicly and wrote about.

Sinha: What about the current political instability in Pakistan?

Durrani: No, this has come up in a few places. Those looking deeply into the situation believe that after Mian Saheb Nawaz Sharif's departure, things calmed down.[2] There may be hype about the Sharif family's struggle with the court cases, but the business community has renewed its activity and seems confident.

The new man, Shahid Khaqan Abbasi, I personally have never been comfortable with him, but he is settling down in the job and handling it well. All my colleagues say he's an institutional man who works from morning till evening. He consults the institutions. The national security committee that he heads has met often. His handling of the difficult relationship with the US is considered good. He gave a good speech at the UN. In an interview at the Asia Society he said the right things.

Tillerson visited but was not afforded an opportunity to say one thing to the politicians and another to the army. They met him together, giving the same message: that instead of being defensive or apologetic, what we do is for our own reasons.

Sinha: Is he totally the army's man and not a politician?

Durrani: He's not been the army's man. Musharraf was frustrated because Shahid Abbasi is the son of a former military man, Commodore Khaqan Abbasi. Musharraf's side tried to woo him away from Nawaz Sharif but Abbasi was loyal to his party leader and went to jail rather than play second fiddle to the army.

On a personal note, there was a time when because of whatever I was, he would be respectful. When I left and Mian Saheb was falling out with the military, Abbasi would avoid me. Despite that, I feel he's tried to do a good job.

Dulat: Interesting. Talking to Pakistani friends I've been trying to get a sense of what will happen in Pakistan. General Ehsan and I spoke in London. He said, it could well be Imran.[3] I said, really? A few weeks later, everybody around the table said Imran now has no chance.

Whatever I heard from my Pakistani friends is that Abbasi is the favourite to be prime minister again in 2018. Because the PML(N) controls Punjab, which is three-fourths of Pakistan, so whoever controls Punjab wins it. The PML controls Punjab, the PPP always gets a look in, and Imran doesn't get too many seats other than in Lahore and other cities.

Abbasi is Mian Saheb's choice. I asked how come he chose him over Shehbaz? The answer was that Abbasi was not expected to stab him in the back.

Sinha: Nawaz Sharif was afraid his brother[4] would stab him in the back?

Dulat: Even if he stabs him, the dagger won't go deep. You said the military, I would like to water that down, like General Saheb uses the term 'institutional', I would say the establishment is happy. Since the PML is in control and the perception is that he's doing a good job, he possibly would be the favourite to be prime minister in 2018. The dark horse is still Imran.

Durrani: He's clever enough to keep saying he will follow Nawaz Sharif's policies.

Sinha: What would be his approach to India?

Durrani: He's not falling over like Mian Saheb each time Delhi called. Right at the beginning he was asked, what role does India have in Afghanistan? He said, zero. It's a different matter that I believe there is an Indian role; his message was that it's no longer Mian Saheb's business.

Dulat: What General Saheb is saying is coming from inside Pakistan. You've seen politics and politicians all over the world. At this point of time he's just filling in for Mian Saheb. If he was to be prime minister in 2018, he would be his own man. Then how he would react to India or to the US, we'd have to wait and see. He's smart enough, well educated, an engineer. He's not anybody's fool.

Sinha: When are the elections?

Dulat: Ehsan Saheb was saying more likely August.

Durrani: Yes, because the new census and constituencies have to be taken into account.

Dulat: There's no rush. A lot of things have to be settled in Pakistan. The Sharif family, the other brother.

20

Good Vibrations, India-Pakistan

—◦—

Aditya Sinha: Can we list the positives of the bilateral relationship? And things that might have endured?

Asad Durrani: Let me rattle off things that are not only positive but can lead us to certain conclusions. First is the Indus Water Treaty. There can always be objections, reservations and shortfalls, etc. This treaty is something that nobody in Pakistan, despite our complaints, wants to give up. India cannot give it up because it's not a unilateral commitment. It has stood the test of time.

A.S. Dulat: Absolutely.

Durrani: Second, as a military man who was a personal participant, if there is an example of gentlemanly war, the two wars against India, in '65 and '71, were it. Both sides deliberately avoided civilian targets.

Dulat: Both wars?

Durrani: Both wars. Third is less commonly known. Soon after the nuclear tests by both countries,[1] the first thing done was to establish a hotline to ensure that no action by either side was misunderstood by the other. A missile test should not be mistaken for a nuclear strike. No surprises.

This is the only line that remains 'hot'. I know other hotlines between the two countries, even between the two armies, that go cold when one side wishes to avoid a prompt response for a couple of hours.

Sinha: Can you give an instance?

Durrani: After a ceasefire violation you may benefit by keeping quiet. Your MO does this. On our side if there is reason not to take the call, it will go unanswered. The nuclear hotline will remain 'hot', however, because of the stakes involved.

Dulat: A lot of positives come out of meetings and engaging, talking, dialogue. The engagement between the two NSAs was positive while it lasted, the Pakistani side says there is nothing now. They talk on the telephone and nothing beyond that, which is unfortunate when you've got a good thing and you like to have a smoke together and sit down and possibly have a drink. Why would you not want to continue that? You've got nothing to lose, and everything to gain.

That was incredible about Vajpayee. When he went to Lahore, Pakistan and the establishment were surprised he wanted to visit the Minar-e-Pakistan. When he visited he made an emphatic endorsement, that Pakistan is an independent country with whom we would like to have a stable and prosperous relationship.

At the much-quoted Governor's banquet Vajpayee delighted the Pakistanis as only he could. 'My partymen did not want me to come to Lahore,' he said. 'When they hear of what I've written in the visitor's book, they'll say, Lahore jana zaroori thha toh theek hain, lekin wahan jane ki kya zaroorat thi, mohar lagane ki kya zaroorat thi.' Then he said, 'Pakistan ko meri mohar ki zaroorat nahin hain, Pakistan ki apni mohar hain'.

After what he said in Kashmir about insaniyat, any Kashmiri will tell you there's been no one like Vajpayee. The question is, did he mean what he said? It's a question of the impact, and it was positive. Like when he went on April 17, 2003 and at a public meeting said, 'I propose to talk to Pakistan.' The crowd went wild.

General Saheb referred to the civility between India and Pakistan even during war. Our friend Showkat the DIG had an interesting story. He was a prisoner of war in '71, before he left the army and joined the police. There was a second lieutenant who looked after the prisoners well. He asked me, can you find this gentleman, he lives in Jalandhar, and I want to meet and express my gratitude.

When we Indians and Pakistanis sit down in the evening, whatever the provocation across the table, and have a drink, it shocks these Canadians and Americans who watch. These swines, they must be thinking, so much mud-slinging happens and yet they get along so well.

Durrani: Talking of prisoners, my unit captured an Indian lieutenant, 2nd lieutenant Sharma and his runner, in the '65 war in the Chamb sector. According to SOP the frontline unit takes down the number, name, rank, and then passes the prisoners of war to higher headquarters. When we captured him, he told us, 'For the last 24 hours we have not eaten anything.' Though we were not serving tea at that time, the chap was straightaway given a cup of tea.

The soldiers were always, kidhar se aaye ho bhai, achha haan haan, my parents come from that side. One of ours who didn't like the other side said Oh Lala e Oye, which is a derogatory remark for Hindu banias. It was the only such remark. Invariably we joked with the Indians that all their soldiers were from Gujarat and Lalamusa,[2] hopefully there were some from India too.

And then, at a higher level, regardless of how the war was going, Manekshaw's[3] favourite unit in the two armies was 6FF (his parent battalion, 4/12 Frontier Force regiment) in the Pakistan army. During the two wars he would ask how's 6FF doing?

And at the highest level is (Morarji) Desai. The Americans were prodding the prime minister to go after the Pakistanis as we were hell-bent on going nuclear. Desai says, I'm not going against my neighbour on your account.

These things have happened for personal, historical or neighbourly reasons. They are the positives.

Sinha: Morarjibhai said this publicly, is it?

Dulat: I don't remember, it was a long time ago.

Durrani: This is the message we got at the time. Desai was known to believe that neighbours should not play games on behalf of anyone else.

We may have problems amongst ourselves but if we do anything against India, that costs India, on prompting from outside, then we are being stupid. Those people are far away, they'll go away, we are left holding the bag.

For instance, after the Soviets invaded Afghanistan, America and Pakistan were allies. The Americans would constantly tell us, don't be so pally with Iran, they've got our hostages. Zia-ul-Haq's response was, always, just as we established contact with China although you didn't like our original reaching out to China, it is possible one day you would like to speak to Iran and we will be the conduit. But even if that does not happen we won't create a problem in the neighbourhood.

What many may not know is that despite American displeasure and a few irritations between Teheran and Islamabad, we continue to represent Iranian interests in Washington.

Dulat: Everybody acknowledges that General Zia was the master of public relations. Cricket diplomacy, landing up here, etc.

As happens in every country, when a dignitary comes, somebody is appointed from the host country to look after his security. In India the Intelligence Bureau does this. General Zia was a big man as far as India went. A deputy director was appointed instead of the usual assistant director—a colleague of ours, O.P. Sharma, who later was Nagaland governor. After his duty he said, 'Bhai yeh gazab ka aadmi hain. So nice, so kind, so courteous, everything, all the graces.' Lo and behold, five days later, there was a personal letter from General Zia, and O.P. Sharma couldn't get over it. He showed us, yeh dekhiye, General Saheb ki personal chitthi aayi hain. I did this duty often, and the most I got from Margaret Thatcher was a photograph. The Prince of Wales' security officer extended to me an invitation to visit Buckingham Palace. Yasser Arafat was more interesting because he would hug you and insist on a photograph together. But no one wrote me a personal letter.

Sinha: Didn't General Zia bestow a medal or honour on Morarji Desai?[4]

Durrani: General Zia was careful, and if this episode happened, General Zia would have recognised it. That is why we consider him to have handled certain affairs well.

You see, there's no end to such episodes.

V

THE FLASHPOINTS

These five chapters discuss the lowest points of recent history, such as the November 2008 attack on Mumbai; the capture of alleged spy Kulbhushan Jadhav; and the surgical strikes by the Indian military across the Line of Control after major terrorist attacks in J&K and Punjab. The two spychiefs also discuss the meaningless Indo-Pak rhetoric like 'talks and terror can't happen together', and the pros and cons of war.

Setting the scene

Kathmandu, March 27, 2016: One night, after a day of intense conversation, we visit an old friend of the Dulats for dinner. Guests are surprised to meet a former Pakistani spychief in person. General Durrani bemoans the fact that the Pakistani rupee is no longer accepted in Kathmandu.

21

Hafiz Saeed and 26/11

Asad Durrani: I don't think anything was in common between Kargil and the Mumbai attack, even assuming each happened during civilian rule. The people were different.

A.S. Dulat: Sir, then why did Mumbai happen?

Durrani: Mumbai remains the only incident in which I decided that I would be available to any Indian and Pakistani channel to say that whoever has done this, be it state-sponsored, ISI-sponsored, military-sponsored, should be caught hold of and punished. It's not only about those 168 people dead, four days of carnage, etc. At the time Pakistan could ill afford its eastern front caught in a war. There were enough problems in the west and within the country. I don't know who did it, but there were questions that David Headley named an ISI major. It created difficulties for us.

Dulat: But the story is that Headley collaborated with Hafiz Saeed.[1]

Durrani: Because all these stories have floated around, people can go ahead and investigate. For eight years both of us have advocated joint investigation, joint trial, intelligence sharing, get on with the anti-terrorism mechanism, etc., for the simple reason that we can't do anything until and unless this is resolved. Till then, Hafiz Saeed, ISI, Jaish-e-Mohammed: it's possible they had nothing to do with it, that there's a third or fourth or fifth party involved.

Sinha: In the last book, Mr Dulat, you mentioned that when the relationship is not moving forward and the Pakistan army feels that India needs a kick, then something like Mumbai happens.

Dulat: Absolutely right. My theory or belief was also that Musharraf would have known about 26/11.

Durrani: But he was out of power. By August-September 2008, he was gone.

Dulat: Yes, but Sir, the planning would have started earlier. Musharraf could have been a party. I stand by what I said, that whenever there is frustration in Pakistan then something happens.

Sinha: Recently,[2] Hafiz Saeed was placed under house arrest. Indian TV news channels say it's the Trump effect.

Dulat: I don't know if Hafiz Saeed is important for Trump. That might have been a coincidence. According to General Ehsan, there was an investigation in which he was wanted, and it was decided to lock him up.

Durrani: He was taken to the courts though they had nothing (new) against him. It is still possible that he was detained to let the storm blow over. In six months he could be out.

Sinha: So Hafiz Saeed's house arrest is also choreographed?

Durrani: What's new, as far as Hafiz Saeed is concerned, is more evidence available? One would expect that there's an arrangement with Hafiz Saeed.

Isn't that what happens most of the time? Modiji in Gujarat—the inquiry report does not absolve him. But the court lets him go, so no one wants to talk about it. A bigger example is Tony Blair. The Chilcot report[4] blames him, yet he still has not been hauled up, with legal opinion split on charging him. The 9/11 report has 28 pages missing because of sensitive information, or because of American inefficiency, or because of possible complicity; some persons had been released as they had business connections or links to the Bush family. It helps the US avoid unpleasant action.

Sinha: So no positive implications for India-Pak relations from Hafiz Saeed's house arrest?

Durrani: There are very few positives on the India-Pakistan front right now. But this can provide breathing space to a country that is constantly under pressure.

Dulat: I don't think this has been done because of India. But, as General Saheb says, it could be used by General Janjua to ring up Ajit Doval and say, look, we've taken action and locked this fellow up for at least six months, so that nuisance is out of the way.

Durrani: In Afghanistan we may be a lesser culprit than the Taliban or Ashraf Ghani or the US. Why is Haqqani network a network? I also don't know. You can keep creating a situation in which the culprit seems to be Pakistan but not the people who have done so much wrong and damage to Pakistan: the US.

Pick up any report by the Americans during the last 15 years, including those of the auditor general, that look at accountability, money spent, civilians killed, and combatants. The reports do bring these facts out but in the end, since punishment could cause political embarrassment, the conclusion is: Pakistan's complicity.

Dulat: How does Hafiz Saeed actually help Pakistan?

Durrani: That probably comes later. What can Pakistan do about Hafiz Saeed?

Dulat: That's another matter.

Durrani: How is it another matter?

Dulat: I agree it's for the courts to decide. But my question is: what is Hafiz Saeed's value?

Durrani: If you prosecute Hafiz Saeed the first reaction will be: it's on India's behalf, you're hounding him, he's innocent, etc. The political cost is big, now.

Dulat: Apart from his involvement, he has nuisance value because he keeps abusing India. But what is his value to Pakistan?

Durrani: The cost of prosecuting him is too great.

22

Kulbhushan Jadhav

Aditya Sinha: What's the story with Kulbhushan Jadhav,[1] the alleged spy that Pakistan sentenced to death? How do countries deal with espionage cases?

A.S. Dulat: General Saheb will tell us because it happened in Pakistan, Sir.

Asad Durrani: Well, you have more experience.

Dulat: I can only say that spooking will never end.

Durrani: Never.

Dulat: It's the second oldest profession. It's conventionally believed that spooking increases when the relationship between two countries improves. The maximum spooking between the Americans and Israelis takes place when their relationship is at its best. But about Jadhav I don't know, Sir, you tell me.

Durrani: No, yes. Essentially it has gone on forever, but I don't agree that spooking is half as honourable as the oldest profession. It's very honourable. Spies take great risks in service of their country. That's why people get caught all the time.

Normally, you don't play it up. First send a message: we know you have two of ours, we now have one of yours. We would like an exchange. You can have your fellow back but we want both of ours, etc. This is the way it is done. Over five, ten years you make exchanges like this.

Also, you don't announce you are looking for more evidence. You've got him, ask about his contacts, network. That's the norm.

This particular case seems complicated. Normally one would be mindful of Iranian sensitivity. And for a long time people have been saying, which is no surprise to me, how everyone who matters is present in Balochistan. Not just the Indians, the Iranians, even the Israelis, the Americans, the Russians, the Afghans...

Dulat: Chinese?

Durrani: ...the Chinese, all are present. It's an important area for different purposes. Some are there to blow up the pipeline Iran and Pakistan want to build, or to sabotage the economic corridor; others because they don't want to miss out on what the first lot are planning. The place is crucial for the 'New Great Game'.

When Pakistan made this revelation (about Jadhav) the idea must have been to counter the Indian threat after Pathankot. Though that famous threat[2] came later, at the end of April, and Jadhav was arrested in March.

Dulat: What was the threat?

Durrani: That India is looking for links between Pathankot and our establishment. So we came up with a counter-argument that we know you've been doing this (in Balochistan).

Second, Pakistan has its hands full in Balochistan, taking countermeasures effectively. The Baloch resistance has mostly been downgraded. Shahbaz Taseer[3] was rescued after Qadri's hanging.[4] Pakistan probably is confident about giving heart to our own people and putting the fear of God in the Indian heart. This is my speculation.

The reality could be different: we too know how to play these games. You caught hold of so many, we now have an important catch. It's one-upmanship.

There may even be a more substantial, sinister reason; that our side suspected the game was going to heat up.

A country like Pakistan at times feels under siege from all directions: relations with India, the Afghanistan situation, or the number of Americans spreading poison about you. When all this is happening, some advocate taking action that conveys to your public that we aren't always on the receiving end, and also it's not always that we can't reveal anything. Here is one.

Dulat: I agree entirely with the boss. I'm surprised that he doesn't know, because I don't know, frankly. We've heard nothing but denials from Delhi, which is understandable; if the guy's a spook it will be denied, and if he's not it'll be denied.

With what little knowledge one has, if this were a RAW operation and he was a RAW spy, then it's a pretty sloppy operation.

Durrani: Hmm.

Dulat: You don't find a senior naval officer wandering around in Balochistan or Chaman, or wherever he was picked up. What the hell was he doing?

Spies get caught, sure, but it may not have happened that way. One of our earlier theories was that he was kidnapped and brought there.

Durrani: Hmm.

Dulat: Still, what the hell was he doing? There's no explanation, surprisingly. Karan Thapar had asked this question on his TV programme and I denied it outright, saying if the foreign office says he's been kidnapped, we've got to see where he was picked up from.

Lo and behold, the next day this fellow was confessing on TV. Karan rang up and said, your man is singing like a canary! I was taken aback. If it was an intelligence operation, it doesn't do anyone any credit.

Sinha: If you had been the chief when this happened, would you have sacked someone?

Dulat: I'm not saying that. I'm not saying I would do it better, but as an intelligence operation it's pretty sloppy. If the guy was a spy.

Sinha: He was from Bombay and had two relatives in the Mumbai police.

Dulat: Yeah, he had, and he was running a business.

Sinha: Someone said he had a boat and was running drugs, as the sea route has become big.

Dulat: I haven't heard that. But that he was into some business.

I agree, it could have been kept quiet. In fact, it could have been used for goodwill. The NSA dialogues we keep hearing about, all General Janjua had to do was call Ajit Doval up and say, we've got your guy but don't worry. He'll be taken care of. In due course you tell us what to do with him.

It comes back to the basic thing, can the Indian and Pakistani intelligence agencies cooperate? And if not, then why not?

Sinha: So Jadhav's case is all around bungling?

Dulat: You can't blame the NSAs, it was on TV before it reached them. Then it was all over the place.

Sinha: So after saying ISI and RAW are number one, we have this bungling.

Dulat: That's how good the ISI is, it put him straight on TV! Like we did during the Kargil war, when we made public that intercept between General Musharraf and General Aziz.

This game is different from politics, and should be kept apart for it to be effective.

Sinha: After the initial fuss, it went quiet.

Durrani: I'm happy if nothing is happening, such shor-sharaba has no place. There's a way to go about it. We should not have broached it with the poor Iranian president while he was an honoured guest. And it was embarrassing that this faux pas was committed by the army chief.

Sinha: We might as well discuss Balochistan. General Saheb?

Durrani: From the very beginning, Pakistan's handling of Balochistan has been faulty. No one understood that it was complex better than the founder himself. Jinnah may not have understood much about many subjects, but he said Balochistan was going to be his province. It's different, so divided, thinly populated. There are divisions between Pushtuns and Balochis. Within the Balochis there are tribes, and on top sit the Brahui.

Balochistan has one of the biggest reservoirs of natural resources. Mercifully not much has been tapped because we're quite capable of messing up. I pray that when we tap it, people will correctly exploit it and not burn it like the Sui gas, or not make it a political tool. The Afghans and Balochis would be interested. It's strategically an important place.

The Persian Gulf, or the Indian Ocean, that's the extension; the Arabian Sea, the Indian Ocean, the Persian Gulf. Everyone is interested in this area, in the corridor, and in the natural gas.

It's no surprise that a few thousand people in Balochistan, which is a good number considering they don't have many millions, are upset. All they needed was encouragement from outside to take up arms and organise a resistance. Without that encouragement some might still have done so.

Their disadvantage is that since they are few and aren't supported by the people—the people are not that sea where fish survive—over a period of time they've been suppressed or overcome. The last was probably the fifth[5] time.

Our force aside or what we did with the Khan of Kalat aside, we put out the insurgency with the snap of fingers in a couple of years. This time it's taken longer because no one thinks of a real solution. If I were to draw a parallel with Kashmir, putting down the movement is one thing but what about their hearts and minds? Here, there isn't enough resources, will, or compulsion.

Musharraf probably wanted to do something serious and even he could not go beyond some patchwork job recruitment. For the Balochis, projects that are supposed to provide jobs do not count. You'll probably be looking at labour from Karachi, which is closer. Balochistan does not have the expertise, it comes from elsewhere.

The Baloch characteristically want more respect and acknowledgement. Don't suspect their loyalty because even Ataullah Mengal, once a dissident, a few years ago clearly said, we've not been handled well but Pakistan remains our least bad choice.

We've bought some, appeased some, and bribed others: Balochistan assembly will always have 60 people from 30 different groups. So you end up making nearly all of them ministers. One man becomes Leader of Opposition and another Speaker. Fifty administrators, small place.

Complexity aside, our ability to manage with the force of arms and a bit of payment at the right places is considerable. In this case the compulsion was to do it quickly to get CPEC running. Quickly because with Afghanistan on the boil, some will exploit it more than we can manage.

Third is probably what led to this episode, the outside factor is a bigger threat than the Balochi. I can agree that you immediately take care of the dissidence and foreign intervention. Addressing people's grievances takes long and is complex, and requires more than Musharraf's song and dance, even though he tried as best he could. He said he knew what to do, whereas the fact is that no one does.

Dulat: I'm glad you compared it with Kashmir. I don't know Balochistan but obviously it's an issue and there is discontent because at several Track-II meetings there have been Baloch boys speaking openly about what's happening there. They've even talked about disappearances, etc. There is an issue that Pakistan has to deal with.

The question that comes up—General Saheb hasn't raised it today, he's in a good mood—is our involvement or interference.

These Baloch leaders are well known. Whether it is the RAW or our diplomats in Pakistan, they would know them, and that's not a big deal. I'm always surprised when anybody says we are fanning discontent, or paying for it, or training terrorists. One allegation was that Jadhav was training Baloch terrorists. I've never heard of this, frankly. I headed the RAW, and it didn't happen in our time. The General has acknowledged that the ISI paid money in Balochistan apart from Kashmir. This is exactly what I had said in my book that money is a tool used by all agencies everywhere.

Sinha: In Pakistan it is alleged that Indian consulates in Afghanistan are used for this.

Durrani: If Indian consulates are used, we'll be happy. There are four consulates and an embassy but we need not inflate their number. In Pakistan some people, who are ill-informed and sometimes silly, will talk of nine consulates, 18; the maximum number I've heard is 23. If the Indians were to conduct espionage from four consulates then we should be happy because then we can keep track. Anyway, espionage is usually not done from there.

A couple of Indian construction companies could employ a couple of Jadhavs. That is difficult to track. Essentially, we exaggerate Indian influence like we exaggerated the number of consulates.

What worried me most about the Jadhav case was the Iranian factor. It has led to speculation in Pakistan, that when Mullah Akhtar Mansoor[6] was returning from some meetings in Iran, Iranian intelligence put a chip in his vehicle that helped the Americans to track him down. Even if this was true I would not talk about it. It's creating problems between Iran and Pakistan.

But regarding Balochistan: espionage happens, people are involved. Second, I've always felt we are overplaying India's involvement. The Americans are more involved. There are others who have more reason to get involved.

Then there's Doval's threats on tape. He was asked about it by the former high commissioners.[7]

Dulat: What did he say?

Durrani: They reminded him that he said, of course Pakistan is not going to be tackled differently, what we can do is cause mischief. He says, yes, but that was when I was a free man, before I took over as NSA. The private view of someone who is now the NSA.

But this debate is unimportant. The important thing is that, of course these things happen.

Dulat: Of course they happen. But the allegation always was that it was happening out of the Indian consulates. As you said, these are not used for espionage.

Durrani: You can do espionage in different ways without it being tracked or traced. A consulate man will have the status to pull strings and lunch with agents. He can be clever so that those people are not caught, or he can do it stupidly. The best thing is that leads should not come to you.

At times I light-heartedly say if India isn't doing anything in Balochistan then I will lose professional respect for RAW. The situation is tailor-made for something.

Sinha: You said like Kashmir?

Dulat: Yes, Kashmir. I first heard this from a Pakistani diplomat, an Afghan expert and a gem of a man, Rustom Shah Mohmand, when at one of the Track-II meetings he surprised everyone by saying Pakistan should first set its own house in order in Balochistan before blaming India for Kashmir. General Saheb has said the same thing in his more subtle manner. When the Baloch boys go out and talk about their treatment and disappearance, it's serious, and it's like if a Kashmiri goes to a conference abroad and says, there've been 7,000 disappearances or whatever. The number may be exaggerated but you cannot say it is not true.

General Saheb is reasonable in saying that the Americans and others are doing more. In the context of the India-Pakistan relationship, the first thing is to blame India. It's said, you guys are meddling in Balochistan. I'm hearing it for the past five-six years.

Durrani: Jundallah is a Sunni group that was targeting Shias in Balochistan. It was supported by the US to carry out sabotage and subversion in the Iranian province of Siestan. I credit someone who is worse than the devil because he's messed up this country, Zardari. Under his watch, whether it was his Shia affiliation or another reason, Pakistan and Iran mounted a joint operation. Abdolmalek Rigi was handed over and executed[8] and ever since, things have quietened.

Dulat: What is the American motivation?

Durrani: One, Iran. Two, if Balochistan remains unsettled they can rationalise their military presence in the region a bit better.

If there is turmoil the US can more effectively play or spoil the New Great Game. It's all about the resources in Central Asia and Afghanistan. Afghanistan's underground resources are supposedly worth a trillion dollars. Balochistan must also figure in that respect.

America, China and Russia are all involved in the region. Another reason to remain interested is to see if you can cut your rivals down. Iran was considered an adversary and America's objection to the Iran-Pakistan pipeline still continues. There are bigger opposing voices to the pipeline; some talk money, others talk about the Shia factor, but this was all for staking an interest and sometimes out of mischief.

Americans are not known to operate surreptitiously and covertly. They bribe and arm people, whether it was Afghanistan even after the Soviets were kicked out, or Balochistan, or lately the Middle East. It is by no means a benign power.

Sinha: An India-Pakistan agreement did not happen in Sharm el-Sheikh[9] because of Balochistan. Does it not make the road to peace a bit longer?

Dulat: Poor Manmohan Singh. A mountain was made out of a molehill with that Sharm el-Sheikh statement. All he said was, okay, if you say there is such-and-such thing, we'll look into it. His point was that we don't do these things, but since you're saying it, we'll look into it. That's fair, instead of saying no-no-no-no-no.

A prime minister is not supposed to know about every little detail, every little operation, or every little happening anywhere in the world. I don't think Manmohan Singh said anything wrong.

Durrani: The other, more subverting factor in play is the media and these political wise-acres. They create an environment that won't allow you to do something honestly or innocently.

Dulat: True.

Durrani: Both of us agree that a joint anti-terrorism mechanism is a good idea. It can still be done. Balochistan, yes, this is all he said. So? What's the harm in saying you'll look into it?

Dulat: Unfortunately, it was Dr Manmohan Singh who said it and not Vajpayee. Some say Vajpayee would never say something like that. Probably Vajpayee's advantage was that he would never be asked something like that. No one would want to embarrass him.

In Dr Manmohan Singh's case, because of his weak position these matters came up from time to time. Despite his good intentions, it made him look weaker. The media played it up: 'Aaah! We've conceded this, we've said that! We've acknowledged this!'

What can a prime minister say? What can a president say? What can any politician trying to build bridges and have a conversation possibly say?

23

Talks and Terror

———

A.S. Dulat: Every now and then when we are not on the best terms with Pakistan, we say, 'terror and talks don't go together'. There's a logic in that, but it can't be that we should never talk to Pakistan. Pakistan has a problem with terror. They've also used terror against us, so then why talk at all?

Once you start a dialogue and on the slightest pretext say terror and talks can't go together, then either you never meant to talk or you're lacking brains. Why did you start a dialogue? Why did you visit Lahore? Why did you start a back channel? Why was Dr Manmohan Singh wasting so much time?

When New Delhi says terror and talks can't go together, it impacts the public. When Vajpayee took the bus to Lahore the mood in Delhi was upbeat. Today, talk to anyone in Delhi about Pakistan and he thinks you're half-cracked if you suggest dialogue. He says, what can we give? And it comes back to the same thing: Can we compromise on Kashmir?

Who's compromising? Why do you use the word 'compromise' when we are talking of cooperation? We're not giving anything away and Pakistan won't give us anything. It's a question of what we have and how far we can cooperate. As Narasimha Rao said, the sky's the limit, once you start cooperating.

Asad Durrani: This statement, terror and talks don't go together, reminds me of other statements that on the face of it seem all right. 'Terror and talks don't go together.' 'We have no option but to talk.' 'Wars do not resolve anything.' 'You don't talk to terrorists.' These statements are made so often that they have become articles of faith for quite a few of us.

Dulat: Vajpayee never made such statements.

Durrani: These statements are not sensible.

You don't talk to terrorists? You actually talk all the time to terrorists. For the agency of any sensible country, these are the most important people to talk to. If you do not have a channel to, let's say, the Taliban, then you're making a mistake.

There's no option but to talk? Sometimes one gets into trouble when others say, you've survived for so long without talking, so why say there's no option?

Wars do not resolve anything? So many questions have been resolved by wars. Certain issues are not resolved because the principal need for war is to create a favourable situation.

So talking and terrorism do not go together? In fact, they go *so much* together.

Dulat: Particularly in our business, General Saheb is right. If you're not talking to the bad guys, then who are you talking to and wasting your time? You don't need to talk to sadhu-mahatmas. If you're dealing with bad guys effectively, you're getting somewhere.

Durrani: It's like early childhood where if you don't know anything you're told to keep quiet. But if you don't know anything you need to learn; and you can only do that by asking questions, which means talking to everyone.

Dulat: That's why I said in the other book that double agents are the best. I was often told, don't talk to so-and-so, he works for the ISI.

I said: That's the guy I'm looking for! If I can't get to the ISI then let me get to somebody who does. Double agents are a great help.

Sinha: But what about from the other side: why not stop terrorism and start talking?

Dulat: This is something the Kashmiri has said many times. If Pakistan wants to stop terrorism, it can do so at any time.

Durrani: Stop what?

Dulat: Militancy in Kashmir. The tap can be turned off whenever Pakistan wants. In that there is sufficient truth. The controls have always been with Pakistan or its military, etc. Kashmiri boys cannot come and go with impunity if you don't want them to.

Durrani: Regarding militancy, I'm sure the State can influence events, though I usually would advise against it. If it does not engage with the Haqqanis' or the Kashmiris' resistance, others from within the country would, and the borders allow these groups to be beyond one's control. It's an illusion that the State is everywhere; we are not a terribly efficient State. Our apparatus does not reach even those against us, leave aside others.

But we don't want to lose leverage; this is what happened in Kashmir in '94 or so. The charge of state-sponsored terrorism caused confusion. Someone had the brilliant idea to pull out, which meant no handle or leverage. That would create an unwanted situation.

Leverage by means like funding Salahuddin's son is a way in which we keep control and can prevent catastrophes.

Dulat: For us terrorism begins with Punjab in the early 1980s. Then it shifts to Kashmir. There was once an apprehension that if these two connected it would be a much bigger problem.

We came across cases of interaction between Sikh and Kashmiri militants in the late '80s. I spoke to some Sikh boys from the Sikh

General Asad Durrani having a chat with the commandant after the Pakistani presentation at the German General Staff Course in Hamburg in 1975.

The commandant greeting General Durrani's wife.

On an exercise with some of his cadets when he was an instructor at the Pakistan Military Academy in 1970.

As Brigade Commander in Pakistan-administered Kashmir in 1984, being briefed on Indian deployment.

General Durrani was once a 12 handicap golfer.

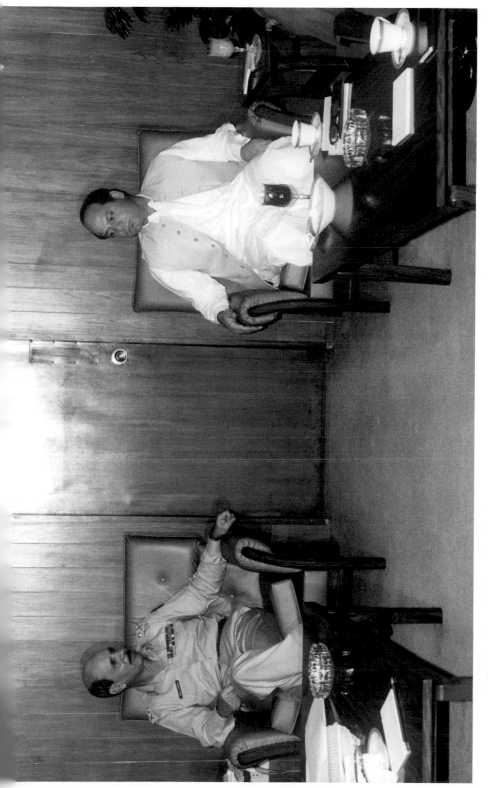

With Prime Minister Nawaz Sharif at the ISI headquarters in 1990, when General Durrani was the DG.

Hosting a former colleague, now a General, at his residence in Germany when General Durrani was the ambassador there from 1994 to 1997.

With then ISI chief Ziauddin Butt and former ISI chief Hameed Gul, along with the Russian attaché, Col Beli, in 1998.

With German President Richard von Weizsäcker after presenting his ambassadorial credentials in 1994.

Attending a national day reception with his wife in Germany when he was the defence attaché.

On a visit to Washington in 1990 as the Director General of Military Intelligence.

Calling on the Defense Intelligence Agency
director during the Washington visit in 1990.

Inspecting the Aviation Command
as the Inspector General Training
and Evaluation in 1992.

Being presented a photo of himself as a cadet on a visit to the Pakistan Military Academy in 1992.

With Pakistani cricketer Imran Khan at a fund-raiser in Germany when General Durrani was the ambassador there.

Students Federation who had been in jail with Kashmiris. Some became informers. I asked why things didn't go further with the Kashmiris. Their answer: the Kashmiris didn't have 'guts'. That was positive from our point of view.

When Kashmir's turmoil started I was posted in Srinagar. Kashmiri boys were going and coming, and we asked locals what was happening. They said crossing the border was normal, no big deal. It started with a handful of guys, five JKLF boys. One thing led to another.

Unfortunately, in December 1989, Mufti Saheb's daughter's kidnapping became a watershed in Kashmir. It gave the boys confidence, that they could get the Government of India to give in to their demands. Kashmiris started believing they might get azadi. They turned their watches back half an hour.

General Saheb conceded that even Pakistan was surprised at how quickly it happened, and at its scale. Pakistan got more involved, leading to the Hizbul Mujahideen's rise.

Militancy hasn't ended in Kashmir. Terrorism has become a part of Kashmir's landscape. The moment things get better, something goes wrong. In a lot of cases, we are to blame.

After the JKLF or the Hizbul Mujahideen, terrorism began travelling south of the Pir Panjal to Jammu. That caused concern.

Then came other tanzeems: Jaish-e-Mohammed, Lashkar-e-Toiba and other names that changed occasionally. There were also bad incidents, like the siege of Hazratbal, the attack on the state assembly, the attack on the tourism centre, etc.

Over time the character of terrorism has changed. At first it was open, these boys were known, they had parades in downtown Srinagar. That's why Robin Raphael[1] insisted Kashmiris were freedom fighters, not terrorists. Let's not forget, the Americans got excited after the Al Faran kidnappings in which five foreigners disappeared. One was beheaded, one escaped from custody, three disappeared.

Terrorism now ran so deep underground that you couldn't tell who was a terrorist. Since 2015 we've been witnessing 40-50 local boys, not large in number, coming overground. These boys take pride in it. The return of the freedom fighter.

Like Burhan Wani, these guys are on Facebook. What happens in Kashmir is a daily occurrence, but what excites us more is an attack on an army cantonment or base, or the threat that it will travel to Punjab, as it has in the incidents at Uri, Pathankot and Gurdaspur.

We blame Pakistan and then ask for help, but as there is no understanding or cooperation or even communication, we live with it. Our side has various perceptions on dealing with it.

Pakistan or Kashmir, there is no better way than engagement. We have hardliners and theorists who say if you want to negotiate, you must talk from a position of strength. Which means we will never talk, because where is that position of strength? When things are all right you don't want to talk, and when they're bad you don't want to talk.

Sinha: Those who attacked Mumbai were by no stretch of imagination freedom fighters.

Dulat: No, the freedom fighters lasted till the early 1990s. This is about creating a threat and keeping up a level of violence. You're right, Mumbai 2008 is attributed to Pakistan and the Lashkar.

Sinha: There is also the category of boys affected by the 2002 Gujarat riots. Indian Mujahideen was born after that. They reportedly get some sustenance or motivation from across.

Dulat: What Muslims went through in Gujarat was bound to have repercussions. Whether the Indian Mujahideen was born out of the Gujarat riots, or out of the Babri Masjid demolition and what followed in Mumbai is a matter of speculation. Yes, some boys did go across to Pakistan. Every now and then we hear of the training or inspiration they receive in Karachi's Binori mosque. An atmosphere was created.

The latest is this ISIS[2] business. It's affected the whole world, Europe more than elsewhere. We in India rake the ISIS up every now and then. But in a country as big as India if 60-70 boys have been to Iraq or Syria, it's a drop in the ocean. It's no big deal.

Despite all the violence and noise, Kashmiris have not been attracted to ISIS. Black flags might come out along with green flags, out of frustration, anger and alienation; but it does not show commitment to ISIS.

The Indian Muslim is a cool Muslim: he's rational, moderate and not interested in getting involved in nonsense. They would rather stay out of this mess. Yet radicalism is growing, perhaps as a result of our muscular policy. Jamaat certainly is growing.

Durrani: The USA's great success is its ability to control the narrative. Our region has produced more terrorists because we call them terrorists. Iraq-Syria is now over. Sikhs, Kashmiris, TTP,[3] the Afghan Taliban, the Baloch dissidents, the sectarian militants: there are ethnic dissidents and political dissidents, but all of them are lumped together as 'terrorists'.

The only definition of terrorist is now the militant. The other worse damage, though, is the terrorism that the State commits. The State targets non-combatants more than non-state actors do. If I don't like you, I call you a terrorist and do whatever I like with you. I can, because you are a terrorist.

As Sikh militants are distinguished from Kashmiris, we found a similar distinction on our western front. The Afghan Taliban told us to keep the 'Punjabi Taliban' away from them. The 'Punjabi Taliban' have no idea how to wage an asymmetric war. Its fighters rise in the morning, offer prayers, and then request their next target. The Afghan Taliban are fine fighters. They've lasted 35 years, not by attacking people every day but by staggering their operations and diversifying their modus operandi.

Kashmiris also lasted after an initial setback in which they were more action-oriented. At some stage, they concluded that militancy alone would not attain their goal. Even if their support base was large, struggle for independence is always a long-drawn affair.

Regarding the Sikh militancy, Indians were naturally grateful for the help provided by Benazir Bhutto's first government. (I was quite surprised that the Indians took so long to make use of it.) But there was the link between the Sikhs and Kashmiris: by helping India, how adversely are you affecting the Kashmiris fighting for their freedom, their rights, and their grievances against the Indian state?

The other parallel with the western front is that Musharraf rounded up sympathisers to the Afghan resistance, or the Taliban, sending hundreds of them to Guantanamo Bay without any due process of law. He[4] admitted this in his book—that he handed over hundreds of such people. Then Musharraf sent the army into the tribal areas. The result is the Tehrik-i-Taliban Pakistan, of 40 different groups: some because we sided with the US against their fellow tribesmen, some for a variety of other reasons. The label that Pakistan gets is of 'terrorism' but it is in fact due to our inadequate policies, our Faustian dealings with the US, and indeed our relationship with India.

To prove the point about foreign support, the equipment that the TTP uses isn't available in the market: sophisticated weapons, electronic equipment, communications, etc. So how is that as an example of terrorism?

On Al Faran, I looked at it from many angles though I didn't have concrete information. I had never heard of this group, it came from some other...

Sinha: Harkat-ul Mujahideen.

Durrani: Yes, absolutely. No one knew Al Faran, and later no one ever talked about it. It was probably a false flag operation by Indian intelligence.

It resulted in anger directed towards Pakistan, and the Kashmiris. No longer were they freedom fighters. They were terrorists because they kidnapped an American, an Englishman, a German and a Norwegian.

We find one of them escapes. Fantastic. But he is picked up by helicopter—in an area covered by forests and snow. The rest were never recovered. Years later, a husband-and-wife team found out and produced a book.[5] They more or less came up with what we thought. Though they found something, it remains a minor account in the big picture. But it led to calling the Kashmiris terrorists, not insurgents.

It's a problem because when everyone is a terrorist, you treat them with the same hammer. One size fits all.

So talking from a position of strength turned out to be a fallacy. But it is an article of faith, especially with the militaries. But what happens if in our efforts to weaken the 'terrorists', they become stronger, like the Afghan Taliban? What happens if they become weaker? The insurgents would wait till they regained strength in five to ten years.

But the worst part of this cliché is when the other side is down and you are in a position of strength you are more likely to refuse negotiations. Like with the Afghan Taliban in 2002, Rumsfeld said they don't exist any more, they're history now. Go climb a pole. The result is that 15 years later, people plead for talks and they ask why: 'Why should we talk? We are in a position to take Afghanistan, the Americans are not going to be here forever.' They are probably wrong. They can't conquer Afghanistan, and while the Americans may not be there forever, for all practical purposes they'll be around for the foreseeable future.

That's 'terror': it's a way to fight a war, and it's a political instrument for the State.

Dulat: I met Adrian Levy a couple of times for a discussion. The first half of *The Meadow* is correct. The doubts are about the second half, based mainly on the account of a senior J&K police officer who is not the most reliable of sources.

Durrani: Who? His name is given?

Sinha: Yes, he becomes the book's hero.

Dulat: Anyway, just that little point.

I forgot the Naxal problem in India. Thankfully, that's one area where we can't blame Pakistan.

Sinha: Mr Dulat, a former PM, Rajiv Gandhi, was assassinated by terrorists who had nothing to do with Pakistan, the LTTE.

Dulat: Of course. Also, he was almost killed on a visit to Sri Lanka, during a guard of honour when a Sri Lankan soldier reversed his rifle and hit him. He was hit but fortunately he was saved.

Sinha: For India, ISI is the bogey.

Dulat: That's why the ISI has to be the best organisation, because everything that happens in India is done by the ISI.

Sinha: In the 1990s I remember IB guys talking about an ISI plan to encircle India. The K2 Kashmir-Khalistan plan.

Dulat: There was K2, there was encirclement, there was a thousand cuts. Colleagues have talked about it. They have also talked about the break-up of Pakistan, which I've always argued won't happen for many reasons. It's not a banana republic, plus no one in the world is interested.

Sinha: Let's ask General Saheb about these plots against India, K2, encirclement. Aap bataye, on the record.

Durrani: As for the so-called Operation Topac, it never existed, even K. Subrahmanyam admitted as much when we met in Islamabad in 1998. (He had come for a round of the Neemrana Dialogue. I met him over dinner at G. Parthasarathy's, who was duly impressed with my support for the nuclear tests.)

Mahmud Durrani[6] once told me to meet Bharat Bhushan, a journalist. When I went for the Pugwash Conference in Delhi, Bharat Bhushan kidnapped me for a couple of hours and took me to a club where I had the best gin-and-tonic and fish tikkas.

He told me he had met Hamid Gul, who was fond of him and had given him a message. After Kargil, Hamid said, India was too big for our comfort so we had no choice but to break it up into bits.

But if breaking up Pakistan is difficult, then breaking up India is beyond us. If Indians themselves decide to break India up then no one can stop them. ISI can't reach Naxalites or the people in the south. It can be blamed; a few officers can feel flattered.

I sometimes ask, you blame us for everything but not when Murli Manohar Joshi[7] insisted on his trip to Kashmir to hoist the flag.

Dulat: That was 1992.

Durrani: Someone said the ISI made the flagpole so that the moment he raised the flag, it fell.

Sinha: Modi was on that trip to Lal Chowk. He organised the Ekta Yatra.

Durrani: Oh! I see. I was heading the ISI at the time.

Sinha: So not only did you not break the flagpole, you could not identify India's future PM.

Dulat: Big failure.

Durrani: Probably that was not our finest hour, but no one blamed us. Probably we broke the flagpole and spared Joshi because he had no chance of becoming the prime minister.

Dulat: The flagpole has a history of problems in Kashmir. On Independence Day, 2017, something similar happened with Mehbooba when she was taking the salute. She ordered an inquiry.

Sinha: Was the ISI's hand found?

Dulat: Who knows, I haven't seen the inquiry report. It might well have been the ISI.

24

Surgical Strike

——◆——

Aditya Sinha: Can you explain the surgical strike, whether it achieved its aims, and its effect on India-Pakistan relations?

Asad Durrani: The starting point, as I saw it in August-September 2016, would be the indigenous uprising in Kashmir. It couldn't be blamed on Pakistan, but it was difficult to control by measures chosen by Modi and his team. There may have been other options that Modi's team found unpalatable. So Pakistan had to be involved. Which it inevitably was, when the spillover came in the form of the Uri attack.

Whether Uri was genuine or a false flag operation is not the point. It provided India an opportunity to give an appropriate response. If it was a classical 'surgical strike' or not, as long as it conveyed the right message—especially at home—it served the purpose.

Your media played the right tune: finally a befitting response. They've saved face; they've salvaged a difficult situation. Kashmir in due course will cool down. Pakistan wisely let India get away with the face-saving, declared the situation taken care of.

A new status quo came into being—indeed till the next time. Will see what happens next!

In military terms, a surgical strike would normally be something like dropping special services 200 km behind enemy lines to carry out a spectacular attack against a sensitive target: a nuclear installation; a GHQ; or Osama bin Laden. Shelling across the LoC and a raid a couple of hundred metres inside enemy territory to kill a few goats would not exactly meet the criteria. But then the bigger purpose—a political one—could be fulfilled. That's why for some it's a genuine surgical strike, for others a political surgical strike, and for yet others a fake surgical strike. In all cases it serves a strategic purpose.

Sinha: So it's a dressed-up hot pursuit being passed off as a political surgical strike?

Durrani: Yes, it's modified hot pursuit. One can legitimately undertake hot pursuit to hit a place from where hostility originates. You don't know where it is in this case, Lahore or somewhere else, but that's not the point; a message has to be delivered to the Indian public.

I was in Herat in October 2016, where someone was happy to see Pakistan in a bad light. No friend of ours. He surprised me by saying, before we discuss Afghanistan may I ask what you think of this so-called surgical strike? I thought, when suspicions have gone that far, where no one is convinced that it's genuine, then not too bad for us.

A.S. Dulat: About this September 9 surgical strike, not being a military man, I don't understand what 'surgical strike' means. I'm familiar with the border because I've been posted in Kashmir and visited many times.

In the background of Mumbai, General Saheb and I were talking one day[1] and he said, there could be a time and situation when you would be compelled to do something. If we have a proper relationship or understanding then we could tell you what to do.

That would be my idea of a surgical strike: okay, now it's necessary for you to do something, so come to somewhere near Muzaffarabad and whatever. You'll say, it's done; and we'll say, yeah, yeah, great, or we could protest but it would be meaningless.

I was not in Delhi when this strike happened, and one of these TV guys called. On TV the DGMO said, we've conducted a surgical strike, it's over, and we don't intend anything more. In the meantime, the Pakistani reaction began, of total indifference, as if nothing had happened.

I thought to myself, and I said on TV that this is the perfect surgical strike. Because we apparently needed to do something, and we've done it. The DGMO says so, and Pakistan says fine. That's the reaction.

That's not how it ended because, as General Saheb says, political mileage had to be drawn. So the media went on and on. We learnt from the Congress and former NSA Shiv Shankar Menon that this had happened many times before.

The point is these sort of things happen on the border. Five years ago, two Indian soldiers were beheaded[2] on the border, and I met the prime minister, Dr Manmohan Singh, who was perturbed by what happened. I said, Sir, these things happen on the border. He said, but it's being shown on TV. His concern was, as prime minister, about what would happen.

Durrani: It's an interesting connection, Mr Dulat, with a likelihood that we considered back when we wrote a joint paper. It was that in case of an episode like the Parliament attack of 2001, or Mumbai 2008, it couldn't be forever that India would not respond. India's reaction would be: is Pakistan going to get away with it? Why do we have a big army? The Indian Army would think about how to respond and come to this conclusion: attack Pakistan.

That's risky for a number of reasons, so they would have to think of something else. That's where the Cold Start doctrine becomes relevant again. It's good thinking because you choose your response. On our side there are self-serving arguments that it can't happen under the 'nuclear overhang'.[3] But it can. Nuclear overhang won't prevent two-three days' exchange of fire. Kargil happened after the nuclear tests.

But Cold Start would lead us to respond with a technique of our own; for instance, a tactical nuclear back-up, which conceptually and technically make little sense except for on the battlefield, because it is unpredictable. In the India-Pakistan context, even tactical nuclear weapons may have strategic consequences. Amritsar and Lahore are not tactical targets, they're separated by only 50 km. There's plenty of India and Pakistan left.

No. The two countries, if they are sensible, will ask their back channel: Mr Dulat, you know Asad Durrani on the other side, let's discuss how to handle it. Both would say, yes, because of India's compulsion there are three-four places where you can bomb, just make sure there's not too much damage.

The term I use is 'choreographed response'. Or, choreographed surgical strike. We understand, India, you have to do something.

Our political compulsion is that we must also respond. So for your ten bombs we'll throw one, don't mind. Without doing much damage on the ground, we can get out of that sticky situation. You give a befitting reply to Pakistan, and we respond by saying, we don't take things lying down. (PS: In the meantime, the West too has caught up with this recipe. Empty bases are being hit in Syria to let the US and its allies claim 'punishment inflicted'.)

Now that's what happened. I'm grateful that my friend today has thought of that connection. Did it happen that way? I do not know and I'm not supposed to. And if I knew, I wouldn't talk.

That's the advantage of a choreographed response. I agree that it's Modi, BJP, and others who hang tough who are in the best position to make peace. With Mian Saheb, they were in a good position for peace, they had a good partner, and the right environment. But it didn't happen. Modi and his team won't do it. Their tough posture will continue.

Sinha: In case of another Pathankot, how would it be managed, or what would the consequences be?

Dulat: Things like Pathankot or Gurdaspur or Uri or Akhnoor have happened many times. There'll be lots of noise and if you ask for a prediction, we'll carry out another surgical strike.

The media causes a lot of problems because everything gets exaggerated.

Durrani: Media is the enemy of peace. If there's peace, mediapeople will lose their jobs, channels will close down. Many who go yap-yap-yap and shout their heads off will not get a second look.

Dulat: If you've been to Kashmir, particularly to the border, many things happen that don't get mentioned and don't need to be known. Many innocent civilians are killed or maimed or are in wheelchairs. People on both sides of the border are suffering because of our callousness. These things will continue to happen.

Like General Saheb said about the Americans in Afghanistan, saying out of boredom, okay, boys, let's go out and shoot some. On our border also, the firing is often unprovoked. Both claim the other side has done it so many times.

Durrani: We've seen a mobilisation after the Parliament attack, and after the more serious Mumbai attack we saw that the Indians probably decided a similar reaction was counterproductive. The next major event took place with the Modi government in place, which has painted itself into a corner.

I don't know why there wasn't any violent kinetic action after Pathankot. Maybe the lessons of 2002, maybe the new government, maybe Nawaz Sharif, or maybe there was an understanding. But after Uri, a surgical strike was announced and applauded, which is why I say painted in a corner. The next episode would bring pressure, that wasn't the surgical strike supposed to prevent any more incidents? Now what?

Either you'll pull your punches or you declare you're under compulsion for something more. This spiral of action-reaction can be contained in many ways but sometimes the dynamic takes it out of your hands. So he's right, we cannot predict.

But I have no doubt that the dynamic of the relationship and action-reaction can be contained depending on who's in charge. Situations build, tempers build. Vajpayee could contain it.

Dulat: General Saheb's right that this government would find it more difficult than Vajpayee or Dr Manmohan Singh to restrain itself, because it's a more hawkish or muscular government. And a more no-nonsense sort.

I'm not worried about a Gurdaspur or a Pathankot or an Akhnoor, but if another Mumbai were to happen, God forbid, then what would happen? Or another Parliament attack. The Government of India would find restraint difficult. I'm sure they would have all this in mind.

Whenever it has happened, the Americans and others immediately arrive and offer support. There are other ways of settling this and during Vajpayee's time there was coercive diplomacy. But when you've painted yourself in a certain image, people around you expect instant retaliation.

Let's focus on restricting it to the skirmishes or the little attacks that happen on army camps or on a police van, etc. That carries on.

Durrani: I'm not being alarmist, but look at the many actors, non-state actors and state actors who are interested in creating turmoil, who are not interested in stability.

Dulat: That's true. Talking at think tanks, etc., when we say we've been at the receiving end of terrorism, we've borne the brunt of it, it's a fact. But look at the poor Kashmiri. You asked why the summer of 2017 was quieter than the year before. Sometimes those state and non-state actors, as General Saheb referred to them, also realise that the poor Kashmiri needs some respite.

25

The Politics of War

———◆———

Aditya Sinha: The last time the status quo was threatened was Operation Parakram in 2002, and Mr Dulat was in government.

A.S. Dulat: Good example, because what did Parakram achieve in the end? In hindsight, it was probably Vajpayee's only option because you can't fight a war, the generals are not ready to fight. What are you going to fight, what will it achieve? So move troops to the border. And we called it coercive diplomacy.

Sinha: How did Pakistan see that mobilisation?

Asad Durrani: Coming soon after 9/11, and God knows what was actually behind the attack on the Indian Parliament, it wreaked so much trouble.

If anyone believed that post 9/11 we were overjoyed at being yet again 'the frontline ally' of the sole surviving superpower—no longer the sole thereafter, and struggling to survive as a superpower—one should get one's head examined. The war next door in Afghanistan, and we were the springboard, was spilling over the Durand Line. Also, India made that famous offer, Pakistan is part of the problem, we'd be a better ally in Afghanistan, etc. Now after that, who would think of accentuating problems on the eastern front? If a lapse happened, it has never been resolved in people's minds.

Regarding the mobilisation, one understood that the Americans had already provided a context for punitive action. After 9/11 they attacked Afghanistan, and after the Parliament attack India found the pretext to follow that line. Invading Pakistan was probably not on Vajpayee's mind, but the minimum political necessity was to be seen to be doing something serious.

How does India respond? That has been a problem from 2001, and we are still looking for a satisfactory way of handling Bombay, Parliament, Pathankot, Uri. I was in Saudi Arabia at the time but I agreed with the assessment back home that there would be no war.

War can become an unintended consequence when things acquire their own dynamic. Like troop movement can acquire a dynamic of its own. Logically, troop movement was the compulsion but war would be by choice; and that choice was not likely to be exercised. Nuclear overhang and US presence would provide Pakistan a cushion. Call it conventional-unconventional strategic paradox.

After the mobilisation takes place and you fall back; then you find it has not produced much, if anything. At the Pugwash-sponsored India-Pakistan rounds, Mani Dixit, Air Commodore Jasjit Singh of the IDSA and others supported my conclusion—presented as a paper, 'The Law of Diminishing Threats' that the Commodore later published—that the net effect seemed to be that both countries' threat cards—Pakistan's nuclear and India's conventional—have been played out perhaps for the last time.

For Pakistan, there was a positive development. Our military had been employed for long periods on non-military duties, and because of your mobilisation, for eight to ten months the entire army was now in battle location. It could now catch up on the much needed refresher training for combat.

Sinha: Did the mobilisation not cause some anxiety in Pakistan?

Durrani: If there is eyeball-to-eyeball contact between two opposing forces, nobody was likely to sit back and enjoy the fun. Chances of something going wrong must have been troubling. I talked to some in the assessment business. Ehsan (ul Haq), who was heading the ISI at the time, said: no, war was not likely. The deployment was a compulsion and had to be done. It had benefits, it had costs.

Not many people who mattered believed that war would take place. But you can count on the media to keep the alarm bells ringing.

Dulat: Yes, I think we agree that war is not an option. It makes no sense. We fought a few in the past and they haven't achieved anything on either side, other than their losing East Pakistan, which was not because of the '71 war but because of other stupidities that happened earlier.

Yes, Vajpayee went to Lahore and said, hum jung na hone denge. Mian Saheb must have been on board with that. After that Musharraf said war was not a realistic option. Manmohan Singh would be the last man to think about war.

But there can always be a madman who gets it into his head that a surgical strike is something routine. So that even if there is no war, somebody can say we're going to teach Pakistan a lesson. Where does that begin or end? It's difficult to anticipate what might or could happen.

The Americans always get excited. In 2001 they worried what might happen after the Parliament attack because Vajpayee said: I tried my best for peace with Pakistan, and despite Kargil I invited somebody who staged a coup and became President, and now this. He was in a difficult situation.

Operation Parakram achieved nothing. It was a waste of money and caused hardship to soldiers who had to serve in inhospitable locations that summer. In Jaisalmer it gets to 47 degrees. And you're sitting on the border doing what? I suppose it was Vajpayee's only option.

Which brings me to the wishful thinking on our side that Pakistan is not a viable country. It'll break up. It was around the time Musharraf took over, some responsible people said we're fond of Pakistan but it's going to break up. I said, I don't see Pakistan breaking up or any sign of that. The world won't allow Pakistan to break up. America would never countenance it.

Durrani: This point about the chances of war, what it ultimately boils down to is the uncertainty, the escalation and unintended consequences.

Dulat: Unintended consequences.

Durrani: One might say: two-three days is understandable, you had your fun, stop firing, go home. Delhi, Rawalpindi, Islamabad, Washington, Beijing would all say, pause before some madman gets his hand on the MAD button. Because then all bets are off.

But then all our assessments and strategies must assume that we are rational actors. Pakistanis are not suicidal. Any nuclear launch from our side would be amply responded. Indeed, the uncertainty that a particular threshold—tangible or intangible—may be crossed serves as the real deterrence.

Sinha: Some philosophers have said that war is a more natural state of man.

Durrani: It at least is easier to start war—any bloody fool can do it—than making and keeping peace that needed everyone who could throw a spanner in the works to come and remain on-board. Then we have those who benefit from war—and indeed we've heard of the military-industrial complex in the US and warmongers elsewhere. They keep nudging us all that some of our opponents only understood the language of the gun. I think nationalism and national interest—an upshot of the concept of nation state—have also contributed to more armed conflicts. Maybe that's the reason Iqbal called nationalism as the new God.

Dulat: Yes, nationalism can become a problem.

Durrani: I agree. You can't have your country's interest at heart if you don't have your region's interest at heart. Like saying: 'No, I couldn't care less what happens in the rest of Pakistan, but in Faislabad this should be done.' To say Pakistan first, or to say we must seal the Afghan border in our national interest, that's a little stupid.

But right now enough numbers of our compatriots believe in it, that they have nothing to do with neighbours, neighbours can fight their own wars, and that we should only worry about Pakistan. When neighbours fight wars, though, it is about Pakistan!

Dulat: At the Karachi 'Aman ki Asha' meet in 2011 that I attended, the most interesting thing was that both the French and German ambassadors to Pakistan spoke. First the Frenchman talked about the effects of war and how Europe came together. The German was brilliant. Without mincing words, he said that after the Second World War, Germany had consciously decided that war was no longer an option. It suffered so much during the wars that it would not go to war again, period.

In 2009, a lot of ambassadors suddenly became Afghanistan experts. One NATO group came from Germany to Delhi, and at a function at Claridges Hotel spoke of nothing but peace and dialogue, etc. So I said, I thought you guys represented NATO, what's happened to NATO?

The world has been changing. Ten years back Henry Kissinger visited Delhi and said, if Iran doesn't fall into line it will be blown off the face of the Earth. Iran is still there, as is everybody else.

Durrani: NATO ambassadors will come and usually talk about peace. NATO is a war organisation.

Dulat: That's it.

Durrani: It's a war alliance, and if there are no wars they would be worried. After the Warsaw Pact dissolved, NATO was expected to follow suit, but it kept inventing new missions to rationalise its perpetuation. Initially it was to keep peace among the Europeans, but after its failure during the Bosnian crisis, as well as with the 'Partnership for Peace' by some of the states of the former Soviet Union, NATO is now breathing easy because it found employment in the unending wars in Afghanistan and elsewhere.

Dulat: In fact, Kissinger also said in Delhi that if NATO fails in Afghanistan, then that's the end of NATO.

Durrani: Recycling NATO doesn't sound good. However, war does serve certain interests, let's not close our eyes to that. Even in Pakistan, a certain small number might disingenuously suggest the need for simmering conflicts—to keep the US engaged with the region. Their rationale varies—from financial dividends to keep Indian 'hegemonistic' designs in check.

Take the Taliban in Afghanistan. Most of them, of course, want the war to end, but some may believe in making the best of a bad situation: getting 500 million dollars every year from NATO.

Without war, though, there are aims that cannot be achieved. Without war, Bangladesh would not have been created. Without the Kuwait war America would not have gained a foothold in the region. Without attacking Afghanistan, the right political response to 9/11 domestically was not possible.

To completely rule out war is wrong. But where war becomes the instrument of policy, and not just an extension of policy by other means as Clausewitz said, it becomes the actual policy. From which the rest must follow.

What does America sell, more than anything else? Weapons. Just a couple of weeks ago there was a seminar attended by a US undersecretary of state. He was here for the strategic dialogue, though the relation between Pakistan and America is not strategic. And he says, Indians are buying plenty of weapons and that makes us happy. It's a true statement, but he also indicated what determines your relations.

Dulat: Why is Pakistan not buying more?

Durrani: We seem to have run out of money.

Dulat: They'll give you money.

Durrani: Even if we want F-16s, they say no subsidies till you go after the Haqqanis. Which would be another suicidal act.

Dulat: Of course, Bangladesh would not have been created without war, but a lot has happened since '71.

Durrani: Yes.

Dulat: War today is a much more serious thing.

Sinha: What about the statement by (then) defence minister Manohar Parrikar about doing away with the 'no first use' policy?

Durrani: Thank you for saying that. It would be nice to hear other voices because professionals, incidentally, do not agree on it. Amongst us there is almost irreconcilable debate as to what it actually means.

Dulat: It means nothing.

Durrani: I agree, and am impressed that a civilian understands this better than many in the military. Declared doctrines are not always the actual ones—in case of nuclear, they're seldom if ever. The reason is simple: ambivalence is the first principle of nuclear warfare. Take, for example, the NFU (no first use) and NNFU (no no first use). India must declare NFU to convey confidence in its conventional superiority. If Pakistan ever said that: not only that it would have no credibility—we acquired it to deter our more powerful neighbour—but would also convey the wrong message to our people.

Remember, the nuclear assets are primarily political and psychological weapons.

Dulat: (Parrikar's statement) was only a political statement.

Durrani: When Zardari said Pakistan should also have a 'no first use' policy, someone said, Zardari Saheb, you may know about commissions on nuclear or other deals, what do you know about nuclear doctrines?

Their political message can create confusion, commotion, anxiety. Parrikar again threatened when you got a new army chief, third or the fourth Gorkha in line or something, that you're talking again of Cold Start. This discussion can go on forever. But essentially, the professional says, under the circumstances a statement was required. It helps the current India-Pakistan tension. But it will pass. Because it doesn't mean as much as people believe.

Sinha: So the status quo remains, and nobody really means anything much.

Durrani: Ultimately, it's every country's domestic politics that matters. American reaction to 9/11 was invading Afghanistan, which can only be justified by the fact that Fortress America was pierced. Americans wanted blood, nothing less than a spectacular attack would have appeased them. Pakistan offered to take out Osama bin Laden, given time, so that the US wouldn't have to come and attack. But that would not have satisfied the Americans.

Sinha: General Saheb, you were in the '65 and '71 wars. What were your thoughts about India during these wars?

Durrani: There is a misunderstanding about soldiers, that since they're fighting each other they must be the worst rivals.

Once an American delegation came over for briefing on our training doctrines. After my stint at the ISI, I had moved to head the Training Branch in the GHQ. One of the visitors asked if 'hating India' was part of our training syllabi. I said, on the contrary, our soldiers are drilled that when the time comes you fight, but remember the other man is doing the same duty for his country. That is our training doctrine. I was angry, so I added, unlike the American army where you are told to kill the 'enemies of the United States of America', all others are motivated to defend their country.

This is the spirit I found on the your side as well.

Our armies are trained that you have to fight; if you miss, the other chap may not. But remember, once the hostilities cease, flag meetings take place, you exchange jokes, tea, coffee.

Dulat: I'm from northern India and we have a lot of family and friends in the army. As youngsters there's excitement about war but what you quickly figure out is that nobody wants war, it's a dirty business. It can be extremely traumatic.

A cousin was in Chamb in '65 and returned traumatised. He narrated how a bullet went through his turban, which he obviously imagined. In some areas it was hand-to-hand fighting. He narrated a story which gave him sleepless nights about a young Pakistani second lieutenant who was killed. 'When I put my hands in his pocket, out came a letter from his fiancee and I felt so terrible,' he said. This guy came and spent a couple of weeks with us after the war, and he used to jump out of bed at night, of nightmares he'd seen first-hand.

Actually, Generals don't want war. That's why an Indo-Pak dialogue between the Generals or armies is necessary. That's why I keep saying intelligence chiefs should also talk, because whatever happens at the diplomatic level doesn't take us far.

Durrani: That's true. Even army education is in this direction. But ultimately, if you're good at your job you try to accomplish it without the use of force. War is more destructive nowadays than before. Previously, a few hundred or a few thousand people died, now a city can be demolished. Winning without fighting has been the ideal military strategy since Sun Tzu's time. These days a good country would follow that advice by many other means.

Dulat: That goes for good Generals also.

Durrani: That's why they preach: be so prepared that the other side thinks many times before they take you on. Plans are based on deterrence, avoidance of war, minimum use of force. The French believe in it, the Germans say that on balance, militaries do not make war. It happens for political or historical reasons, but not because a military is raring for war.

The American army is an exception. When they are offered a non-military solution it says we haven't created this mighty machinery for nothing. In their culture, what caused your cousin sleepless nights might actually amuse them, as they've been doing in Iraq, taking pot-shots. In Afghanistan they say they're suffering from boredom, so how about today going out and shooting down civilians, since the Taliban is too tough a cookie. That's why the distinction between the training of American soldiers and soldiers elsewhere.

But India and Pakistan are different, they have mutual respect.

Sinha: What about the '71 war?

Dulat: '65 was the more serious war.

Durrani: The '71 war broke out somewhere else and I rushed to my unit in the desert. The desert campaign did not go well. From a soldier's point of view, and one who had recently learnt the art of war as I was in Quetta doing the staff course, it was a tremendous source of learning. From your own mistakes you learn.

The desert was where my unit was. We went very close to Jaisalmer, it was desert, khula hai, then returned because the operation could not be logistically supported.

Dulat: When I was in the PMO I was regularly called to the National Defence College to talk on Kashmir. During one talk, a senior officer said, why did the politicians prevent the army from going to war in 2001? We had every provocation. I said, what makes you think the politicians stopped the army? How do you know it was not the Generals who didn't want to go to war?

The public doesn't get to hear of these things, so there's this silly perception that we all want to go to war and fight. Whereas war is the craziest option.

Durrani: Even those two former Mossad chiefs in Berlin at that Pugwash Conference repeatedly said, going to war against Iran was the stupidest idea.

Dulat: My Mossad contemporary, Efraim Halevy, was a votary of dialogue and peace. Two-three years back he was in Delhi, and we spoke the same jargon on dialogue. People were surprised that a Mossad chief said that. But Halevy, who was chief for five years, was that kind of guy.

VI

NEW GREAT GAME

Given the fact that India's and Pakistan's neighbourhood has historically and also lately been of great interest to countries pursuing global power, the discussion looks at Afghanistan. Durrani speaks on what he believes happened in the climax of the USA's search for Osama bin Laden, and he and Dulat discuss why Afghanistan is unsortable at the moment. They also assess how Donald Trump will treat the region, and examine how Russia, which was once India's best friend, is now cosying up to Pakistan.

Setting the scene

Bangkok, October 29, 2017: We sit in the 13th floor lounge of our hotel to hold our conversations where we try to shake off the general negativity that characterised the previous day's Track-II dialogue. Coffee and cookies and Mr Dulat's unshakeable optimism rescue the project from futility and surrender.

26

The Deal for Osama bin Laden

<hr/>

A.S. Dulat: I credited Pakistan with managing things in the past, choreographing things. Whichever way you look at Osama bin Laden's capture,[1] it was huge. I felt Pakistan cooperated in some way, but even if it didn't, and somebody could enter your country and take out whoever they want, then Pakistan managed the thing well.

Aditya Sinha: That's what Seymour Hersh says.

Asad Durrani: I got a call from BBC on May 2, 2011. I was in Abu Dhabi for a high-profile Afghanistan-related Track-II. The call was about a special programme on Osama bin Laden who had been killed the previous night. I didn't know much, but I was invited on the show because for a few years I had been saying Osama bin Laden could not be in the tribal areas but in a big city. Since I was proven right they probably assumed I knew something.

It was just an assessment that for Osama bin Laden to hide in the tribal areas was not feasible. I wasn't interested in knowing where he was. They said it was going to be a special episode of HardTalk because unlike the usual one-on-one it would have former British military chief Michael Jackson and maybe their former foreign secretary David Miliband. In a way they were conveying that I would be defending Pakistan.

At the studio there was no Miliband. A former deputy NSA from the US took his place. I said, I don't know but I think Pakistan has cooperated. Without cooperation the operation would have been risky. The risk was so high that the other consideration, that we would alert someone, was sacrificed in return for our cooperation.

Then why are you not owning it? For political reasons, I said it will not go down well in Pakistan that we cooperated with the US to eliminate someone many Pakistanis considered a hero.

There was no uproar over my version. Two years later, I probably repeated myself elsewhere but by this time another curse had caught up with the world, called the social media. I was on Al Jazeera in Oxford, an audience of 400, and the moment I gave my assessment that Pakistan cooperated, 400 messages went out of that hall, most distorting what I said. They said: General Durrani, former head of the ISI, says Pakistan was harbouring Osama bin Laden. I didn't say that. I said we probably found out at some stage and cooperated, handed him over in a way that they got all the credit.

Seymour Hersh, whom I had met a couple of times and was in touch with, called me. Again I was out of the country on a Track-II meeting. He said, I have evidence that Pakistan and the US cooperated but no one here will buy it. What can we do together? I said please send me whatever you write, I'll send my comments. He did.

The US control of this narrative and media was marvellous. Hersh is a famous, respected and accomplished investigative journalist. He's written books on Vietnam and Abu Ghraib, for which he's been duly acknowledged. But no one in Washington openly endorsed his report on Osama.

There are several other investigations of Osama bin Laden's assassination, by Hersh and by Gareth Porter; one by a retired Pakistani, Brigadier Shaukat Qadir; and one by a retired Brigadier living in Canada. All make the same point about cooperation. For Pakistan, being blamed for incompetence was more acceptable than complicity; how could it not know the US helicopters ingressing 150 km inside the country?

The last point, important for India, Pakistan and all those who deal with the US, was that after the operation, America did not honour its commitments.

Nothing unusual. It's always been like this. Some time in the 1960s when Ayub Khan was in power, Kennedy himself told him that if he helped the US create assets in Tibet and East Pakistan, directed at southern China, they would do something about Kashmir. This is documented by Bruce Riedel, who is by no stretch pro-Pakistan.

After Ayub Khan reluctantly agreed, America did not fulfil its obligation. Post-Afghanistan, post-Osama, there are so many instances of unfulfilled commitments. It's in their DNA. They admit it: when it comes to honouring commitments, parachutes are better.

The four-five months after the Osama raid was a particularly bad period in Pakistan-US relations. We did manage some sort of normalcy in 2012. It's not over. Their criticism in the region continues because of the difficulties in Afghanistan.

Dulat: So what was the deal on Osama?

Durrani: I do not know. This was only my assessment. The then army chief was Ashfaq Kayani. He was my favourite student at the NDC. Professionally sound. Though retired, he is keeping away from me lest I ask if he made a deal.

I don't think there is any reason for him, or for Pasha who was heading the ISI at that time, for keeping quiet. Get the secret out because we've been getting the worst of both worlds. We are blamed for incompetence, for playing a double game; and what did we get in return? That is what I want to know.

But on that BBC programme they asked me what the deal was. I didn't know, but I presumed it must have been about exiting Afghanistan.

Money isn't the main factor. Once you have Osama bin Laden, if there's any sense at the helm, and Ashfaq Kayani was sensible, you settle for nothing other than an agreed, reasonable exit strategy. Vali Nasr,[2] who was on Holbrooke's team, also spoke of an exit plan.

If Kayani settled for some farms or a billion dollars then I myself will start a campaign against him, who I once liked and feel was one of our thinking chiefs.

Dulat: A couple of days before Osama was lifted, Kayani met with somebody, where was it?

Durrani: On a ship.

Dulat: Or at an airbase. There was a meeting which I thought significant in the context of what happened days later. Why did Kayani go to the meeting? Who was the US commander in Afghanistan then?

Durrani: In 2011? (David) Petraeus.

Dulat: It seemed like too much of a coincidence[3] because two days later, Osama was bumped off.

Durrani: I agree, it's a reasonable deduction that these meetings concerned the raid. My criticism of the Pakistani side is that just a few months earlier, another deal made by Kayani and Pasha[4] was not kept. A CIA contractor, Raymond Davis, shot two Pakistanis in Lahore.[5] Once he was safely out of Pakistan's airspace, a drone attack on a jirga in the tribal areas targeted non-combatants, to send us a message.

Panetta, the obnoxious CIA director and later the defence secretary, was our ill-wisher and one reason I didn't want Hillary Clinton elected. After the attack he was asked: that was a tribal jirga, why did you hit it? He heartlessly responded: it was not a glee party. He had to give us a message: how dare we keep their guy in prison for six weeks.

Dulat: What was the role of the doctor who's locked up?

Durrani: Under the cover of a polio programme he found where Osama bin Laden was.

Dulat: So he was working for the Americans. It seems to me that the Americans found Osama via the doctor, and told Kayani that now we know. Are you willing to cooperate or should we do it on our own?

Durrani: Yes, they said play ball. Kayani says, we will do it in this manner, and what do we get in return. They found out not only because of Dr Afridi. I have no doubt that a retired Pakistani officer who was in intelligence walked in and told the Americans. I won't take his name because I can't prove it and also I don't want to give him any publicity. How much of the 50 million dollars he got, who knows. But he is missing from Pakistan. I should know.

Dulat: He must have got some farms.

Durrani: Yes.

Dulat: There was a story of a CIA mole in the ISI. You're saying he's a retired officer.

Durrani: At the time he was not with ISI. After retirement he had a petty business and stumbled on this, or worked on this operation. My charge against the two is not that they worked for the US to track down the world's most wanted man. In our business, the worst crime a person can commit—especially the walk-in, a military man, an intelligence man—is to work for another country's intelligence agency. Even a friendly country.

Sinha: That's why poor Dr Afridi is in jail.

Durrani: Pollock remained in US custody for years, and could not be released because he was working for another country's intelligence agency, even though it's the most allied ally. The second crime (Dr Afridi) committed is that because of his fake programme, polio vaccination[6] got a bad name and children were going without it. Some polio workers were even targeted.

Dulat: Polio programme was a fake?

Durrani: It was fake. But on that pretext he went around, knocked on many doors and asked if there were any children.

Dulat: And that's how he found Osama.

Durrani: He found Osama.

27

Selfish Self-interests in Afghanistan

—◆—

Aditya Sinha: Could Afghanistan be a CBM between India and Pakistan?

Asad Durrani: Once upon a time I did believe that if there was an area where both countries could meaningfully cooperate, it's Afghanistan. Why isn't it taking place? It's, amongst other reasons, because of the mindset.

A.S. Dulat: Ahmed Rashid said if India and Pakistan can sort out Afghanistan, then Kashmir would be a cakewalk.

What intrigues me is our policy in Afghanistan. When I was in service it seemed that we put most of our eggs in the Northern Alliance basket. The Northern Alliance, Russia, Iran, they were cooperating in whatever little we were doing. Now there's no Northern Alliance left and the Russians and Iranians are still around, but we don't have a proper connect with them either.

The civil war in Afghanistan will continue endlessly unless the main party, the Taliban, is involved in talks. Talks are essential. Even the Americans have come around to that view.

We missed out because when the Taliban was in power, we refused to recognise them and then again in 2000 or 2002. We will never have the clout that Pakistan has, because Pakistan is right there.

If we had links with the Taliban and other leaders in Afghanistan, it would have helped.

Even the Americans agree that Pakistan is key to this dialogue. It won't happen or progress without Pakistan. Because key players are with you and so you hold the key cards.

Why have we been squabbling in Afghanistan? Why are we not cooperating?

I'm clear that however much we have done or invested, we are handicapped and that's why it makes sense to work together. If the younger brother is the more active brother in the game, then why would I not concede that to my younger brother? Let's move on.

Durrani: We are time and again blamed for wanting to keep our backyard free of Indian influence. I know that Indians have influence, their cultural influence is great. To think we're playing the game to keep the Indians out is not smart. Though enough number of people believe in it.

The main issue is that the US—regardless of its aims and objectives that have been discussed elsewhere in the book—wants us to go after the Taliban and the Haqqani network who are fighting against—according to them—the 'foreign occupation'. The problem is that even if we could—that is if the insurgents were on Pakistani territory—it would be a bigger disaster than when we first employed the military in our tribal areas in 2004, which led to the formation of TTP. There is sympathy amongst our tribesmen as well as the general public for those resisting the American occupation. And then by going against them, we would not only turn some more of our own people against us but also these groups who have never harmed us.

They do hold a grudge for when we joined the US-led coalition in 2001, but they're prepared to forget that as they understood our compulsion. After a couple of years, Pakistan did try to help with whatever was possible despite the pressure. To lose that capital would be something from which you may not recover. We are still suffering from the blowback of 2004.

If that happens, we will harm ourselves more than either India or the US ever can.

The Bollywood influence in Afghanistan is tremendous. Some speak to me in my language because of Bollywood. When Aziz Khan and I were in Herat in 2015, a ten-year-old girl overheard us speaking in Urdu, so she turned around and did this (palms joined together). I said, kyun bhai kahan se sikha. TV per dekhte hain na, she said.

You're right, we have clout. Our geography is God-given. Pakistan is the strategic depth that Afghans have, even those who don't like us.

This is where Afghans come and find work. Karachi has been the world's largest Pushtun city for many years and is now the second largest 'Afghan' city with maybe 2.5 million Pushtuns. They come and go. Those who do Paki-bashing in the morning, by evening are in Peshawar for the dentist or business or family. Some of them have told us that they have a car with a full tank and loaded boot, and they don't use it except occasionally to start the engine to keep the battery alive. 'If something happens, we're making a beeline for Peshawar,' they say. There are hospitals in the north that treat Afghans for free. Those who can afford come to Peshawar because they trust the hospitals there more.

When Aslam Baig said Pakistan provides strategic depth, he meant it militarily. Like we used to talk of Iran as a relief zone, that we would in case of an Indian attack shift our air force to Iran, as the Iraqis did in the 1991 war. People thought he wanted to occupy Afghanistan. See what happened to the mightiest armies that tried; Pakistan would be foolish to even think about it.

We light-heartedly say we now know what to do with India. If the Indian army attacks, we'll get out of the way and let them march through to Afghanistan, for that is where all big armies get buried.

The classical strategic depth is that whenever Afghans are attacked by a foreign army, they come to Pakistan. They continue to stay, work, get absorbed. This has happened over a period of time; even my own clan came from there 150 years ago, in a different context, went to Kashmir, and some of them travelled as far as south India.

It isn't true that Pakistan's Afghan policy is India-centric. The complexity of the Afghan situation is such that I keep revising my knowledge and assessment every six months.

Dulat: Why has President Ashraf Ghani suddenly turned hostile to Pakistan?

Durrani: He was always hostile. The problem with him, an imported and imposed president surrounded by whiz-kids who are Western-educated and ambitious, is that they do not belong in Afghanistan and don't have a firm footing or a constituency. This government can't sustain itself without American military, financial and political support.

The Taliban, on the other hand, have withstood the world's mightiest alliance for over 16 years. It's an important factor and an intra-Afghan settlement will be on its terms. One can talk to the Taliban, as has been done in two rounds of Doha[1] and last year in Murree.[2] No wonder the Americans and the Kabul regime scuttled the second Murree round.

Dulat: Like you said, Ashraf Ghani had on his own crash-landed of the GHQ.

Durrani: That was an unhelpful gimmick. I thought, my god, this man has created a situation for poor Raheel Sharif,[3] a simple soldier, that will be difficult to sustain. Some Pakistanis are so stupid they considered Ashraf Ghani brave because he knocked at the gates of the GHQ.

After all, others have ruled Afghanistan before Ashraf Ghani, and even those installed by the Soviets, be it Daud, Hafizullah Amin or the Tarakis, whenever Moscow told them to tighten the screws on Pakistan, they would show reluctance, and some of them lost their jobs; others, their heads. Ashraf Ghani has no such inhibition. He bad-mouthed us in Amritsar.

Ashraf Ghani is more harmful to Pakistan than Karzai[4] ever was. At least Karzai, for whom I have sympathy and admiration, had his feet on the ground and knew how to play these games. He even had the guts to tell the Americans what he thought of them even though he was president for 13 years, dependent on US money and security. Lately he even accused the US of launching and supporting IS.

Dulat: Do we take it for granted that Ashraf Ghani is an American man?

Durrani: He is.

Dulat: That's how he got elected?

Durrani: Yes, but worse, he belongs to Zalmay Khalilzad's group.[5] An Afghan, representing Khalilzad, dependent on US military, political, and financial support. He's a big disaster for us and for Afghanistan too.

Dulat: If he is so American, why should he be hostile to Pakistan?

Durrani: Because America is not happy with Pakistan's policy in Afghanistan. Every US report on Afghanistan talks about US deficiencies, but the last few pages will focus on how they would have succeeded but for Pakistan and its complicity with the Taliban, its double-game, etc. They continue to do that though we've offered many times, let's work out a strategy so that you can leave and blame Pakistan for the mess you would leave behind, just so long as you get the hell out, because your continued (military) presence means: war continues.

Dulat: They may not be happy but the Americans can deal directly with you. Why use Ashraf Ghani?

Durrani: Ashraf Ghani will probably continue to use them as the bad cop. This Afghan president, after meeting Raheel Sharif, next went to the US and said, please don't leave in 2014. Just for that alone he put off the Taliban, whose sole precondition for negotiation and settlement is a firm US commitment to withdraw. Worse, he said he'd like to express his gratitude to the American military's sacrifices in Afghanistan.

Even the anti-Taliban Afghans were upset, and so was I. The Afghans have in the last ten years lost 300,000 people to US bombing, compared to the 2,000-3,000 Americans 'sacrificed'.

Ashraf Ghani is an embarrassment for Afghanistan. It's difficult to consider him Pakistan's friend. Six months later he told us we haven't played our role: 'I made a political sacrifice coming to you, Pakistan is unpopular in Afghanistan,' he said. Six months! The Afghans in six months don't even start moving. They have plenty of patience and time. Anyone who knows the Taliban also knows that they will wait six months to see how serious you are.

For Ashraf Ghani to think that after one visit to Pakistan, he could turn the region on its head is fatuous at best. We have no reason to keep Ashraf Ghani in good humour.

Dulat: How do you see Afghanistan playing out?

Sinha: Any realignments with Trump?

Durrani: Realignments have been taking place the past five-six years. In 2011, for example, one could see a new axis emerging: Pakistan, Iran, Russia and China. During my visit to Moscow in 2012, I could see these countries closing ranks on coordinating policy on Afghanistan. Both the Iranians and Russians are talking to the Taliban. The Chinese have essentially said, you lead the way, and if it led to the regional countries coming together, then we can probably play a role.

Let me also mention here that in mid-2016, I was on Al Jazeera with Michael Flynn before he briefly became Trump's NSA, for a discussion on Afghanistan. When he said, Pakistan and the US were pursuing their 'selfish self-interests'—a double negative must be the American way to emphasise a point, like 'you don't know nothing'—I thought here was an honest man one could do business with. He was known to be rabidly 'anti-Muslim', but the Russians too must have missed him when he was fired.

Dulat: The obvious thing is the Indian side cosying up to Trump to countervail against this Gang of Four, which came into being even during Obama's time when we had a special relationship with the US. The India-US relationship will get cosier. Whether we gain anything out of it, I don't know because we have been losing, other than the nuclear deal. We still have the same policy on Afghanistan. We are becoming overdependent on the US. Like Ashraf Ghani, Indians are not happy if the Americans leave because we seem to think America provides relief or support for us there.

The moment the Chinese announced they were prepared to talk to the Taliban, I've wondered where we figure in this. So many years and opportunities to begin a relationship with the Taliban and we've not done so. We don't in the belief that whatever the Americans do is right and everybody else is wrong.

Sinha: So India does not follow selfish self-interest?

Dulat: No, we are also confused about this selfish self-interest. It makes no sense, not even selfish sense.

Who was that friend of ours, that tall fellow, whom you sent to Abu Ghraib (Guantanamo?)? Mullah Zaeef. Aziz used to say Zaeef is third class, but where is he now, in Kabul?

Durrani: Zaeef is in Kabul.

Dulat: We had a long conversation at Pugwash in Berlin and even he said India doesn't seem to take interest, doesn't bother. Now there was that that Brit who's been declared persona non grata, the bearded fellow, 'Lawrence of Arabia'? With a Pakistani wife?

Durrani: Yes, yes, Michael Semple. He is an Irishman.

Dulat: Well-informed about that area. I asked him at that Berlin meeting if it was worth talking to Zaeef. And he said, yes, Zaeef's stationed in Kabul to listen and report.

Durrani: On India's Afghanistan policy, Bhadrakumar, another man with considerable experience in regional affairs, is also worried. Indeed, it is an upshot of our bilateral rancour. In case Afghanistan settled down, Pakistan of course would be a huge beneficiary.

Whenever I tease the retired Indian diplomats during our Track-II encounters that they were still in Kautilyan mode, the violent reaction clearly indicates that one had touched a raw nerve—unki dum par paer aa gaya. Using Afghanistan to needle Pakistan is absolutely in line with 'a neighbour's neighbour' concept, first floated by Chanakya. They lose no opportunity to tell the Afghans that their problems were with no one except with Pakistan: 'they want you as their fifth province'. I've been dealing with Afghanistan for the last 25 years, directly or indirectly, and no one in his right mind ever talked about the fifth province. We have enough problems with the existing four.

One of your former foreign secretaries is indeed the master of the craft. He has repeatedly told the Afghans: 'You have ruled over us for 200 years (or was it 400?), so we have no problem with you; only these Pakistanis vainly believe that they were the real inheritors of the Muslim rule over India.' Regardless of the reality, this approach works better with the Afghans. We may have done them a favour or merely fulfilled a good neighbourly obligation by hosting millions of Afghan refugees, but when we demand gratefulness from them, all our investment goes down the drain. I'm waiting for another refugee influx—Taliban, Daesh, or hunger-driven—to make up for our previous deficits as hosts.

Dulat: Thinking Pakistan can be wished away from Afghanistan is like Pakistan thinking we have no role in Nepal. Afghanistan is as crucial to Pakistan as Nepal is to us. If Pakistan were to meddle in Nepal, it would be a matter of concern. I served in Kathmandu for four years, and always looked at Nepal as a country very close to us. But even that relationship of late is not so great.

Durrani: When I was the ambassador at Riyadh and I visited Yemen, which I remember often after the Saudi misadventure, I was well looked after in the Taj hotels in Sanaa. There were all Indians and they said, ambassador from Pakistan is here.

Sinha: India has no policy-making on Afghanistan?

Dulat: It has been too dependent on American policy. As long as the Americans are there, we're fine. We never believed the Americans would start withdrawing. If Trump were to say, okay, out, then India would get a shock.

Durrani: India has created autonomous assets. Media to some extent, journalism to a large extent. Herat culturally, since it is distant.

Dulat: India has every right to try and build influence in Afghanistan, the way you are free to try and build influence in Nepal or Sri Lanka.

Durrani: Policy-wise they may be keeping a couple of cards up their sleeve, but on the whole, Indian policy in Afghanistan is neighbour's neighbour...

Dulat: Enemy's enemy is my friend?

Durrani: To return to the Trump administration, there's no change in its Afghan policy. None. Previously Obama spoke softly and the stick was delivered by the minions he sent across, the Secretary of State and the Generals, etc., who came and read us the riot act. The same message comes across loudly now because it comes from the President.

The core of the actual policy in Afghanistan remains: keep the bases. The way they're built, as underground fortresses or silos. They've spent billions on these huge fortresses, and the idea is to hang on to them because they'll never get another chance in Afghanistan, a place that armies have historically crossed through. Geopolitics terms it 'the heartland'. It provides the ability to influence developments around Afghanistan, in Pakistan, in China, in Iran, and in Central Asia, all important places. This is the world's best nodal point.

For America the rest doesn't matter: Iran, Afghanistan, Panjsher Valley, whether there's peace in and around Helmand. So long as you are there and you have a client in Kabul and a friend in Delhi, it'll be all right. That is the policy, and I don't see any change.

Sinha: Tillerson spoke of an enhanced role for India, and a century of Indo-US partnership.

Durrani: India has a role, and space was provided, not by the US but because of India's clout, culture, financial assistance. America's ability to provide an enhanced role is a scam we have suffered. Yes. It can't even provide an enhanced role to its friends in Kabul. They remain confined in their fortresses. If anyone expects India will send boots on the ground because of Trump's desire, the Indians are too clever to get militarily involved. It would start a downward trend in India-Afghan relations.

Dulat: It's interesting and makes sense that the Americans play carrot-and-stick, I'm sure General Saheb is right. I also see no change in American policy. The only difference is General Saheb looking at those deep-dug bases, that's no policy at all.

I sense the Americans have been desperate to talk to the Taliban but don't know how to get there. I've been to London twice (in the summer of 2017) and I think they'll use the Brits much more in Afghanistan. The Brits are sharper, more experienced, in dealing with these things. Even in their own country they deal with these problems better than the Americans do. The CIA and MI6 have this thing where what we can't do you please do for us.

The boss is wrong in underestimating Pakistan. The Americans know you can't move in Afghanistan without Pakistan's help. I don't know how they've become India's buddies when there is a long-standing US-Pakistan relationship. In a sense, the Pakistanis have the Americans by the balls.

The sad part is many have said that India's strength lies in its soft power. When we try to be muscular or demonstrate our hard power, we are missing a trick. Somebody said the most important thing is your smart power. By not using our smart power, we get the worst out of Pakistan.

Durrani: About bases being no policy, hope also isn't a policy. Ultimately the message must be that things can happen. True, there's no point in spreading doom and gloom. That's why people are eager to listen to Mr Dulat when he speaks on anything, on Kashmir, on Pakistan or on India, his book is all about these themes.

But if you ask me why this is the policy, for me there just might be a rationale. The US is the only world power with a truly global reach, not just with money but also militarily. It is a country like no other. China is in a different class and plays things differently. India is certainly a power and plays things differently.

America also knows in which regions it can't exercise the influence it wants to. Europeans are willing allies, some unwilling. India has an alliance of convenience with the US. But the Middle East and Central Asia, with Pakistan and Afghanistan at their junction, are regions where American influence has some serious limitations—acceptance, for example.

Even in a NATO ally like Turkey, 95 per cent of Turks are historically anti-American policy, not anti-America. For a long time in every poll, 80-90 per cent Pakistanis did not like American policy, even though they wanted to go and work in America. Like the Afghans who spew venom against us but want to come and work in Pakistan.

Ever since America became the sole superpower, has it not preferred confrontation over a negotiated settlement in these areas?

In Afghanistan, Taliban wanted to reconcile with America, and in 2002 made the first move. Each effort by the Taliban to reach out and each effort made by Pakistan to facilitate it was spurned. Rumsfeld refused. Obama wanted an exit policy and negotiated settlement, but the Deep State subverted it.

The latest occasion where the effort was to reconcile Kabul and the Taliban came after the first Murree meeting. Then (Afghan intelligence chief Rahmatullah) Nabil revealed that Mullah Omar had died two years earlier but the news was under wraps in the interest of the Taliban unity. That was around July 30, 2015, just before the second round, which got scuttled.

Then Mullah Akhtar Mansoor, the man who had sent Taliban delegates to Doha, on record, who sent the delegates for the first

Murree round on July 7, 2015, who took over after Mullah Omar's death was announced, and was getting ready to bring the Taliban to the table again. Instead, on May 21, 2016, he was eliminated by an American drone. Negotiations once again stalled.

It's quite clear that the US will not allow a negotiated settlement in Kabul. Ashraf Ghani has no constituency and virtually no choice but to submit to Washington. Karzai, Sayyaf, Dostum and others are confident of their position, and therefore they don't mind a settlement. The US does, because it is only in conditions of conflict that it can play one country or a faction against the other(s).

Turmoil also helps the US in another crucial area. If there's peace in Central Asia, the minerals can be exploited by China, which is close by, the Russians who have influence, and India has cultural influence, even India because of historical and, in due course, reasons of proximity. America has none of this. In the New Great Game, America loses—if there's peace.

Dulat: You have been a believer, and I'm a follower in this, that without talking to the Taliban there is no other way. But I don't believe the American policy in Afghanistan is just to dig holes and stay there. If it is, and Indian policy in Afghanistan is so dependent on American policy, then it's sad.

I learned from you and Rustam Shah,[6] who's a great believer in Afghanistan, that the only way out was reconciliation. What other way is there? This civil war will continue endlessly unless the main party is involved. The Talibs are prepared to take everyone on board provided the goras get the hell out.

Durrani: No disagreement on that. It's the core condition. You make a commitment to leave, we'll sort out the rest.

Dulat: Mullah Zaeef told me, we know how to do it, we'll get the Tadjiks, Uzbeks, everybody in it.

28

Donald Trump, Nudger-in-chief

A.S. Dulat: I'll tell you of my experience of the American role in India-Pakistan relations. How much do they nudge both sides, how often is it done? If they tell you something would you do it?

In the PMO this was a question I was asked—even, intriguingly, by Americans: Are you guys pressurised in any way? I said, I've never felt that anybody in the PMO was under pressure or that the Americans were putting pressure.

My job was different, and pressure might have come on Brajesh Mishra, if anybody, not me. But the nudging happened occasionally. Sahay and Ehsan acknowledge it, saying that when the 2003 ceasefire took place and they met, there was an American hand.

I got a lot of messages asking why we didn't talk to the Pakistanis. I said to Brajesh Mishra: 'Why don't we give it a try? So many are suggesting it.'

He said, 'Nahin, abhi time nahin hain, abhi ruko.'

My only direct evidence was when Cofer Black, the director of the CIA's counter-terrorism centre, visited Delhi. He had come to meet Brajesh Mishra, who passed him along to me. As usual, the RAW gave a presentation. He said, 'I want five minutes alone with you.'

We went and had a cup of tea. 'We're putting pressure on the Pakistanis to behave, so we hope you won't do anything silly,' he said.

'No we don't do those things,' I said. 'Only the Pakis do those things.'

Then it's okay, he said.

I was thinking of it in the context of Modiji's visit to Raiwind. Could it be that in his hug with Barack, Obama may have said why don't you go hug Mian Saheb?

How much of this happens according to you?

Asad Durrani: It happens probably all the time.

Dulat: All the time. Ah. That's what I wanted to hear.

Durrani: All the time. They are pressuring, requesting, suggesting. It goes on forever. But that's not the important thing.

Dulat: I know your 'buts', Sir! It means it doesn't affect us one bit.

Durrani: Essentially it is about the state of our country and our leader's bent of mind. Some can take pressure, others succumb. But whenever it affected our core interests, our core policies, we always resisted, and succeeded.

An example of managing pressure was President Ghulam Ishaq Khan, who would not even concede what had already been done in the nuclear programme. Jo banana tha, that had already been completed. And he would still say: 'No, we will not even cap it, there is no question of going back.' This is the hard ball that one plays.

Aditya Sinha: If Trump withdraws from the world, how does a strategic partnership work for India?

Dulat: Even now it's not working to any great advantage.

Durrani: I give Mr Dulat credit that he said Trump is likely to win the election. I was wishy-washy about it though I wanted him to win, because he was one of those who could shake up the establishment. The establishments in the US, Pakistan and India are usually working for their own good rather than for the good of their public. Shaking them up might not be a bad idea.

Two, I considered Hillary Clinton a known disaster. Get rid of the known disaster and even if the other option was to be a bigger disaster. At least that's not known yet.

It soon became certain he would also be a known and established disaster.

Dulat: The day the results were out, General Saheb called me. It was an interesting conversation. Frankly I was disappointed with the result. But he said, 'Good result. For both of us.' I replied, yes absolutely. Good for you has to be good for us.

My hunch was because I was in London when the Brexit vote[1] happened. It surprised the Brits and shook up London. What the countryside or the North voted is another matter. If (David) Cameron could be defeated in a referendum that wasn't needed, it made sense that Trump could be elected.

My question to General Saheb would be, how do you propose to deal with Trump? Whichever way he plays it there will be pressure on Pakistan. The targets will be terrorism in general and the Haqqani network, etc., whatever specifically they have in mind. Possibly that pressure will do Pakistan no harm because when you deliver on or focus on something that they want, you'll also get something in return.

There might be pressure on us as well, logically. Pakistan is bound to say, what about those guys? That's how it usually happens. Will Trump appoint another Holbrook? Has he got a General in mind? When Holbrook was appointed, India was a part of his beat. We protested and said no, how do we come into this, this is AfPak. So India was left out, but who knows what might happen this time. The guy's nuts, no doubt about that.

Sinha: But Trump doesn't operate according to old templates.

Dulat: It'll be both known and unknown. On our side people are gung-ho. Prime Minister Modi in particular thought his own buddy was in place, somebody much like him.

Trump appointed a businessman as Secretary of State, a pleasant fellow apparently. That might be fine because Mr Modi may not have a problem dealing with a pleasant businessman. But there are also tough Generals in the team, and that's where Pakistan will have an advantage, ultimately.

These Generals have worked in Afghanistan, so there's a theory that they know what Pakistan is up to, etc. But we also know that for years Pakistan has had a good relationship with the Pentagon. (Secretary of Defence James) Mattis was Centcom chief, so he's known to Pakistan.

South Block forgets that traditionally there is a special relationship between the Pentagon and the Pakistani military. That relationship is still there and still solid. When George Tenet visited Pakistan soon after Musharraf took over, whatever message he might have carried he also went because there was once again a General in command.

Durrani: If Trump doesn't deliver on his disengagement from foreign military ventures, or with doing things differently, it would increase chaos, disorder, confusion and internal strife in the US and with the allies. Sceptically seen, that's all right for us because it means no more big brotherly attitude.

With the Generals it can play both ways. They know of our problems in Afghanistan and why we can't do openly what is asked, which over time some have recognised. Mattis served in Afghanistan, and I expect him to continue playing double games: you're helping us, you're not helping us. I've understood the whys and the limits of their pressure, and the limit of what we can do.

I don't think this type of relationship is forever, but I hope ASD is right and the American Generals have a sympathetic view of Pakistan, not just because of our past relationship but also from a realistic assessment of the AfPak situation. In their system, however, good cops are always followed by bad cops.

Yes, ultimately there will be pressure. But others can only pressure you to the extent that you allow them. If you don't, beyond sound and fury, what can they actually do? A few bombs here and a few drones there. In 2011 and 2012 we stopped their ground line of communication, the Americans returned to the table to work out an arrangement.

Dulat: Pakistan knows how to build a relationship with the Americans, it's been doing so for long, it knows the American weaknesses.

Pakistan is also able to hand over someone like Osama bin Laden and then get as many dollars as they want in return. That, again, excites India. Something like that will happen, and it won't be one-sided.

This is our problem. Everything looks hunky-dory but we're not too good when it comes to a relationship. Now we're supposed to have a special relationship. What have we gained out of it? In the bargain you've screwed up your relationship with the Russians, there is none with the Chinese, and there's no great relationship with any neighbour.

We're supposed to have a strategic relationship with the US. Probably what the Americans have in mind is that India will provide a counterbalance to China. This also is wishful thinking. Because (a) we're not in a position to do so, and (b) no government in Delhi would offend the Chinese beyond a point. They won't play proxy for somebody else.

Sinha: What if there is a major terrorist attack on US soil, what would Trump do with regard to Pakistan?

Durrani: If it originates in Pakistan his response will be drastic. To come and bomb a few places can even be choreographed; it's possible that India is asked to tighten the screws on Pakistan. They can cut off aid whenever they want. I suppose they know that no country can be held completely responsible. After 9/11 the Saudis were not attacked, though there was political pressure on them behind the scenes.

An invasion or spectacular attack is usually against a weak and indefensible country that can't retaliate. What can Pakistan do? We need not talk about that. But seeing the power that Pakistan has within the country and region, I doubt an Afghanistan-type attack will take place. A few bombs here and there we'd expect.

A disengagement also lowers the possibility of a terrorist attack. Of the few Americans focussed on the subcontinent, a few go overboard on the subject of a possible terrorist strike whose roots are traced to Pakistan. They talk of making Pakistan a no longer functioning state. Not only is that idiotic, it means Afghanistan and Iraq may not be terribly functioning but they ceased to be properly functioning states. I believe Pakistan can weather a possible storm, but the point is to put a worldly fear in our heart.

Dulat: I used to often say to the Americans, enough is enough, why don't you put pressure on the Pakis? They would reply, we do put pressure but there's only X amount we can do. Beyond that, we're helpless.

Durrani: True, and therefore I believe there is a big fallacy in Pakistan, that the US can get our issues with India resolved. Because even if the Americans were to be serious and sincere, if Delhi tells them to buzz off they will.

Dulat: You're right but I can't imagine anyone in Delhi telling the Americans to buzz off.

Durrani: You don't say it like that.

Dulat: Because we haven't had the kind of relationship with the Americans that you had. We think we have a special relationship, so I don't think Modiji would say buzz off.

Durrani: Buzz off is not said in that way, what is said is…

Dulat: Sir, he will not say that talks and terror don't go together. That he will say to you. That's what I'm trying to say.

Durrani: He will say many things to Trump but essentially it will mean, depending on how he says it, thank you very much for all your concern.

Dulat: If you think that Prime Minister Modi thought Barack Obama was a buddy, he now thinks Donald Trump will be a bigger buddy. So how would he resist or deny him anything?

Durrani: By saying, you are a great friend, thank you very much, and now that you have told us we must work hard. Foreign secretary, begin work on what the President says and let me know what screws we can tighten on Pakistan. In Musharraf's case, for example, the pressure put on him after 9/11 amounted to: you'd better behave and cooperate. He wanted to, but he knew there would be flak back home. So he made up a story. What could I do? I was threatened; Pakistan was to be bombed; the Kashmir cause was in danger; our nuclear assets would have been taken out; and our economy was in ruins. That's why I accepted it.

Of course, he was not threatened in that sense.

Dulat: He was read the riot act publicly. Bush said, either you're with us or against us.

Durrani: Yes, but it was also expected that along with cooperating, Musharraf would negotiate some of their demands. A couple accepted, a couple denied, and the rest negotiated. That's how it should have happened.

Dulat: But as you mentioned, the first casualty was General Mehmud. The Americans said he's bad news, off with his head!

Durrani: Bilkul theek hai, correct.

Sinha: Will Trump do a deal with the Taliban?

Durrani: His people will. Mattis is supposed to be sensible and has been putting pressure on Pakistan and the Taliban for the past ten years. They will try and find a way without saying they had succumbed to the Taliban.

Dulat: The Americans have been talking to the Taliban.

Durrani: All the time.

Dulat: If Trump thinks talking to the Taliban has been the right policy then being a doer he'll say let's get down to business. Do the deal. What is it that they want, and what is it that we want?

Sinha: He can sell it easily as a deal-maker.

Dulat: Trump sees himself as a deal-maker, so at the start I wondered: would the deals be made through the Generals, or by his daughter and son-in-law? If you have a son-in-law as advisor, it's an advantage and a disadvantage, so it depends on how it pans out.

Durrani: I'm not aware of anyone who does not make deals. Even the Pakistanis make deals.

Dulat: Even the Israelis. Everyone makes deals.

Durrani: Trump as a deal-maker may want a business-like deal, it isn't about business-like deals. It is about negotiating hard, public threats, conveying other messages.

Dulat: For America, though, it's easier to nudge Pakistan, because when required to deliver, you deliver.

We're able to explain the nudging as a success of our diplomacy, that, see, we got the Americans to intervene. But the fact is, a nudge is a nudge.

Durrani: Post-9/11 we tried to deliver but found nothing was good enough. They always demanded more, even if it was against our national interest or beyond our capability.

But the Indians will not even make a symbolic gesture. No pressure on India will come from the US.

Dulat: If Pakistan is being nudged, then logically India will be nudged. Pakistan is bound to say: What the heck, why don't you tell the Indians? Look at what they're up to in Kashmir. Why are you blaming us? If there is increase in turmoil, it is the Indians who are in control, and they refuse to talk to anyone. They think they are a breed apart, because of their relationship with you.

Sinha: What would be the Americans' interest or role in Kashmir?

Durrani: They show an interest in every possible place, but their ability to contribute anything in Kashmir is limited. One, they can't do anything. They have often failed to arm-twist Pakistan. They can't make India do what India doesn't want. Two, God forbid we ever got into war and accepted the US as mediator. They will favour India.

Dulat: Whatever interest the Americans had in Kashmir, and there was a lot of American coming and going in the 1990s, it all stopped after 9/11. That was a game-changer, something as serious as Pearl Harbour. It shook the Americans up. Even the jargon on terrorism changed. Freedom fighters became terrorists. The US ambassador in New Delhi made it a point to say nobody from the embassy visits Srinagar any longer. The same ambassador and one of his predecessors earlier made it a point to lunch with Shabir Shah on a houseboat, got him sacked from the Hurriyat.

My only difference with General Saheb here is what I heard from Kashmiris: that the Americans have the capacity to arm-twist Pakistan. But that may be an incorrect perception. I would generally agree that both India and Pakistan are beyond arm-twisting.

Durrani: In any case, we must remind ourselves that when we invite outsiders to mediate our disputes, the settlement would be in their favour and on their terms. Remember the fable of the monkey who was invited to broker a piece of cheese between two quarrelling cats, and ate all of it.

Dulat: I agree, the Americans are happy to see khatpat continuing between India and Pakistan. So the most positive way of seeing it is that there is much going for India-Pakistan to think together in the right direction. And I like what General Saheb said, that it would be on our terms.

Durrani: One should not forget Henry Kissinger's famous, most-quoted statement: being enemies with the US is dangerous, being friends is fatal. It's been proven in cases like Musharraf, Saddam, Mubarak, Shah of Iran, and it will continue. Even with Europeans, at times.

29
Pakistan's Pal, Putin

———————

Aditya Sinha: Can Russia play a role to help Pakistan and India move forward?

A.S. Dulat: Russians can, but they won't, whatever one knows of them and of the great Putin. He would be happy watching the tamasha.

We used to have a great relationship with Russia. I'd like to believe that there's still a relationship but I don't know. There have been Russian ambassadors who've served forever in Delhi. One died recently, (Alexander Mikhailovich) Kadakin, and most who stayed long had a KGB background. Kadakin had. Before him, Trubnikov had. Like Putin has.

Things began to change in Yeltsin's time. The Cold War warriors, as they were called, felt they were losing their importance. These old KGB guys were used to living in style, in dachas, etc., with luxuries and privileges. In Moscow, a lane in the middle of the road is reserved for these elitists. Only those with better cars can drive there.

The old Soviet Union went out of its way to support India, like in the '71 war. The relationship was best under Indira Gandhi. It may have slipped a bit with Rajiv Gandhi but even during Vajpayee's time it was good.

When I visited Moscow, Trubnikov was the intelligence chief and he said, how would you react to a Russia-India-China axis on intelligence? I said that it's a great idea; between us there's no problem, but how would the Chinese react? Trubnikov laughed and said: you leave the Chinese to us, just think of how the Pakistanis would react. We laughed and left it at that.

When I went to China, I mentioned it. The Chinese in their typical style said: 'Very good idea. We must examine it.' As if it had to be sent to the university for research.

The Russians always made much of our relationship. Trubnikov was in the Izvestia in Delhi, then years later he returned as ambassador; in between, he was the intelligence chief in Moscow. When Putin took over from Yeltsin, Trubnikov was kicked upstairs and made minister of state in the foreign office. He visited Delhi and I was in the RAW. I said, chief, you've become supreme chief, how does it feel? He said it didn't feel good, it wasn't the real thing.

Trubnikov visited Delhi as intelligence chief and was keen to meet Vajpayee. I told him, Vajpayee doesn't meet intelligence chiefs. He said, have you forgotten I took you to meet Putin? You have to tell Vajpayee you knew me and interviewed me when I was with Izvestia. Vajpayee was kind enough and met Trubnikov, who was delighted.

What has gone wrong is that we have made so much of our relations with the Americans after the nuclear deal that the Russians feel as if we've forgotten them. With Putin in power, some say the most powerful man in the world, he's not going to be bullshitting. All right, if you think you have a special relationship with the Americans, we'll make friends with your friends.

Sinha: What was meeting the most powerful man like? Is Putin the only spook to head government?

Asad Durrani: Andropov.[1] Senior Bush.[2]

Dulat: Putin was prime minister. Quiet, correct and didn't say much. Trubnikov was interpreting, so out of 30 minutes, you're only talking for about ten-twelve minutes. What a special relationship we have, how much we value friendship with India, that kind of stuff.

What struck me in Moscow is how important power is. Trubnikov, despite being in the KGB, had become close to Yeltsin. One day in Delhi we were to have lunch at his hotel, the Taj. From the morning I got messages that Trubnikov had an upset stomach. At 1:30 I was told his stomach was better. When I got to the Taj I asked if he was all right. I'm fine, he said, today is Yeltsin's birthday and I had to speak to him before I spoke to you.

That's the thing with the Russians: they've always looked to where power is. The controls are important. In fact, Trubnikov asked me a peculiar question: Do you control the sale of armaments? I said no. Well, we do, you should too, buying and selling armaments should be under your control.

That's how powerful these guys are. Somewhat better, more effective than the CIA.

Sinha: How did you slip in, General Saheb, considering you bruised them in Afghanistan?

Dulat: There are no permanent friends or enemies in this business, Putin and Pakistan realised.

Durrani: ASD is a fascinating storyteller in the tradition of Qisa Khwani Bazaar in Peshawar or Alaf Laila in Baghdad. Incidentally, I also met Trubnikov at a Pugwash Conference in Astana that ASD was unfortunately unable to attend. Much to the discomfort of the Kabul regime's representatives, Trubnikov supported the Pakistani narrative in the India-Pakistan-Afghanistan session.

We in Pakistan knew about the chemistry between the Soviets and the Indians from various accounts, including our Leftists (surkhas) like Ibrahim Jalees, who offered to buy Raj Kapoor a round of drinks in Moscow. Raj Kapoor declined, saying he had plenty of money in that country because his films were popular in Russia. Incidentally, his films were also popular in pre-revolution Iran, and in Afghanistan they act as a force multiplier against us. I also recall watching a film with Prithviraj Kapoor on a river cruise up north and crossing path with a Russian ship. The film was famous for its lead song.

We had a problematic relationship with the Soviet Union because, to offset the advantage of our bigger neighbour, we joined the Western bloc. After the '65 war, when the Soviet Union played mediator at Tashkent, our relations were on the mend; but then we played bridge between the US and China in 1971, and of course they opposed us in the '71 war.

The Soviet invasion of Afghanistan in 1979 pitched us against each other like never before, and after the Soviets withdrew across the Oxus and then their empire unravelled, there was naturally rancour against Pakistan, even though we helped their troops withdraw.

But nothing is forever. Moscow has recovered. It has made up with China and revived the old Shanghai Five[3] to provide equilibrium against the sole superpower. After 9/11, with a powerful Western alliance sitting in the heart of Asia, it found more allies in the region. Other developments in the Middle East made Russia reach out to Pakistan, and the ISI responded positively. With India seen as closer to the US, it could not block closer Russia-Pakistan relations.

The relationship has evolved over the past decade, and I have been a beneficiary. During two visits for mega-non-proliferation conferences in Moscow in 2012 and 2017, I gave my views on the New Great Game. Right during the first visit, I could sense that our bilateral relations were on the mend.

Dulat: One other thing that's important to the Russians has been the Congress party relationship. The Congress was in power for so long in India that there is a natural friendship. Now, the Congress has become more of a centrist party. The bilateral relationship is a message to the Congress party on where it is headed, what it stands for.

No matter how big Modiji is, the Russians would feel uncomfortable. What General Saheb was saying coincides with our US nuclear deal. The communists didn't support that deal, and Sonia

Gandhi had strong reservations for a while because she didn't want to antagonise them.

All this has impacted our relationship. How India fits into Putin's thinking is difficult to say, except it's not that cosy a relationship. That's obvious.

Durrani: When invited to conferences, there were only four places where I was able to take my wife along. To Delhi in 2004 because we didn't want to miss the chance of seeing the Taj Mahal. Then the Dead Sea in Jordan, where she first met the Dulats. In December 2016 we went to Uzbekistan, on the invitation of the ambassador, where even my wife got a lady translator. Presumably that was for our historical, ideological, intellectual and lately our geopolitical links.

Twice my wife went to Russia on the insistence of my hosts. On both occasions my talks at the civil and military universities found a surprisingly enthusiastic audience. It gave me the rare opportunity to impress my wife.

Incidentally, on no occasion in Russia did anyone show interest in India-Pakistan acrimony. Unlike the Americans who take pleasure in pitting countries against one another, the Russians seemed pained that we went for each other's jugular.

Sinha: You passed on an article by a Russian academic/expert about the CPEC, which has emerged for India as a matter of concern. The article itself was positive and saw Pakistan as the fulcrum of various relationships.

Durrani: I was pleasantly surprised in 2015 when I received these two articles. One was by Andrew Korybko at the Russian Institute for Strategic Studies. His take on Pakistan is positive, no doubt about that. The other was by Polina Tikhonova, a London-based writer who took us by surprise by saying there's a new superpower axis emerging, of China, Russia and Pakistan. She also mentioned Iran in due course.

Over the last few years I felt that these four countries were trying to create an understanding amongst themselves. The articles took a more optimistic view than any of us would. And no, they're not hired by the ISI, which isn't in a position to hire such people.

Sinha: General Saheb, tell us about your most recent Russia visit (just before our final session).

Durrani: The Russians were keen to talk to me. They invited me for a nuclear conference in 2012, but before that we met in Dubai and it was made clear the nuclear conference was a cover, for they wanted to discuss post-Soviet Afghanistan. This time when I was invited I asked to see St Petersburg as well, and they arranged a talk at Petersburg State University which Putin attended. The university is alma mater to the majority of Nobel Prize-winning Russians.

I gave a talk, came to Moscow, attended a nuclear conference but spent more time talking to the Afghan hands at the military university. Foreign Minister Sergey Lavrov was there. I might also point out that while Pakistan had the third largest delegation at the nuclear mega-conferences after the Russians and the Americans, both in 2012 and in 2017, India was represented by a single delegate. On the first one, it was Lieutenant General V.R. Raghavan, who ran a think-tank. Marvellous man, sound professional, and useful to talk to. This time India sent someone from the foreign office.

Dulat: The General said a lot of meaningful things, and I can't help reiterating that in Afghanistan we've lost the plot.

Putin is the world's big toughie with a muscular policy, that we'll show you what we will do; that's how he keeps testing Trump. He takes great pride in it, he recorded congratulating his intelligence officers. He's even congratulated Russian illegals who live around the world. He's maybe a variation of Modi.

Durrani: True. Putin has played his cards well. America has helped him regain muscle. He was getting unpopular domestically. Even in Petersburg, his home constituency, they didn't seem too happy with him.

Dulat: People are opposed to him but no one is challenging him.

Durrani: The opportunity to regain popularity came when he annexed Crimea. Ukraine and Crimea are of premier importance not only historically but since many Russians are there. It helped Russia gain influence in the Levant, to the extent that even the Turks, after they shot down a Russian plane,[4] patched up. Putin has played his cards so well that he is regaining ground amongst his own people as well.

Dulat: During Yeltsin's time many of these old KGB hands mellowed. But Putin hasn't. It may not be called the KGB, but his boys are still around for both muscle and dirty tricks.

Durrani: True.

Sinha: Xi Jinping in 2017 consolidated power for another five years. China has ambitious plans for the future. Putin is merely trying to recapture past glory. Isn't Xi actually the world's most powerful man?

Dulat: I can't disagree with that. The Russians and Chinese have a good relationship and understand each other well. The difference is that the Chinese are not in a hurry. Xi is looking ahead and has planned lots of things. With Putin it is now, today, yesterday, tomorrow. I'm going to make things happen now. He's all over the world; look at Syria. The situation is such that even the Americans realise that unless we cooperate with the Russians, we can't move in Syria. You can't put boots on the ground, the Russians are in control. And because of Russia-Iran relations, the Iranian spread has become more noticeable in Iraq, Syria, the Gulf. Suddenly, Trump is threatening them again.

Durrani: China and Russia play their cards carefully. They don't become euphoric because today they are on one platform, and they don't become hostile. Their reactions are slow. I don't think the two of them ever trusted each other. But their interests coincide to the extent that now, it's not only SCO but bilaterally too they don't want to split. They won't act as we do, immediately bringing our swords out. Even if they have reservations they take their time, otherwise America would get a foot in the door.

Sinha: So India-Pakistan should be more like Russia-China.

Durrani: Yes, why not? Easy and relaxed, patient, do not on the second day come out with a big statement and then retract soon thereafter. This is what we do.

Incidentally, the theme of the non-nuclear conference I attended was North Korea.

Dulat: I was just about to say that North Korea is doing whatever it is doing because it knows that behind them are the Russians and Chinese.

VII

LOOKING AHEAD

The final chapters look at the various ways to break the impasse between India and Pakistan. The two former chiefs have differing approaches: Dulat favours confidence-building measures while Durrani favours durable structures for a long-term breakthrough. The wildest ideas are discussed; these are so out-of-the-box that hawks in both countries may feel surprised. In conclusion, there is one unmistakable point of agreement: that the madness between the two nations must end.

Setting the scene

Bangkok, October 30, 2017: The last session of our discussions wraps things up on a positive note (and we even meet an intriguing Russian gentleman), so we celebrate with lunch and then some Thai ice cream.

30

Forge Structure or Break Ice?

———

(Note: For a way forward, both former chiefs were asked to submit a roadmap. These are reproduced first, followed by the discussions.)

A.S. Dulat:

- Encourage/facilitate people-to-people contact.
- Ease visa regime—consider visa-on-arrival not only at airports but at Wagah as well.
- Increase flights to Lahore/Islamabad/Karachi from Delhi/Mumbai.
- Encourage cultural, arts, literary, sports meets.
- Cricket could be resumed between India and Pakistan in a third country, if necessary. Pakistani players could be included in IPL. Former cricketers/commentators spend time in India, so why not youngsters?
- Greater Punjab-to-Punjab interaction/trade.
- Confidence-building gestures—why is MFN held up when it was a done deal?
- Increased communication by opening/softening borders.

- Kashmir gets priority in confidence-building in trade, currency, banking.
- Kashmir should be addressed first; terrorism, low-hanging fruit like Siachen, Sir Creek, etc. would automatically follow.
- Let's talk, both Indo-Pak and India-Kashmir, without one-upmanship.
- Foreign secretary-level talks and more importantly NSAs, intelligence chiefs, army chiefs should meet, institutionally. As there's no dialogue—why not invite Ajit Doval?
- Intelligence cooperation would be a confidence booster—let the station chiefs be open posts in both countries.
- Facilitate regional cooperation—SAARC must consider revival of the Gujral Doctrine.
- We could consider cooperation in even international forums. Our Muslim population ought to give weight in Islamic forums.
- Open media on both sides. More Indian cinema. More Pakistani actors in Bollywood.

Asad Durrani:
- Formalise the 'on-again off-again' back channel. It should be hidden from the public limelight.
- Instead of a confidant of each prime minister, a team headed by someone considered suitable by the major political parties, the foreign office and the military (to ensure their long-term relevance). He should select a small team with expertise on foreign, security and regional affairs.
- Its primary tasks would include regular communication with the other side, exchange of ideas on crisis/conflict management, establishing rapport to gain the confidence of decision/opinion makers, and pre-empt/prevent panic reactions by either side.
- In a bad situation—e.g., the Mumbai attack—the team should make imaginative new suggestions on which the two countries could cooperate—e.g., a hydel project in Kashmir or on

Afghanistan—to assure both sides that detractors did not have a handle on the process.

- In crisis situations it should prevent any harmful moves that may be seen as politically expedient.

- Conceptually, it isn't different from the conventional wisdom of tasking wise-men to arbitrate between conflicting parties. It can be considered a modified version of OSCE,[1] a Cold War body created to prevent conflicts in Europe which had representatives from both sides of the East-West divide. All countries including the Warsaw Pact gave it the mandate to act as mediator. It can also be considered a manageable form of the traditional Jirga that used to facilitate reconciliation between squabbling parties.

- If it is well selected, has relevant support, and kept intact over time both to learn the ropes as well as establish trust with the other side, this body could evolve an incremental process to move from conflict management to conflict resolution.

- The members must not promise too much, score brownie points, or seek the limelight.

- This body's most important attribute would be to not be stuck in an ingrained approach or preconceived objective; and it should calibrate its assessment to evolving circumstances.

Durrani: Like a military man I have given a structured answer.

Dulat: Structures have screwed us, Sir.

Durrani: Simply saying we should do this-that has not helped. You may ask, how? What's the way? The way is in a concrete construct, and a mock-up. We've done it before.

Dulat: You're right, while you have provided these models I've talked of gestures, and you'll tell me that I've come back to my bloody gestures. You have to break the ice somewhere. This bloody ice is so solid that you need to take people by surprise. That's why at the time I gave full marks to Modi, although some in Pakistan, including you, called it gimmickry and called him circus-man.

I said full marks, he had the gumption to go to Raiwind. The Pakistan media was gung-ho.

Durrani: Woh toh paagal hain.

Dulat: Hum sab paagal hain.

Durrani: Look at the structure suggested. It's not for the first time, but not ancient either. I don't say that after five or ten or 20,000 years of human history we can come up with something novel. I've suggested it in Afghanistan, in Doha during the US-Muslim World dialogue. In India-Pakistan's case, faceless people are behind the scenes, preferably as advisors to chief executives, whose ears and confidence they hold. And they can also reach out to the other side.

Dulat: Would you then advocate that instead of our six-member dialogue, we reduce it to two?

Durrani: In a wargame you can have two or four, that does not matter; the people and their role is important.

Dulat: Why don't you take the gestures seriously?

Durrani: It needs a context. After Mumbai, for example, when both governments were stuck, I sympathised with the Indian government over what should they do. Even with best intentions and the best leadership in Delhi, they can't say forget about Mumbai and get on with Pakistan. That's when this group gets into action, communicate, and say that the environment is such that no visible movement is possible. However, let's think of something not diversionary but at least another track on which to start moving.

For instance, at the time someone could have suggested, since Kashmir is an issue as is terrorism, why not a joint project in

Kashmir, to benefit Kashmiris and downstream Pakistanis? It would have lowered temperatures a bit, and provided you another talking point.

Call it a fire brigade, call it wise-men behind-the-scenes to keep matters on track and prevent the process from derailment. Instead of an out-of-box solution, I say out-of-box arrangement. In tribal society this is the way of resolving things, though their conflicts are more serious; they're deadly and go on for hundreds of years. Yet when reconciliation happens it's because of two-three people, with credibility on both sides, who can reach out in both directions and prevent things from getting out of hand.

An international example is one that the Saudis led, though I'm no great fan of how they handled Yemen. Post-9/11, the focus is on terrorism, Afghanistan and the Middle East. Prince Abdullah,[2] who later became King, said four weeks after 9/11: We should be prepared to recognise Israel provided this-that, etc. It was nothing new, but unbelievably for many months people talked of his formula. He sprung it at the right time, created the right effect, defused pressure on the kingdom and put pressure on America and Israel.

Dulat: So why don't you accept my suggestion and invite Ajit Doval to Lahore?

Durrani: I'm not making that gesture, not for Ajit. I'll be happy if someone else does but right now the ball is in your court.

Dulat: It's the same thing when we say we'll play hockey, not cricket. And we've played hockey. But the whole world now plays cricket with Pakistan amid terrorist and security threats. But we are cussed about it: why should we play cricket with Pakistan, of all people?

Likewise, General Saheb says, why should we invite Ajit Doval? The psyche is the same. Why should I do anything for that so-and-so?

Durrani: This is dependent on a person and I'm talking of a permanent structure in which no new leader will come and disband it. They may change personnel but not destroy the citadel. That body or system is institutionalised.

Dulat: So you would suggest someone like Sati Lambah?

Durrani: Sati Lambah should serve for as long as he's creative, constructive. Once he runs out of ideas and is close to 70+, bring another man. He's not there for perpetuity, the structure is. The changeover doesn't take place in one go. We have suggested it to our own government, not India-related, but establishment-related.

Aditya Sinha: You spoke about doing things away from the limelight. But in India one needs public support behind a policy. If you suddenly spring something on them, will it work?

Dulat: It will if you have faith in it. Before Vajpayee took the bus to Lahore he didn't publicise it. He just decided and took along a lot of people including Milkha Singh, Kapil Dev, Dev Anand; as if every Punjabi was taken to Lahore.

Durrani: You work out a conclusion or a provision and then think of how to get the feedback. That strategy should also be up to this group. If you put it to the public or media before finalising anything, you can be certain some of them will shout, 'sell-out of falana, a reversal, now a U-turn'.

Sinha: It sounds like a perpetuation of status quo for the next 50-100 years.

Dulat: I'm not at all for perpetuation of the status quo. I'm saying one must do something.

Durrani: It's not going to be easy to break the status quo. Probably each of us is suggesting that yesterday's status quo need not be tomorrow's, which may look better.

Sinha: It could still be a stable stalemate.

Dulat: And it could also look worse.

Sinha: Let's talk about your list.

Dulat: General Saheb's suggested a way to do it, whereas I've said these are easy things that should be done.

For instance, in March 2014 when Abdul Basit had just arrived, I said, 'High Commissioner, I hope you're bringing good tidings from Islamabad.' He said, yes, good news was in the offing. I heard it was the announcement of the MFN. But the BJP got into the act, and some businessmen went to Lahore and Islamabad, and this thing was stalled. It still hasn't happened. Now our guys in Delhi say, what's the big deal about MFN? We don't need it.

There's a cussedness here but the question is, if it was a done deal in 2014, then why has it still not happened? Yet this is typical of India-Pakistan, sadly.

My list is a list. It has basic things that are easy.

Like facilitating people-to-people contacts. We keep talking about it but it doesn't happen because even getting a visa is painful. At one time it was suggested that senior citizens get visa-on-arrival. These would be great if Pakistani senior citizens, on arrival in Delhi or Mumbai or at Wagah, would get a visa. And vice versa.

Now flights have almost totally stopped. Even when there was a PIA flight, it was just a PIA flight. The high commissioner said he talked to Jet and to Indigo and they're ready to fly. But nothing happens.

Sinha: What's the stumbling block on flights?

Dulat: Cussedness. If Air India doesn't fly, why should Jet or Indigo? It's rubbish, nothing more.

Sinha: Your list gives us a profound sense of the cussedness. They're all so do-able.

Dulat: And they've been talked about umpteen times. But never done.

Interestingly, if a Kashmiri wants a visa like any other Indian he won't get it in a hurry. But if Geelani Saheb or the Mirwaiz recommend a visa, it'll come through. My wife can possibly get a visa easily, but I may not.

Sinha: You can always go to Geelani Saheb for a recommendation.

Dulat: Someone actually suggested that. I said: 'Shaayad hume visa na mile.' He said: 'Hum dila denge Geelani Saheb se bolenge. Unki sifarish se ho jayega.' It's as mad as that.

Sinha: Cricket teams don't even play.

Dulat: Yes, it has to be resumed. If the Brits and Australians can feel secure, what's so special about us? If we feel that insecure, why don't we play Pakistan in England? Or in Abu Dhabi?

Sinha: They held a T20 league match in Lahore without incident. People joked there was more security than spectators, but they did it.

Dulat: Yes. If we hesitate going to Lahore or Karachi, what's the problem in inviting the Pakistan team to India? They're prepared to come.

Now we've had this circus called IPL on for the past seven years, and there are some outstanding Pakistani cricketers who'd be great entertainers. Afridi has probably retired, but people come out especially to watch him bat. But such players aren't included in the IPL. What's the reason? The reason is cussedness: Why should a Pakistani make money?

The irony is some senior Pakistani cricketers live in India almost all the time, like Zaheer Abbas, who's married to an Indian. Or commentators like Wasim Akram and Rameez Raja. Wasim Akram even manages the Kolkata Knight Riders. If they can be around, then why not youngsters? And some of them are exciting players.

Sinha: Why the cussedness?

Dulat: Who knows? If you sat a German friend of General Saheb's and a Frenchman here and let them listen to this, they'd be astounded.

Then why can't we open or soften the borders? We have borders in Punjab, Rajasthan and Gujarat, and all could be considered for easier movement of people.

I suggested Kashmir be given priority in confidence-building. Mufti Saheb had suggested a common currency.[3] A common currency would make banking important. People don't realise that the J&K Bank has been an asset not only in Kashmir but other parts of India as well. One thing I learned after the UP elections was that one reason for backwardness among Muslims is that no banks are available in Muslim localities. Banking is a big problem.

Sinha: So are you saying the State Bank of Pakistan should come and open branches in India?

Dulat: And the J&K Bank in POK. I agree with General Saheb that the starting point should be Kashmir. Let's sit down and talk Kashmir. There needs to be an India-Pakistan dialogue, an India-Kashmir dialogue, and a Pakistan-Kashmir dialogue. Like what happened informally during Vajpayee's time.

Then the more formal diplomatic talks. Foreign secretary-level talks, General Saheb's favourite composite dialogue. Why should it not be revived? But set that aside for now since we aren't talking at all, and whatever is happening is between the NSAs, in a hush-hush manner.

General Saheb has mentioned how we should go about it. For me, the starting point would be that let Doval go to Lahore. When civility returns, the next special guest at our Republic Day should be the prime minister of Pakistan. In fact, the Pakistan prime minister should be a regular guest in Delhi. When the weather's good, he should be having lunch with Modiji at Hyderabad House.

SAARC has been stalled and should be revived. The Gujral Doctrine needs to be taken into consideration.

If the relationship got going we could even consider cooperation at the international level. It's often forgotten that our Muslim population is, what, second in the world? So why shouldn't India be a member of the OIC?

Sinha: India has never been invited?

Durrani: Once.[4] Pakistan objected. We said, why India? This conference is for Muslims and they'll have a turbaned Sikh sitting here.

Dulat: If you can have turbaned Muslims then why not a poor turbaned Sikh?

Durrani: Funny things were said, but the idea was that we would not let India stall us in this forum.

Dulat: Last was the opening of the media. We can't watch Pakistani TV though they can watch Indian TV. Even that has dropped of late. Bollywood films are popular in Pakistan, as is Indian music. Pakistan has good actors and some were coming to Bombay. Now it's been stopped.

People at large would appreciate cooperation in this. Our higher society's most hawkish love Pakistani serials.

Sinha: The additional problem is that whoever wants to do these things has to prepare public opinion.

Dulat: That's why what General Saheb has written is important, because he says let's not make it public, let's do it quietly.

Sinha: General Saheb's turn.

Durrani: That these things don't happen has been discussed so often that I take it for granted that for now, these good ideas won't make an impression on the decision-makers. There must be hurdles, and these begin with the bureaucracy. They are by training nit-pickers. They play safe. In our environment, it pays to play hawkish. And they forever look over their shoulders—at their own colleagues, who are ready to bring down anyone going 'soft' on the arch-adversary.

Still, the decision has to be taken by the political leadership. Manmohan Singh, even with his heart in the right place, was vulnerable to flak from his political opponents, the media, and his own peers. We could get lucky and get another Vajpayee, who could overrule the establishment, though even he could be scuttled by implementers, or fall victim to developments on our side.

To illustrate the system, Sharat Sabharwal, who had the good of the region at heart, had a talk in Islamabad a few months before he left. I asked him about the Gujral Doctrine. Let me just say that whatever his answer was would not have caused problems in his hierarchy.

That's why we've spoken of a process away from the limelight. It would comprise people who would think of small yet substantive steps that aren't vulnerable to the system's shenanigans. My favourite recipe is to create a council of wise-men: people of status who are patient, discreet and know the art of sounding out the right ear at the right moment.

Dulat: Peter Jones has done us a good turn while doing himself a good turn as well. There are three former intelligence officers from each side who sit down and have a good time. They carry back messages to their sides, because we have people who have this potential or capability.

So my suggestion is, suppose we reduced this to two each, and instead of doing it for Peter Jones we did it under the supervision of Ajit Doval or General Janjua.

Let's start quietly, addressing important issues that are acceptable to the two gentlemen. If something emerges it could be put out in the open, or to the prime ministers. Then we could have forward movement.

Durrani: It's certainly a good way of going about it, but this is one way. I agree that once we're back we can convey this message to our respective NSAs. It's a possibility.

Dulat: I'm not saying it's a possibility, I'm saying it's a possibility worth exploring.

Durrani: Trusted means trusted by Ajit Doval.

Dulat: Trusted people for Ajit Doval, people that Ajit may trust.

Durrani: And Janjua appoints two whom he trusts. I'm sure Ehsan will be one of them. I'll be happy if my name comes up, but he can suggest others.

Dulat: Once we've made a beginning with the two NSAs, and when they have two lieutenants each, they can temporarily rope in experts for specific subjects. Both countries have no dearth of experts.

Durrani: There are too many.

31

Council of Spies

———

Aditya Sinha: Intelligence agencies operate in 'grey' areas. Other government departments have defined dos and don'ts. How does this fit into your idea for intelligence cooperation?

A.S. Dulat: We do talk from time to time, so why shouldn't it be institutionalised when we talk to everybody else in the world? You always seem to have issues with your neighbours, especially Pakistan, so why not talk to Pakistan?

They also have this big issue, terrorism, which by itself calls for cooperation or at least institutional interaction. Because when you sit down the first thing you say is let's talk about terrorism: what are you guys up to? If that be the case, should we not be doing it on a regular basis? Someone would have some explaining to do, but interacting makes it easier to simplify things.

I've been pleading that the station chiefs in Islamabad and Delhi should be declared open posts. That would make it easier for the gentleman to ask for meetings and interact more easily. These things, in this day and age, are known, who's who. Every intelligence agency has officers in embassies which aren't declared open, so the open post could be the station chief or his/her number two.

From the Indian point of view our chap has a tough time in Islamabad, where the surveillance is far more aggressive than it is in Delhi. Some of them end up doing nothing. So why have an officer in Islamabad if he's doesn't achieve anything? By the same logic, not many want to go to Islamabad though our best officers should be going there.

General Saheb and I in our paper did mention the grey areas. Many things can be done that aren't in the open glare and aren't immediately accountable, though with political backing; we don't have autonomy though the ISI might. Would you agree with me?

Asad Durrani: Absolutely. The more complex the situation, the more is the need for this. These are the only people who can, at a moment in difficult conditions, ensure some sanity.

There are problems, however, of sharing or cooperating in the field of intelligence, even within a country. Not only because you want to take credit for a certain operation, but at times you're not sure whether one should share doubtful intelligence with others. It would be embarrassing and also mislead the other party.

But it is in that critical field where cooperation would help against certain groups that are out to derail any efforts at peace. It would be better than the cooperation given to so-called friends.

Dulat: The reality is that a lot of what goes wrong, and terrorism, does come from Pakistan. But if we have an understanding or interaction between the agencies, then this would be easier to handle. Let us say the ISI runs or maintains the Lashkar. They may not hand over Hafiz Saeed but if we were cooperating, other things could happen.

Sinha: Like what?

Dulat: Imagine whatever you like, it's not difficult.

We earlier spoke of liaison with foreign services. The important point that General Saheb made is that while you have great liaison and have long analyses of things, rarely does an agency share anything worthwhile or operational. On the other hand, the way we function in South Asia, it would be much easier to share this kind of information and help one another.

If the US had got a hold of Kulbhushan Jadhav, for instance, it might be impossible to get him back. It's not so difficult from Pakistan. A senior RAW officer defected[1] to the US in 2004, and we have no trace of him though some say he's living on a farm in Virginia or even dead. It might seem ironic but with Pakistan it would have been easier to get him back.

Durrani: I agree with my friend that Jadhav would eventually be back, despite the poor handling of his case by us. A better way would have been to send a message to the RAW that we had him, extract all the overt and covert benefits, and at some stage return him 'at the right price'.

Sinha: If there can be intelligence cooperation then why not just end the use of terror? Why not just stop Lashkar in your territory? Why not just hand over Hafiz Saeed? Or is it just a lubricant for when things get hot?

Dulat: It's not a lubricant, but it would help when things get hot. Hafiz Saeed is an extreme case and I don't think Pakistan would hand him over.

With cooperation we could sit down and say, why are we taking terrorism or infiltration, etc. so far? Why can't we contain it or stop it? Keep it to a certain level. In 2003 India and Pakistan agreed to a ceasefire. Both C.D. Sahay and Ehsan ul Haq claimed their two meetings brought the heat down on the border.

In an institutional arrangement, the station chiefs in both capitals would be open posts. The ISI officer in the high commission in Delhi would be known and in regular communication with the RAW or IB chiefs. Or with Ajit Doval.

When you are in regular communication, a lot of things are possible. Today we can't even get a visa. I've been to Pakistan four times and it never occurred that I may not get one. Recently I feel that I may not get it. General Saheb was keen to visit Delhi in the winter and wanted an invite. I spoke to colleagues and they said the time now is not right. It's an unfortunate atmosphere.

Durrani: We know their guy and they know ours, so open posts for contact makes sense.

Dulat: Open posts will clear a lot of air.

Durrani: True. In the case of Hafiz Saeed, for example, we may come to an effective understanding and then let the court solve the problem. There are others like his case that are less complicated.

Dulat: There's Masood Azhar. Every time his name comes up in our discussions, Ehsan immediately says Masood Azhar is wanted but not traceable. If true, here's a prominent militant wanted by both Pakistan and India. This would be a natural case for cooperation. Even if Pakistan did not transport him to Delhi, once they had him, someone from IB could go and talk to him. It should not be a big problem.

These things can happen once you have confidence.

Durrani: True, it would also be important in that China would stop vetoing the action on Masood Azhar at the UN. If he was wanted by both of us and we provided joint direction, it would no longer be an issue. China does the veto as a favour to Pakistan but I'm sure it feels embarrassed by it.

Dulat: As a result of our not talking or cooperating, when the Pakistanis and Chinese get together they bitch about India, and when India and the Americans get together they bitch about Pakistan. We all think we're buddies, that we have a great relationship with the US, that Pakistan has an all-weather relationship with China, not realising that our own relationship could be the best relationship of all.

Durrani: Yes. It's pathetic at times when reasonable countries like ours invoke the big brother card in our relationship.

Dulat: They wouldn't then be desperate for an all-weather friendship.

Durrani: It could be done without changing any policy. You needn't say Kashmir is no longer in the limelight. It can continue to remain whatever status you prefer.

Dulat: Instead we have an impasse when six officers from the Pakistan High Commission were sent home, and five-six from ours were sent home as well. The Americans and Russians were good at this during the Cold War but they still never stopped talking.

Talking makes more sense than not talking, however adverse the circumstances. In fact, the more adverse the circumstances, the more reason for talking. If Uri happened, as General Saheb earlier said, we would talk about a surgical strike. Due to this lack of communication and understanding, the media pounced on it, saying now we have the capability to blow Muzaffarabad up, etc.

Durrani: I agree, on both sides the people managing the surgical strike could have given statements to keep tempers down. The Falklands war is a good example. England goes some 18,000 km and takes back the islands from Argentina. Well done. Afterwards, the English said, it's over and there's nothing more to be done, no compensation, end of episode. They didn't want to rub it in so that it would flare up again ten years later. This is the mature way to settle it, but we would not.

In the case of Jadhav, it's pathetic how much shouting from the rooftops there was, as if it was a cricketing victory. We just cannot contain ourselves. I have no good words for our media, at least yours is better organised.

Dulat: Our media is worse than yours.

Sinha: Maybe it's something in our common DNA that makes us too emotional.

Dulat: When we had problems in Punjab and then in Kashmir, there was cooperation from the agencies, more in relation to Punjab. It happens if it suits both sides or whoever is giving the information. In the case of 26/11, the Americans provided us intelligence but nothing happened. When did they provide it? What did they provide? Why was no action taken?

The guy involved in this operation, David Headley, was working for the ISI, he was working for the Americans; and when he lands in jail in the US, he confesses. These inputs obviously didn't figure in whatever was given to or shared with us.

Tell me General Saheb, when the Mumbai attack happened and it was announced that the DG ISI would go to India, why did he not come?

Durrani: I don't know the details, but it was a silly statement by Zardari that the army should send the DG ISI. All he had to do was tell the chief he wanted to make this statement; the chief would have agreed and then sent someone suitable. If you mention the DG ISI, all attention would focus on him. Then it becomes a precedent for every such incident.

Dulat: So all Zardari or Gilani had to say was we are sending our intelligence chief.

Durrani: Intelligence chief would mean the head of ISI.

Dulat: Not necessarily.

Durrani: The IB chief or the DG…

Dulat: His number two, three, etc.

Sinha: A missed opportunity.

32

Akhand Bharat Confederation Doctrine

A.S. Dulat: I'm an optimist and I say you can't give up on this. Otherwise there's hopelessness: just sit back and say, forget it, nothing can happen. You were asking about the status quo for the next 20 years, but we'll remain like this the next 100 years because we are destined to remain us.

General Saheb says we can't rise to this occasion, but you can't give up trying. Vajpayee always said: this madness cannot go on indefinitely. I can say, having watched closely for five years, that Vajpayee had more problems during his time than Manmohan Singh or Modi did. Yet despite that, Vajpayee continued to try and move forward.

One must keep trying, and the most basic way of doing this is that you never stop talking. Even if it is to abuse each other.

Asad Durrani: Your description of madness is interesting. Now I know why you're good friends with Hamid Ansari. He said to me: 'Yeh deewangi kab khatam hogi.'

Dulat: When you said India-Pakistan can't rise to the occasion, it implies that neither country has gotten over the baggage of 1947. We

286

were one country. Why does the Punjabi get excited about people-to-people, etc.? Because there has been closeness, but it's the same baggage that weighs you down. 'Do you know what these fellows did in '47? How many people they killed? Do you know what happened to my family? Do you know what happened to my town? I had to leave all my property there. I couldn't bring my cart even. Hum toh kapron ke bagair aaye.'

This is the narrative that continues.

Durrani: But in Kashmir, it was started by Kashmiris. It had nothing to do with Punjab.

Dulat: It was started by Kashmiris where there had never been a riot. In 1947, Mahatma Gandhi said if there is an island of peace on the subcontinent, it is Kashmir.

Durrani: Nothing is forever. That's why I suggest that '47 may not be forever. For example, the Bengalis revolted against Pakistan, and people had said, oh yeh Bengali, yeh toh violent nahin hai. They can agitate or crib, but not be militant.

Aditya Sinha: General Saheb, can we discuss Gujral Saheb's approach to India-Pakistan relations?

Durrani: The Gujral Doctrine[1] had so much of sense in it: if you can't improve your relationship with every country then start with the smaller countries. And even with Pakistan you could start by improving relations at the lower levels: sub-regionalisation between the two Punjabs, the two Kashmirs and across the border.

One precedent is Bavaria and Austria, which are much closer than Germany and Austria. They're neighbours, they come and go. The Bavarian will even sometimes threaten Berlin that if you one day decide to change Bavaria's status from the State of Bavaria to another province of Germany, we'll join the Austrians, who we are more like anyway. It has brought Europe's neighbouring communities together.

Sub-regionalisation means giving autonomy to the two Punjabs, the two Kashmirs, etc. Aapas mein cricket, hockey khelni hai; even across the LoC put up a net and play volleyball. People are capable of coming up with things like this. Once they do, confidence comes and they say, we can live like this too.

But no one wants to even talk about Gujral's sub-regionalisation any more. Your Maharaja (Amarinder Singh) and Shahbaz Sharif were for a time doing the two Punjab thing without realising Gujral had suggested it.

It stopped on the Indian side because of the establishment's paranoia. Delhi might lose control over its border regions; the people would happily speak to each other in Punjabi or exchange Kashmiri dishes. The establishment fears giving them latitude, in their eyes even traders are unreliable, along with Christians, Kashmiris, Punjabis. They can never be trusted, they'll go out of control.

Dulat: He was talking SAARC or only India-Pakistan?

Durrani: My understanding is that the two Punjabs have more to do with each other, Sindh on our part and the areas bordering Sindh on your part.

Dulat: Yes, you could do that.

Durrani: Then the two parts of Kashmir. Without ruffling feathers if you start with that you ultimately find that the regions that have come closer to their counterparts produce a synergy. The bus could have synergised the process, but then: Huee mudatt ke mar gaya Ghalib, par yaad aata hai, woh har baat pey kehna, ke yoon hota to kya hota. That is what I understand about sub-regionalisation.

Dulat: The last time the Congress lost an election to the Akalis in Punjab, though the Maharaja was a good chief minister you could see he was going to lose. His admirers said, just open the border with Pakistan and he'll win hands down. Because he had done a lot for

Punjab-to-Punjab relations. He even came back with a horse from Shahbaz. There were inter-Punjab games. A lot happened.

Sinha: General Saheb has also been talking about Akhand Bharat.

Dulat: Akhand Bharat is a crazy, impractical idea. It has emanated from the extreme right, and at some stage Advaniji subscribed to it. The one who set it to rest was Vajpayee, during his visit to Pakistan in February 1999, when he visited the Minar-e-Pakistan.

The NDA after that didn't seriously talk about Akhand Bharat. But now we have a gang that is more to the right and has this obsession. I don't blame it entirely on Modiji and his adviser Amit Shah. It's a worldwide phenomenon, this mad obsession with nationalism.

Sinha: It's possibly an electoral card for the future.

Dulat: It is, but it is also that we are a great power. We're not the softies of the past. Modi is a different kind of prime minister.

Durrani: Akhand Bharat isn't a fantasy that nowadays some are thinking. Enough used to say M.A. Jinnah's uncompromising objective was not Pakistan, that he floated this idea to get the best deal for the Muslims when the British were leaving. He felt the best formula was maximum autonomy for the regions with a Muslim majority. This is essentially what *The Idea of Pakistan* by the best India-Pakistan hand in the US, Stephen Cohen, says. He says that the division of India was not inevitable.

Many people would call Partition a mistake, in that what did it gain for Muslims? In united India they were a big minority; would they have been threatened? Would they have been able to negotiate their position? Even minorities in Iraq, Bahrain or South Africa could not be oppressed.

Partition, or trifurcation, led to many problems: Bangladesh, the Kashmir problem. And now the countries are forever fighting, whereas if they did not, they could benefit from peace in Afghanistan, or the gas pipeline from Iran.

I mentioned the Tehelka dialogue I attended in London in 2008. The co-host was a Sikh restaurant owner who provided us dinner and also invited us to his own place. Marvellous hospitality. At one point, in my presence, he asked: 'Why don't you Pakistanis press home the fact that Jinnah accepted the Cabinet Plan?[2] Indeed, he was trying to prevent the violation of a united India. It's actually the Congress who created Pakistan, thinking it would not survive, jaana kidhar hain.'

I'm glad the credit of breaking India up still goes to the Indian National Congress.

Dulat: Maulana Abul Kalam also argued that Pakistan or Partition was not inevitable, in his book *India Wins Freedom*. He said our own leaders were responsible for Partition, that they were not fair to Jinnah. He did not want the extreme step, but that the Congress took a rigid position.

Sinha: Pakistani historian Ayesha Jalal says Jinnah was the sole spokesman for his people, trying to bargain the maximum gains for them within India.

Durrani: Partition led to certain problems but it isn't possible right away to do away with borders and create a united India. Pakistanis enjoy their independence and in a combined India would perhaps not be dependent but certainly would not be enjoying the same independence. You cannot undo history.

My idea was that if we understand the reservations on certain things, that we are trying to resolve through back channels, we can address them. We cannot go back to pre-1947 but we can gradually create a situation in which those concerns are addressed. We can also address the desire of those who say, Bharatmata ka pata nahin kya ho gaya.

So we create a situation in which all these requirements, not entirely but partially or predominantly, are met. Right now it's impossible to create a coalition or a union like the European Union, whose relevance is itself in doubt, but at some stage we can think of a common currency, or laws applicable to when we develop the new South Asian Union: a Confederation of South Asia.

We can do it at least as well as the Europeans have. If not, we can be content that some of our disputes are sorting out, and it benefits Punjab, Balochistan, Kashmir, Tamil Nadu, etc. This is thinking aloud, we might reach a common minimum consensus.

Maybe we're not ready for such a big project but we can work on its elements, by softening the India-Pakistan borders, as in Kashmir, and make them irrelevant over time. Then five or ten years later, we'll look at the next step.

Delhi as the capital of a Union. Armed forces integrated. Reduction of forces numbers by ratio. In a hundred years most of the demands of an Akhand Bharat may have been met.

The reason one should discuss this is to not rule out any possibility. For West Germans the reunification of East and West Germany did not seem possible in their lifetime.

The same corollary holds when I talk about a unified independent Kashmir. I know it's unpopular in both countries, probably more in India, it's a bigger political and sentimental issue. Pakistan has lived without it for 70 years, but you haven't, so how do you conceive of it?

I spoke of Amanullah Khan. I'm sorry I never gave enough thought to his idea of independence. Now I assess that if not a majority then certainly a considerable number of Kashmiris, possibly on both sides but certainly on your side, will say: 'Pakistan, aap logo ka locus standi kya hai, we've had enough of both of you, pox on both houses, we want independence.'

It's not possible, however.

Yet if there's a sentiment, why not war-game it? Now let's look at an independent Kashmir, on whose side will it stand or will it bounce between India and Pakistan? For the last 70 years it has been in India. They may likely say, no, we've suffered enough with India, we should see what we can do with Pakistan.

But what if it becomes a hub of international conspiracy? All this can be discussed. And when a discussion begins, questions and ideas will emerge. One day it may be an inescapable reality neither Islamabad nor Delhi will be able to resist.

Dulat: Though my idea of Akhand Bharat is different, I would endorse what he suggests. A union or federation between the two Punjabs—can you imagine? Maharaja Amarinder Singh ruling from Lahore? As a military man, his regret was that in '65 India didn't take Lahore. Today he would have other emotional or sentimental reasons for wanting Lahore.

Durrani: Jinnah's dreams did not materialise but he said, okay, if in the bargain this is what has happened, I'll take it. So Akhand Bharat walas would have to say this is not exactly what we wanted, but we'll take it.[3] It's not unprecedented.

In my own moments of madness I threaten some of my Indian interlocutors that Pakistan was prepared to rejoin and undo Partition, so that we can destroy India from within. They'll say, that's not what we mean by Akhand Bharat. Two persons won't have the same view. In any case, conventional wisdom is that you don't always get what you want.

By the way, what is their view of Akhand Bharat?

Sinha: Akhand Bharat extends from Persia to Indonesia, or something.

Dulat: The new Indian Caliphate.

Durrani: The poor Da'esh envisioned a Khorasan caliphate, but didn't get it. You ask for it and hope that you will get in its place— Sy-raq. Syria and Iraq.

Dulat: These sorts of things have been debated at the UN, where someone concluded that changing boundaries should not be encouraged.

Good old Musharraf and Dr Manmohan Singh talked along these lines. Musharraf may have had different reasons but he said, now you can't change boundaries. Dr Manmohan Singh endorsed that.

Durrani: There is debate on what they discussed, but the fact is, there is a constant adjustment of borders throughout history. Three years ago, Ukraine's internal borders changed, and Crimea was carved out. No one knows where the borders in the Levant will be. Don't forget Bangladesh. Sikkim's international borders disappeared.

To claim that we will not let this happen is nonsense. Boundaries change. Manmohan Singh once said that borders can't be rewritten in blood. It is a political statement that does not stand scrutiny because borders have always been rewritten in blood.

Dulat: No, they won't be rewritten in blood. When you're talking peace, as Manmohan Singh and Musharraf were trying to do, then it's not easy to redo these boundaries.

Durrani: Therefore, neither had a sense of history. Borders are drawn, redrawn, and re-redrawn. If you're trying to make peace, then at times peace will come if you agree to redraw borders.

My point is why aren't people even ready to discuss it, academically or theoretically? Today we do that and tomorrow it may become reality. If the situation is so tenuous that it can become reality then I rest my case.

Dulat: If you look at it realistically, then if Kashmir were to go, life for Muslims in the rest of India would be difficult. That is a reality that you have to face. Already some at the drop of a hat say, send him to Pakistan. If Kashmir were to go to Pakistan or become independent, a lot of people will say send this baggage along.

Durrani: This argument is made about the plight of Muslims but I don't think they can become hostage to the situation. The Kashmiris are paying the price.

Dulat: That's the unfortunate part. Kashmiris are not willing to pay the price, and Muslims in the rest of India are also not willing to pay a price for Kashmir. I've raised this matter with Indian Muslims and said, you guys debate many things but never about Kashmir. They are your co-brethren.

Durrani: Let me switch tack for a moment and talk about an independent Pashtunistan. There are twice the number of Pashtuns in Pakistan than in Afghanistan. The chances of an independent Pashtunistan are slim because all Afghans would choose to remain within Afghanistan's present boundaries, and Pashtuns virtually run my country. But if it happened, it would become a province of Pakistan with Peshawar, or even Kandahar, as its capital. I've always believed there were more chances of an Af-Pak confederation than an Indo-Pak one, the idea is 50 years old.

Dulat: What's the conclusion in all this? Akhand Bharat, no Bharat, independence for Kashmir?

Durrani: The conclusion is nothing is forever and it pays to keep an open mind.

Remember that Advani, when he visited Karachi (in June 2005) made conciliatory noises. Such a thing can set the stage. His party began breathing down his neck, that's another matter; but for us it became an example to follow.

Sinha: What specifically did he say?

Durrani: Not so much on cooperation but he had words of praise for Jinnah. Jaswant Singh's book on Jinnah made him a persona non grata in his party. But these people had the right idea, that's the important thing. We do not have to say, where will you start?

We start by addressing the humanitarian problem, which does not ruffle any feathers. No one has to change positions, that is important.

Dulat: I fully endorse the boss. In a sense it is a diluted version of Musharraf's four-point formula, which is a good way to start.

Sinha: Musharraf is now a fugitive.

Dulat: His ideas don't need to be fugitive.

Aziz Saheb is not here and these days he's in a different frame of mind, but I remember when he was high commissioner in Delhi, we discussed Kashmir umpteen times. He said: 'Why doesn't Delhi understand that if we meet the Hurriyat we're only helping you, because what we tell the Hurriyat is that it must talk to Delhi.'

Sinha: When it comes to dialogue, isn't the General looking for a way to keep the establishment on ice? Whereas you want the establishment to get into the act.

Dulat: I'm saying that the poor Kashmiri is so rattled that if you were to tell him to go ahead and do what you like, he won't believe it. He will say something's fishy.

Durrani: The establishment has to be involved because it will send the message that if you want to do something, go ahead. But being in the room during the process, that's not for the establishment.

Dulat: We wanted a stage to come, which had actually started, this coming and going, and trade. People in Kashmir were happy.

Durrani: These actually impede establishment goals. The establishment weighs whether each thing is more in favour of India or Pakistan, and that's where it applies brakes, refuses visas and permits.

Dulat: Is there an Amarkot in Sindh?

Durrani: Umerkot, yes, in Pakistani Sindh.

Dulat: It has a substantial Hindu community.

Durrani: True.

Dulat: Mainly Thakurs. One of our girls from Jaipur is married there and I met her father-in-law few years back in Delhi, a towering man with a booming voice. I almost said, Thakur Saheb, you need a silencer, you can be heard way down the corridors.

He said: We Hindus dominate that area as big lords. We have no problem. We celebrate Holi, Diwali, like in Rajasthan. All our leaders come, all PPP supporters.

What's India's problem? Why not settle?

Durrani: Jo cheez aaj na ho, woh ye na kahe ki kabhi na ho.

Dulat: I would love to meet Maharaja Amarinder Singh in Lahore. He would think he's following Maharaja Ranjit Singh.

Durrani: Who will accompany him as Maharani?

Dulat: Our Maharaja already has a Maharani.

33

Deewangi Khatam

—◆—

Asad Durrani: The idea behind my enthusiasm for this project is based on differing perceptions. Ever since my retirement I've been exposed to what people outside said, and how it differed from information I was privy to. I reflected on it. Sometimes it was very different and at times the variance was due to a deliberate twist or spin.

Whatever version people want to accept is not the problem. I just want to convey that this was how I saw things. People can take it or leave it.

Aditya Sinha: Well, we're hoping for reason to be a bit more optimistic.

A.S. Dulat: It's been a privilege talking, many a times arguing, with the General. It's been a great idea, we spent time together, we talked about things.

My only reason for getting involved in this is the same as being in Track-II: India-Pakistan relations. It may be just a dream but I believe, as Vajpayee used to believe, that this madness between India and Pakistan has to end. This book will be about that, and that in the India-Pakistan relationship, going forward, things will improve.

We've talked about a lot of things, but our main theme has been that India and Pakistan need to realise and get together because there is so much to be gained by understanding each other.

That's why we yapped about intelligence cooperation and we've given it a lot of time and focus. That's one of the main things. How important it is for people who are in a position to be constantly talking. Do you agree, Sir?

Durrani: Absolutely. This point about madness. I want to tell you of one episode. In 2015, we made a joint call on Hamid Ansari. I reached five minutes early. As soon as I did, hello, hello, the vice-president, a very fine man. His opening salvo was, 'Yeh deewangi kab khatam hogi?' Such a profound sentence, and a mandate for our book.

Dulat: That's exactly what I have stressed on throughout.

Sinha: From your discussions it seems, Dulat Saheb, that even more than the people of India and of Pakistan, you want to do something for the people of Kashmir.

Dulat: When I talked about the people of India and Pakistan, it includes the Kashmiris. Kashmir has always been in my mind, it's become an obsession. The theme of my last book was that there was no other way but to talk, and that is why I get elated whenever somebody is appointed to talk to the Kashmiris. It gives me hope.

Most of all, this book, when it is out, will excite Kashmiris. They hear, and word does travel from Istanbul or Bangkok or New York, etc., that these two madcaps are meeting and keep meeting, so something is up. Something is up between India and Pakistan. When they see photographs of the two of us together, or when they hear of the two of us together, they get excited.

Yes, one of the motivations is that this book is also about the Kashmiris.

Notes

1: 'Even if we were to write fiction, no one would believe us'

1. *Kashmir: The Vajpayee Years* by A.S. Dulat with Aditya Sinha, 2015, HarperCollins India, New Delhi.
2. The Pugwash Conferences on Science and World Affairs bring together academics and public experts to offer solutions on global security.
3. A US-sponsored security meeting of US, Indian and Pakistani retired officials, in Pakistan.
4. Foreign Secretary, India, 1995-97.
5. A Strategic Security Initiative focussed on India and Pakistan. This one was sponsored by the Jinnah Institute.
6. The guerrilla resistance which fought for Bangladesh's independence from Pakistan in 1971.
7. Vikram Sood, Secretary, RAW, 2001-03.
8. Also referred to as 26/11. On November 26, 2008, ten Lashkar-e-Toiba (LeT) terrorists came from Pakistan by sea and attacked several points in Mumbai. The attack ended after three days, leaving 164 dead and over 300 wounded.

9. Former diplomat and an academic at the University of Ottawa who organised the 'Intel Dialogue' meetings of retired intelligence chiefs from India and Pakistan.

10. Mufti Mohammad Sayeed (1936-2016): India's Union Home Minister (1989-90), Jammu & Kashmir chief minister (2002-05, 2015-16). Founded the People's Democratic Party (PDP).

11. Mehbooba Mufti, Chief Minister of J&K, daughter of Mufti Mohammad Sayeed.

12. Farooq Abdullah, Chief Minister of J&K (1982-84, 1986-90, 1996-2002). Son of J&K National Conference leader Sheikh Mohammad Abdullah.

2: The Accidental Spymaster

1. The Union of Soviet Socialist Republics (USSR) invaded Afghanistan at the request of the local communist regime in December 1979. The mujahideen resistance, supported by ISI, the USA and Saudi Arabia, forced the USSR to withdraw a decade later.

2. General Mohammad Zia-ul-Haq, military ruler of Pakistan (1977-88). He was killed in a plane explosion in August 1988.

3. Benazir Bhutto (1953-2007), former Prime Minister of Pakistan, head of the People's Party.

4: Pakistan's Deep State

1. See Chapter 26.

2. Agha Mohammad Yahya Khan (1917-80), Commander-in-Chief, Pakistan Army (1966-71); third President of Pakistan (1969-71).

3. Sheikh Mujibur Rehman (1920-75): The central figure behind Bangladesh's liberation from Pakistan.

4. Z.A. Bhutto (1928-79): Pakistani prime minister from 1973 to 1977, deposed in a military coup.

5. In July 2007, a confrontation developed between the Government of Pakistan and terrorists inside Islamabad's Lal Masjid. It took commandoes eight days to end the siege; the government claimed 154 militants, security personnel and civilians were killed.

6. On December 16, 2014, terrorists attacked the Army Public School in Peshawar, killing 141 including 132 schoolchildren.

7. DG, ISI, 1987-89.

8. Secretary, RAW, 1987-90. He and Gul met in Interlaken, Switzerland, to discuss Khalistan and Siachen.

9. *The Bear Trap: Defeat of a Superpower* (1992) by Mohammad Yousaf and Mark Adkin.

10. Akhtar Abdur Rahman Khan, DG, ISI, 1979-87. He perished in the same flight as General Zia-ul-Haq.

11. Amanullah Khan (1934-2016), one of the founders of the pro-independence Jammu & Kashmir Liberation Front, the group that started the 1989 militant insurgency against India.

12. To mark in protest the day in 1947 when India sent troops to Kashmir after J&K ruler Hari Singh signed an instrument of accession. Pakistan would stop the protest at the Line of Control whenever it happened.

13. Actually, on November 3, 1988, the Maldives experienced an attempted coup d'etat. President Abdul Gayoom requested India's help, and the Indian Army foiled the coup attempt.

14. Prime Minister of India, 1984-89.

15. Nepal and India's negotiations on a transit treaty broke down at the same time, leading to the embargo.

16. J.N. Dixit (1936-2005), High Commissioner to Pakistan (1989-91), Foreign Secretary (1991-94), National Security Advisor (2004-05).

17. Abdul Qadeer Khan, father of Pakistan's nuclear programme, dismissed after the US suspected his involvement in a nuclear components' black market.

5: ISI Vs RAW

1. Indira Gandhi (1917-84): Prime Minister of India, 1966-77, 1980-84.

2. Independent India's 2nd Director, Intelligence Bureau (1950-1964).

3. Ram Nath Kao (1918-2002): Founder and Secretary (1968-77) of the Research & Analysis Wing.

4. Director, IB (1987-89, 1991-92); National Security Advisor (2005-10); Governor, West Bengal (2010-14).

5. Director, IB (2004-05); NSA (2014—current).

6. All Parties Hurriyat Conference was a 30-plus conglomerate of Kashmiri separatist groups, formed in 1993.

7. Dawood Ibrahim, fugitive wanted by India for the 1993 serial bomb blasts in Mumbai which claimed 257 lives and over 700 injured. He is on the FBI's 'world's ten most wanted' list.

8. Chief of the Jama'at-ud-Da'wah, co-founder of the Lashkar-e-Toiba. The USA has a bounty on his head for masterminding the 2008 Mumbai attack.

9. Founder and chief of the Jaish-e-Mohammed, Maulana Masood Azhar was one of the terrorists freed by India in exchange for the passengers held hostage by the hijackers of flight IC-814. India holds him responsible for the 2001 Parliament attack, and the 2016 attack on the air force base in Pathankot, Punjab.

10. Hizb-ul Mujahideen, the pro-Pakistan terrorist group in Kashmir. It took over the separatist movement from the pro-independence JKLF in 1990.

11. See Chapter 6.

12. Shyamal Datta, Director IB.

13. Field Marshal Mohammad Ayub Khan (1907-74): President of Pakistan (1958-69).

6: The CIA and Other Agencies

1. USA Deputy NSA (1989-91); Director of Central Intelligence (1991-93); Secretary of Defense (2006-11).

2. Vladimir V. Putin, KGB officer (1975-91); President of Russia (2000-08, 2012-current); Prime Minister (1999-2000, 2008-12).

3. A series of terrorist attacks took place in London on July 7, 2005, killing 52 and injuring over 700.

4. On March 22, 2017, a terrorist drove a vehicle into pedestrians near Westminster, London, killing four and injuring over 50.

5. James Woolsey, Director of Central Intelligence (1993-95).

6. *Shariah: The Threat to America*, 2010.

7. Leon Panetta, Director CIA (2009-11), Secretary of Defense (2011-13).

8. George Tenet, Director of Central Intelligence (1996-2004).

7: The Intelligence Dialogues

1. Gauri Shankar Bajpai, Secretary, RAW (1990-91).
2. C.D. Sahay met Lt Gen Ehsan-ul Haq; P.K. Hormis Tharakan met Lt Gen Ashfaq Pervez Kayani.
3. General Mahmud Ahmed, DG, ISI (1999-2001), took over after Musharraf's coup, was transferred out after 9/11.
4. See Chapter 15.
5. End-January 2017, Intel Dialogue in Bangkok, Thailand.
6. C.D. Sahay, Secretary, RAW, 2003-05.
7. Former IB Special Director, served in Kashmir as additional director, 2000-02.
8. October 2017.

8: Status Quo

1. See Chapter 15.
2. The ruling alliance in J&K since March 2015.
3. Burhan Muzaffar Wani was a 21-year-old Kashmiri militant commander of the Hizbul Mujahideen, whose death in an encounter with security forces in July 2016 led to several months of unrest. Over 100 residents were killed and thousands injured by pellet-shots.
4. Chief Minister of J&K (2009-15), son of Farooq Abdullah, grandson of Sheikh Abdullah.
5. In June 1961, US President John F. Kennedy and Soviet Premier Nikita Khrushchev went for 'a walk in the woods', alone with interpreters, to defuse a crisis over Berlin. Two months later, construction of the Berlin wall began.

9: The Core K-word

1. Capt. Liddell-Hart's 1920 paper on the Expanding Torrent System of Attack: Like flowing water, an attacking army looks for a breach against a defence of depth. That breach is widened as the penetration is deepened, by automatically progressive steps, enlarging the deployment.

2. The Heart of Asia—Istanbul Process is an annual discussion between Afghanistan and its neighbours. On December 3-4, 2016, it was held in Amritsar, India. In his statement, Afghan President Ashraf Ghani said: 'Taliban insurgency would not last a month if it lost its sanctuary in neighbouring Pakistan.'

10: Amanullah Gilgiti's Dreams of Independence

1. Syed Mohammed Yusuf Shah, contested the 1987 J&K assembly election from Srinagar, then headed Hizbul Mujahideen from the other side of the LoC.
2. Sardar Mohammed Abdul Qayyum Khan (1924-2015). For much of the post-1947 period he was either Prime Minister or President of Pakistan-administered Kashmir.
3. J&K's socio-religious organisation that favoured Kashmir accession to Pakistan and was thus able to take the post-1989 movement over from the pro-independence J&K Liberation Front (JKLF).
4. Article 370 of the Constitution of India guarantees J&K special status, with certain exclusive rights, such as on state residentship.
5. One of the early leaders of the JKLF in Kashmir, charged with murdering Indian Air Force personnel in 1990.
6. Ravindra Mhatre was a 48-year-old Indian diplomat kidnapped and murdered by the JKLF in Birmingham, UK, in 1984.
7. Mirza Afzal Beg was a key lieutenant of Sheikh Abdullah. He formed the Plebiscite Front after his leader's removal (as J&K prime minister) and arrest in 1953.
8. Syed Ali Shah Geelani is the seniormost Kashmiri separatist. He was for long the head of the J&K Jamaat-e-Islami. He was also thrice a state legislator from Sopore.

11: Kashmir: The Modi Years

1. The J&K assembly has 87 seats, so 44 meant a majority for government formation.
2. In April 2017, assembly elections in Uttar Pradesh produced a three-fourths majority for the BJP, and a government was formed under religious hardliner Yogi Adityanath.

3. Rex Tillerson, US Secretary of State, 2017.
4. Jammu is the winter capital of J&K from November to April. The other six months, the darbar moves to Srinagar.
5. Professor Abdul Ghani Butt is a leading founder-member of the All Parties Hurriyat Conference.

13: Take What You Can Get

1. The negotiations took place at Camp David, hosted by US President Bill Clinton. Arafat has been blamed for its failure as he made no counter-offer to Barak's concessions.
2. In March 628 (6 AH), this treaty called for a ten-year peace and authorised 'The First Pilgrimage'. It was significant in the formation of Islam.

14: India and Pakistan: 'Almost' Friends

1. Lalu Prasad, Indian Railways Minister (2004-09), Bihar Chief Minister (1990-97).
2. L.K. Advani, Deputy Prime Minister of India (2002-04).
3. On December 24, 1999, IC 814 from Kathmandu to Delhi was hijacked. One hostage was killed, the others released in Kandahar, Afghanistan, on December 31, in exchange for three terrorists lodged in Indian jails.
4. India and Pakistan agreed to a bus service between Delhi and Lahore. The first bus arrived in Lahore on February 20, 1998 with Vajpayee on board.
5. In early 1999, Pakistan infiltrated armed personnel into the Kargil heights overlooking the Srinagar-Leh highway. It led to a military conflict from May to July 1999, when Pakistan withdrew. Also see Chapter 21.
6. Vajpayee and Musharraf had a summit on July 14-16, 2001. It produced no agreement, however.
7. Lt Gen (retd) Naseer Khan Janjua, NSA, Pakistan, 2015-current.
8. In the midst of civilian agitation over the death of Burhan Wani, on September 18, 2016, four terrorists attacked an Indian army brigade camp, killing 19 soldiers. Eleven days later, India quietly conducted

a surgical strike on suspected terrorist camps on the other side of the Line of Control in Kashmir.

15: Lonely Pervez Musharraf

1. Lt Gen M.L. Chibber headed Northern Command of the Indian Army.
2. Lt Gen (retd) Iftikhar Ali Khan, Pakistan Secretary of Defence (1997-99).
3. Lt Gen (retd) Sikander Afzal was DG (analysis), ISI, in the mid-2000s. He was initially part of the Ottawa process.

16: Modi's Surprise Moves

1. Sujatha Singh. After the Modi-Sharif meeting she stated that India expected Pakistan to prevent terrorism and show progress in the trial on the 2008 Mumbai attack.
2. Nepal hosted a SAARC summit in November 2014, where Modi and Sharif, amidst tense relations, shook hands.
3. Modi and Sharif stayed at the same hotel in New York during the UN General Assembly in September 2015, but did not meet.
4. Modi stopped in Pakistan on December 25, 2015, on the way back from Russia to India. During a stopover in Kabul Modi informed Pakistan of his proposal for a brief visit. It was Sharif's birthday and the two leaders proceeded to Sharif's Raiwind Palace for Sharif's granddaughter's wedding.
5. Burhan Wani's death in July; Uri attack in September; surgical strike across the LoC announced in October.
6. Modi criticised Pakistan for fomenting terrorism in the region, in a speech at Dhaka University in June 2015.
7. On the way back from Russia and before he landed in Lahore, in December 2015, Modi stopped in Kabul where he criticised Pakistan for its role in terrorism in the region.

17: The Doval Doctrine

1. India's first Consul-General in Karachi, 1978-82, later joined the Congress party, served as minister in different governments.

2. John le Carré, 2017.

3. In April 2016, the Ananta Aspen Centre organised a Track-II with six former Pakistan high commissioners and nine former Indian high commissioners in Delhi. The group also met various functionaries and dignitaries.

4. Lambah was Prime Minister Manmohan Singh's special envoy to Pakistan, 2004-13. He was High Commissioner to Pakistan, 1992-95.

5. Bangkok, end-October 2017.

18: The Hardliners

1. Government of India building on Raisina Hill in New Delhi, housing the foreign office, the defence ministry and the Prime Minister's Office.

2. Bangkok, October 2017.

19: BB, Mian Saheb and Abbasi

1. Rajiv Gandhi visited in July 1989. He had already been to Islamabad once in November 1988 for a SAARC summit.

2. This is from the session in Bangkok in October 2017, before the November siege of Islamabad by the religious right.

3. Imran Khan Niazi, former international cricketer, head of the Pakistan Tehreek-e-Insaf, member of Pakistan's National Assembly.

4. Mohammed Shehbaz Sharif, chief minister of Punjab (2013-current).

20: Good Vibrations, India-Pakistan

1. India conducted nuclear tests on May 11 and 13, 1998. Pakistan conducted tests on May 28 and 30, 1998.

2. A city in Gujrat district, Punjab, Pakistan.

3. Field Marshal Sam Hormusji Framji Jamshedji Manekshaw, 1914-2008, Indian Army chief during the '71 war.

4. Morarji Desai is the only Indian to be bestowed the Nishan-e-Pakistan. It was conferred by President Ghulam Ishaq Khan in 1990.

21: Hafiz Saeed and 26/11

1. Hafiz Saeed founded the LeT and is amir of the JuD.
2. This part of the conversation took place during February 1-3, 2017, in Bangkok.
3. He was released on November 24, 2017.
4. The report of the UK inquiry into the 2003 Iraq invasion, published in 2016, found Tony Blair guilty of exaggerating the threat posed by Saddam Hussein and of going to war before exhausting all peace options.

22: Kulbhushan Jadhav

1. On March 3, 2016, Jadhav, an ex-naval officer, was either arrested in Balochistan or snatched from Iran. Pakistan said he was from RAW and charged him with aiding the Baloch insurgency. India denied this. Pakistani authorities released a video in which Jadhav confessed to espionage. India said it was made under duress. Pakistan sentenced him to death on April 10, 2017. The International Court of Justice stayed the execution on May 18, 2017.
2. By India's NSA in New Delhi. See Chapter 17.
3. Son of assassinated Punjab Governor Salman Taseer. Shahbaz was kidnapped in August 2011 and was recovered from Balochistan four and a half years later, on March 8, 2016.
4. Malik Mumtaz Hussain Qadri, Salman Taseer's bodyguard who shot the Punjab Governor in January 2011. Shahbaz was a witness in the trial. Qadri was sentenced to death and hanged in February 2016.
5. List of insurgencies: 1948, 1958-59, 1962-63, 1973-77, 2003-current, though the intensity waned after 2008.
6. Mullah Omar's successor as Supreme Leader of the Taliban. See Chapter 27.
7. See Chapter 17.
8. A member of the Baloch Regi tribe, Rigi was captured and executed by Iran in June 2010.
9. An agreement was almost reached at the Egyptian resort in July 2009 between Prime Ministers Manmohan Singh and Syed Yusuf Raza Gilani.

23: Talks and Terror

1. Former US assistant Secretary of State for South Asian Affairs, who in 1993 became unpopular in India.
2. Islamic State of Iraq and Syria, also known as IS (Islamic State) or Da'esh (in Arabic) or ISIL.
3. Tehrik-i-Taliban, Pakistan: a pro-Taliban umbrella group of anti-State terrorists operating along the Afghanistan border.
4. Donald Rumsfeld, Secretary of Defense (2001-06), author of *Known and Unknown: A Memoir*, 2011.
5. *The Meadow* by Adrian Levy and Cathy Scott-Clark, 2012.
6. Mahmud Ali Durrani was NSA, Pakistan, 2008-09.
7. BJP president during 1991-93. He undertook an 'Ekta Yatra' to Srinagar in 1992, when militancy was at a peak.

24: Surgical Strike

1. See Chapter 1.
2. In January 7, 2013, after a confrontation just inside the border near Mendhar, two Indian soldiers were beheaded.
3. As defined by Air Commodore Jasjit Singh, the sheer existence of nuclear weapons with both adversaries imposes major limitations on the way force and violence can be used against each other without risking a nuclear war.

26: The Deal for Osama bin Laden

1. Osama bin Laden, head of al Qaeda, was killed in a raid by US Navy SEAL commandoes at his house in Abbottabad, Pakistan, on May 1, 2011.
2. Vali Reza Nasr was senior advisor (2009-11) to Richard Holbrooke, Obama's special envoy for AfPak. His book *The Dispensable Nation: American Foreign Policy in Retreat* goes into how Holbrooke and team unsuccessfully pushed for a peace plan (involving the Taliban) to end the war in Afghanistan.
3. US officials who met Kayani in April 2011: Centcom chief General James Mattis on April 8; Chairman of the Joint Chiefs of Staff Admiral

Mike Mullen on April 20; US commander for Afghanistan General David Petraeus on April 26. On April 28, President Obama signed orders for Petraeus to be the next CIA director. On April 29, Obama signed the order for the Osama raid.

4. Lt Gen Ahmed Shuja Pasha: DG, ISI (2008-12).
5. January 27, 2011: Davis was released after paying 'blood money' to the kin of his victims.
6. Dr Shakil Afridi has been charged in Pakistan with running a fake Hepatitis B vaccination programme. Other Hepatitis B workers have been targeted after the Osama raid.

27: Selfish Self-interests in Afghanistan

1. Qatar allowed Taliban to set up an office in Doha in 2013, for quiet diplomacy. Two rounds of talks with the Afghan government have taken place there.
2. The first round of the Murree peace process, between the Afghan government and the Taliban, took place on July 7, 2015.
3. Pakistan army chief, 2013-16.
4. Hamid Karzai, President of Afghanistan, 2001-14.
5. Former US ambassador to Afghanistan (2003-05), to Iraq (2005-07) and to the UN (2007-09). He is a Pushtun.
6. Rustam Shah Mehmand served as Pakistan's High Commissioner to Afghanistan and as Chief Commissioner for Afghan Refugees.

28: Donald Trump, Nudger-in-chief

1. On June 23, 2016, 51.9 per cent of the UK electorate voted to leave the European Union.

29: Pakistan's Pal, Putin

1. Yuri Andropov (1914-84) headed the Soviet Union from 1982 till his death. KGB chairman, 1967-82.
2. George H.W. Bush, US President, 1989-93. Director, Central Intelligence, 1976-77.

3. The Shanghai Five was created in April 1996 comprising China, Russia, Kazakhstan, Kyrgyzstan and Tajikistan. In June 2001 it became the Shanghai Cooperation Organisation, of which India and Pakistan became full members in June 2017.

4. On November 24, 2015, Turkey shot down a Russian Su-24M military aircraft near the Syria-Turkey border. Putin accused the Turks of wanting to 'lick the Americans in a certain place'. In June 2016, Turkish President Recep Erdogan sent a letter to Putin expressing sympathy and deep condolences.

30: Forge Structure or Break Ice?

1. Organisation for Security and Cooperation in Europe.
2. Abdullah bin Abdulaziz al Saud, King of Saudi Arabia (2005-15).
3. For the two parts of Kashmir.
4. The OIC was founded in 1972 but was preceded by an Islamic summit in Rabat, Morocco in September 1969. India was invited through Ambassador Gurbachan Singh. Delhi decided to send a delegation led by Fakhruddin Ali Ahmed. President Yahya Khan refused to attend saying that Pakistan had agreed to the participation of the Muslims of India, not its government, as represented by the non-Muslim Gurbachan Singh.

31: Council of Spies

1. Rabindra Singh. He was under investigation and slipped out via the land route to Nepal.

32: Akhand Bharat Confederation Doctrine

1. The five-point Gujral Doctrine sought to remove quid pro quos from diplomacy with India's neighbours: (1) With neighbours like Bangladesh, Bhutan, Maldives, Nepal and Sri Lanka, India does not ask for reciprocity, but gives and accommodates what it can in good faith and trust. (2) No South Asian country should allow its territory to be used against the interests of another country in the region. (3) No country should interfere in the internal affairs of another. (4) All

South Asian countries must respect each other's territorial integrity and sovereignty. (5) They should settle all their disputes through peaceful bilateral negotiations.

2. The 1946 Cabinet Mission Plan of the British Imperial government sought to keep India united by proposing a power-sharing arrangement between Hindus and Muslims. It envisioned India comprising three groups of provinces with strong decentralisation of power, and Delhi controlling nation-wide subjects: defence, currency and diplomacy. The Congress Party, however, wanted a strongly centralised government.

3. See Chapter 13.

Index

About the Authors

A.S. Dulat was Secretary of the Research and Analysis Wing, 1999-2000.

General Asad Durrani was Director-General, Inter-Services Intelligence directorate, 1990-91.

Aditya Sinha is a writer and a journalist living on the outskirts of Delhi.